Globalization and the BRICs

Also by Francesca Beausang

THIRD WORLD MULTINATIONALS: Engine of Development or New Form of Dependency?

Globalization and the BRICs

Why the BRICs Will Not Rule the World for Long

Francesca Beausang
Senior Economist, 4CAST

First published 2012 by
PALGRAVE MACMILLAN

Palgrave Macmillan in the UK is an imprint of Macmillan Publishers Limited, registered in England, company number 785998, of Houndmills, Basingstoke, Hampshire RG21 6XS.

Palgrave Macmillan in the US is a division of St Martin's Press LLC, 175 Fifth Avenue, New York, NY 10010.

Palgrave Macmillan is the global academic imprint of the above companies and has companies and representatives throughout the world.

Palgrave® and Macmillan® are registered trademarks in the United States, the United Kingdom, Europe and other countries

ISBN: 978–0–230–24314–9

This book is printed on paper suitable for recycling and made from fully managed and sustained forest sources. Logging, pulping and manufacturing processes are expected to conform to the environmental regulations of the country of origin.

A catalogue record for this book is available from the British Library.

A catalog record for this book is available from the Library of Congress.

10 9 8 7 6 5 4 3 2 1
21 20 19 18 17 16 15 14 13 12

Printed and bound in Great Britain by
CPI Antony Rowe, Chippenham and Eastbourne

Contents

Tables

Figures

Preface

It is the year 2050. An astronaut steps out of his spaceship. He has been out of contact with the earth since 2010. He is surprised that the delegation sent to meet him is using roughly the same iPhone as he had 40 years before. He is surprised by the obvious poverty and inequality that he sees as he travels on the high-speed train (which seems to be travelling more slowly and much more unsafely than trains did 40 years before). And he is surprised that he cannot understand his hosts. But then, he had never bothered to learn Mandarin. He has landed on the planet of the BRICs, where innovation has died and inequality has bloomed.

'What could have caused this state of affairs?' he wonders. The future had seemed so full of promise when he left. Although developed nations had been struggling under a heavy load of debt, the BRICs seemed poised to take up the baton and lead the world forward. But all around him the world looked the same, not better. And people looked poorer, not richer. What had happened?

In this book I analyse why the BRIC miracle might not turn out exactly as planned.

Acknowledgements

I am greatly indebted to the critical eye of my husband, Christopher Hunter, so much so that I have contemplated adding him as a co-author! This book is the culmination of both my academic knowledge of Brazil, Russia, India and China and my practical experience of their financial markets. In that sense, my thanks go to the great thinkers who inspired me during the years I spent as a lecturer at the London School of Economics Development Studies Institute. Their influence helped in shaping my interest in the meaning of economic development, which this book is very much about. But my thanks also go to the traders, economists and analysts with whom I have engaged as a financial analyst for the last eight years; they have given me a sense of the real challenges which the BRICs face through globalization today.

Every effort has been made to contact all the copyright holders for tabular material in this book. If any have been inadvertently omitted, the publishers will be pleased to make the necessary arrangements at the earliest opportunity.

Abbreviations

BRIC	Brazil, Russia, India, China
CFIUS	Committee on Foreign Investment in the United States
CIC	China Investment Corporation
EU	European Union
FDI	foreign direct investment
FED	US Federal Reserve
GDP	gross domestic product
ICT	information and communication technologies
IMF	International Monetary Fund
ISI	import substitution industrialization
LDC	least developed country
M&A	mergers and acquisitions
NAFTA	North American Free Trade Agreement
NIC	newly industrialized country
NSI	national system of innovation
OECD	Organisation for Economic Co-operation and Development
OPEC	Organization of the Petroleum Exporting Countries
PPP	purchasing power parity
R&D	research and development
SEZ	special economic zone
SWF	Sovereign Wealth Fund
TFP	total factor productivity
UNCTAD	United Nations Conference on Trade and Development
WTO	World Trade Organization

Introduction

The aims of this manuscript are (1) to provide an overview of the recent ascent to economic and political power of Brazil, Russia, India and China – the BRIC nations, or simply BRICs; and (2) to provide a vision of their future prospects. The signs of the BRICs' ascent are many. Whether one looks at the Eurozone calling on the BRICs to salvage it from indebtedness or at the US Senate passing a law which imposes sanctions on countries with undervalued currencies, such as the Chinese yuan,[1] it would appear that the BRICs have acquired significant economic and political importance. Yet this could all be a matter of perception. In an effort to set the record straight, this book gathers the facts embodying the economic and political ascent of the BRICs. It then moves beyond the facts and onto the speculative plain, in what may be seen as an alternative, unorthodox scenario of future BRIC decline. While the necessary concrete evidence for this scenario of decline will not exist for another 20 years the scenario is rooted in the unsustainable nature of two key characteristics of the BRICs: their excessive inequality and their insufficient innovation capability.

The history of the Third World concept

In the 1950s, the French demographer Alfred Sauvy coined the term Third World to describe those countries which were neither aligned with the communist Soviet bloc nor with the capitalist bloc of the North Atlantic Treaty Organization. As he noted, 'the Third World is nothing and wants to be something'. The tone of those who wrote on the Third World was very pessimistic; many will remember Frantz Fanon's *The Wretched of the Earth* as a sombre depiction of the Third World's struggle to emerge from its past as a victim of colonialism. With the end of the Cold War and hence of the 'Second World', Third World was discarded as a term in favour of a more neutral cat

---

egory based on income levels; that is, the category of 'developing countries', those of low and middle income. Then, out of nowhere, the 'emerging markets', especially Brazil, Russia, India and China (BRICs), invaded the public's consciousness. Myriad articles and books celebrated their advent, and the wretched of the earth were conveniently forgotten. What a difference half a century makes!

The rise of the BRICs in historical perspective

Before presenting an overview of the BRICs' ascent is shown in overview, a brief step back in time can give a sense of the change in the public's perception of BRICs and other equivalent 'special groupings' which existed before it. At the end of the 1990s, when I wrote my PhD thesis on Third World multinationals,[2] the concept of a multinational enterprise from the Third World seemed like a contradiction in terms, a freakish institution with no future. How could such a symbol of wealth, profits and economic success be associated with an adjective denoting inferiority and poverty? Yet with the turn of the century, 'Third World' started to conjure positive associations, as the focus shifted to a celebration of 'emerging markets' – those Third World countries with the greatest economic potential (see box on right). By the end of the 'noughties', emerging market multinationals were all the rage. (Maybe my book would have sold more copies had I called it *Emerging Market Multinationals* rather than *Third World Multinationals*.) What had happened? There was an extreme change in perceptions, one at least partially triggered by the financial crisis experienced by the West but also based on a genuine increase in the emerging markets' economic significance,[3] in particular that of the BRICs.[4]

   The BRIC grouping is not a natural, historical, cultural, political or linguistic construct. It is entirely an economic concept, first popularized in an economics paper from Goldman Sachs.[5] In retrospect, the choice of Brazil, Russia, India and China is nothing but a focus on the four emerging markets with the largest GDP (at purchasing power parity (PPP), see box on right) and on their four big populations becoming more productive. Indeed, the father of the concept, Goldman Sachs's Jim O'Neill, writes in *The Growth Map* (2011), his latest reflection on the origin and evolution of the BRIC category, that the two most important determinants of GDP are demographics and productivity. In terms of demography 'more working people make an economy easier to grow, unless of course they are extremely unproductive. More people produce more output. More people earn wages and income, which is the basis for their consumption'.[6] As for productivity, 'the more a group of workers can produce with a given set of inputs, from time to materials, the faster their economy will grow'.[7] Hence, in a 2001 paper[8] for each BRIC, Goldman Sachs' economics research group blended the growth rate of investment, demographic projections on the growth rate of the working-age population and projections on the growth rate of total factor productivity (TFP) to predict that by 2050 'the BRICs economies together could be larger than the G6[9] in US dollar terms'.

Purchasing power parity (PPP) is a statistical method which takes into account the relative cost of living of the countries being compared. The rationale behind PPP, as opposed to simple US dollar comparisons, is that GDP in, for example, Mexico and France may include many similar goods but their prices will be higher in France; hence, they contribute more to GDP in France than in Mexico. In addition, many countries restrict exchange-rate movement, which also makes GDP comparisons in dollars problematic. PPP controls for these factors. While one can be sympathetic to the argument that emerging markets have lower prices precisely because they are poor and hence the lower GDP in dollars resulting from lower prices reflects the country's economic state, GDP comparisons between emerging and developed countries are invalid if made in dollar terms. For that reason, PPP comparisons are preferable, although one should bear in mind that they overstate the GDP of emerging markets. For an excellent summary of the dollar terms versus PPP debate, see George Magnus, *Uprising* (London: Wiley, 2011, 80–1).

While it is difficult to predict exactly what the world will look like in 2050, there is no doubt that a 'great economic convergence' is taking place between the economies of the developed and emerging markets. In the year 2000 the GDP, in terms of PPP[10] (see Figure I.1), of the United

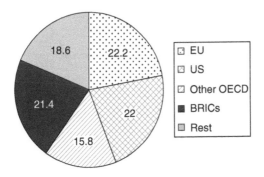

Figure I.1 Percentage share of global GDP at PPP in US$, 2000
Source: IMF World Economic Outlook, May 2001.

States at 22 per cent of world GDP was slightly larger than the 21.4 per cent of the combined BRICs. Ten years later, the combined GDP of the BRICs was US$12 trillion, or approximately 25 per cent of world GDP, larger than the US contribution of 20 per cent (see Figure I.2). This change in the BRIC's contribution to the world GDP was accomplished by consistently high growth rates in the BRICs, particularly in China and, to a lesser extent, India (as can be seen in Figure I.3).

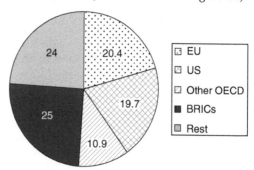

Figure I.2   Percentage share of global GDP at PPP in US$, 2010
Source: IMF World Economic Outlook, October 2011.

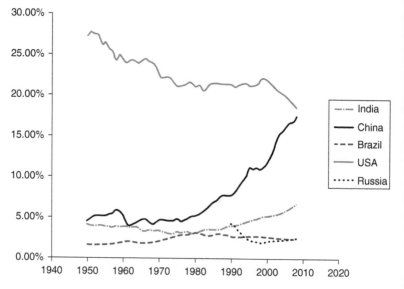

Figure I.3   Percentage of world GDP
Source: Angus Maddison, http://www.ggdc.net.

According to Magnus, China's claims to being a global power rest on the following facts:[11]

1. It is the world's largest creditor nation;
2. its economy is sufficiently large to have a material impact on the global economy;
3. it has engaged forcefully with global trade and capital markets;
4. it is a major consumer and participant in global energy markets.

Ultimately, China's economic power also seems grounded in the scale of its foreign reserves. At US$3 trillion, Chinese reserves dwarf Brazil's US$352 billion, India's US$310 billion and even Russia's US$525 billion. The importance of this factor is illustrated by the widespread expectations in October 2011 of a Chinese contribution to the Eurozone's bailout fund.[12] Another way to see the dominance of China within the BRICs is to observe the exponential growth trajectory of the Chinese economy relative to the slower pace of the other BRICs, especially Brazil and Russia, as captured by Figure I.3. Yet as is argued below, the quality of that exponential growth – or of the productivity and innovation behind it – will determine whether such dominance is more than a passing phenomenon.

Furthermore, there is an important factor which the above data do not highlight. While emerging markets are catching up, their performance in terms of GDP per capita is much less impressive, as shown in Figure I.4. Even if emerging markets are growing at staggering rates,

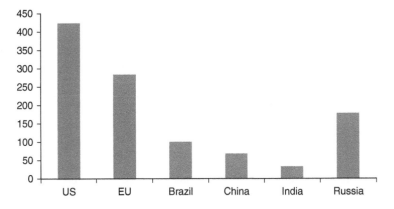

Figure I.4   GDP per capita relative to world average (%)
Source: World Bank.

their massive populations mean that, in terms of GDP per capita, individuals still have a long way to go before they actually experience 'the great convergence'. China and India represent a joint 19.1 per cent of world GDP, but due to their giant populations, their respective GDPs per capita – US$7,535 and US$3,585 – are dwarfed by that of the United States, US$47,083. Even the predicted high growth rates of China over the next 40 years will not suffice to eradicate this difference. In the Goldman Sachs 2050 prediction, Chinese GDP per capita will only be 37.5 per cent of the US level (NB: these figures are not PPP-adjusted; hence the ratio would be higher at PPP). This important point brings some perspective to the recent BRIC mania.

In the specific case of China, another approach to making growth projections is to examine the development experiences of Japan and South Korea as Chinese benchmarks, based on the statistical data series on GDP per capita in 1990 international dollars at PPP of Angus Maddison.[13] This is what is done in Figures I.5 and I.6. The raw data on Japanese GDP per capita are presented, and the South Korean and Chinese data are lagged to account for the fact that those nations are at different stages in their economic development. Empirically, in terms of absolute GDP per capita, China is 42 years and South Korea is 18 years behind Japan. In terms of the ratio of its GDP per capita to that of the United States, China is 57 years and South Korea is 28 years behind Japan. India is further down on the economic development ladder,

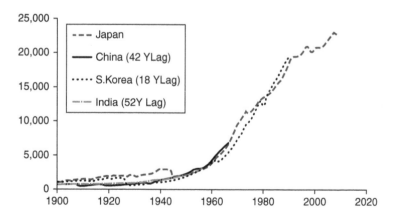

Figure I.5   GDP per capita series: Japan, China (lagged 42 years), South Korea (lagged 18 years) and India (lagged 52 years)

Source: Angus Maddison, http://www.ggdc.net

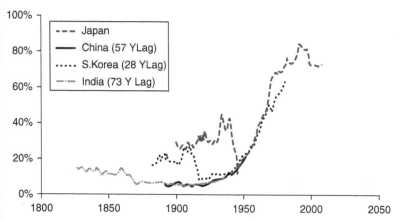

Figure I.6 GDP per capita ratio to US: Japan, China (lagged 57 years), South Korea (lagged 28 years) and India (lagged 73 years)

Source: Angus Maddison, http://www.ggdc.net

being 52 years behind Japan on GDP per capita and 73 years behind Japan on GDP per capita relative to the United States.

These charts give us a sense of the evolution of absolute and relative Chinese GDP per capita. On the basis of the above lag, the Chinese GDP per capita series ends in 1966 and Japanese data end in 2008; so China's absolute GDP per capita would be expected to be 22,000 in 2050. On a relative basis, since the lagged series on the ratio of Chinese GDP per capita to the United States ends in 1951 and data on the Japanese ratio end in 2008, Chinese GDP per capita would be expected to reach 70 per cent of the USA's in 2065 (alternatively, since Japan already reached a 70% ratio in 1975 for the first time, which implies a difference of 24 years with the end of the Chinese series, Chinese GDP per capita would therefore reach a similar ratio in 2032).

On a related note, the demographic factor introduces a similar sense of perspective into the BRIC debate. The UN forecasts that India's population will continue rising beyond 2050 (possibly nearing two billion by 2100) and Brazil's will peak in 2040 (at 220 million). However, Russia is expected to see its population decline steadily (to 116 million by 2050), as it has become a net mortality society, one that steadily registers more deaths than births.[14] In particular, Russia's share of the global working-age population is projected to drop from 2.4 to 1.6 per cent between 2005 and 2025.[15] Similarly, China's population is expected to peak relatively soon – in 2030, at 1.46 billion – and include a significant share of elderly citizens. In China, between 2010 and 2050, the over-sixties are expected to rise from 12 to 31 per cent of the population. Combined with low fertility, this rise is likely to have significant reper-cussions on the labour force, which is expected to fall by 10 per cent over the period. According to Magnus, 'at the very least, the decline in the labour force and the significant rise in old age dependency could knock 2% off the country's current long-term growth rate of about 7–8%'.[16] For the time being, China's pool of rural migrants should con-tinue to offset these negative effects on the labour force. Yet instead of being a foundation for short-term growth, demographics can also be seen as one of the threats to the long-term sustainability of China and Russia's economic miracles. Since the demographic threat has been examined carefully elsewhere (for instance in chapter 6 of Magnus's *Uprising*), this volume will focus on other limitations to sustainability, which apply across all four BRICs. Still, it is worth pondering demog-raphy's influence on the scope for realization of hyperoptimist growth forecasts for China.

The decline of the west?

The consensus view on the ascent of the emerging markets is aided by reports of the death of Western civilization. As with any tragedy, numerous books provide post-mortems. One diagnosis, put forward by Dr Moyo,[17] amongst others, finds that the patient died of its own struc-tural flaws – primarily, misallocated capital, labour and technology, although gridlocked democracy[18] and globalization both played a role. Another diagnosis, set out by Dr Ferguson,[19] maintains that Western civilization has ruled until now due to its exclusive possession of six 'killer apps' (applications):

1. competition;
2. the Scientific Revolution;
3. the rule of law and representative government;
4. modern medicine;
5. consumer society;
6. the work ethic.

Ferguson argues that these killer apps were the key to Western ascend-ancy but since they are no longer the monopoly of the West, its dominance is no longer assured. That being said, he notes that there is still some hope for the West because Western civilization is above all a 'package' made up of these killer apps and the West still has a monopoly on the total package. For instance, he notes that the Chinese do not have political competition, and while Russians have a vote, they have no functioning rule of law. He even suggests that in these two countries, it may be the absence of the full Western package of killer apps that prevents the development of innovation capacity – a hypothesis highly relevant to our analysis of BRIC innovation. However, he ends the book on a pessimistic note for the West. Beyond his material focus on the possession of killer apps, he suggests that 'maybe the real threat [to Western civilization] is posed not by the rise of China, Islam or CO_2 emissions, but by our own loss of faith in the civilization we inherited from our ancestors'.[20]

It will be left to others to examine the specific prospects of the West. This book contends that any threat to Western domination from emerging market ascendancy is offset by the fact that the latter is itself constrained by a set of limitations.[21] Indeed, it suggests that while economic forces are clearly placing emerging markets at the helm of the global economy, they will soon lose their dynamism due to two significant limitations:

1. high income inequality
2. lack of innovation

First, while the 'great convergence' may have resulted in a reduction of the global inequality between the average incomes of the richest and the poorest countries,[22] domestic economic inequality ironically continues to plague many emerging markets. Domestic inequality may be preventing these countries from 'graduating' from emerging to developed status. Worse, it could end the emerging market miracle. For example, the long-term upside structural pressures of food inflation on the poorest segment of emerging market populations could result in destabilizing social unrest, leading to a pull-out of foreign capital and immediate repercussions on the core of the emerging market miracle – economic growth. Put otherwise, inequality implies that the emerging market economic miracle is fragile.

Second, the paucity of ideas originating from emerging markets makes their ascent unsustainable. Yes, the Chinese and Indian people are capable of applying the stock of knowledge globalization brings to them. The mere fact that the Chinese have developed both a supercomputer industry and a high-speed railway industry without having any outright domestic innovation policy until very recently speaks for itself. In fact, they copy too well for their own good. The limits of the emerging market miracle will become visible when it becomes obvious that emerging markets cannot create such knowledge themselves. The inability to innovate will threaten their economic domination, as innovation is the crucial engine of long-term economic growth. In sum, inequality and lack of innovation place limits on the sustainability of emerging market economic domination, especially that of the BRICs, as will be explained below.

The perspective

The investment banks, which created the concept of emerging markets, are concerned with them as an asset class. This book, however, will look at emerging markets as success stories in terms of their implications for development and, in particular, will try to understand the conditions for the sustainability of the development miracle they represent. This requires an interdisciplinary perspective, which touches upon economics, politics and sociology, because development is simultaneously a process of economic, social and political transformation that takes place within the context of a specific developing country. The book will also analyse power in terms both of the rise and fall of nations and of its historical explanations. In sum, this book combines political economy and development and historical approaches to explain the ascent of the BRICs and examine the scope for its sustainability. Hence, it should be of interest not only to economists but also to political scientists, as it examines development from the perspective of the global political economy. Furthermore, its approach is relevant to the general public, which is interested in the broader question of whether the BRICs will rule the world. To cater to the general public, Chapters 1, 3 and 5 start with a summary providing background on the main theoretical debates on, respectively, economic approaches to development, international relations approaches to power and economic approaches to innovation.

The structure

While 'emerging markets' can be defined as those developing countries with the largest economic potential, this book focuses mainly on a subset of emerging economies – the BRICs[23]. The two reasons behind the focus on the BRICs are far from original.

1. Solely by virtue of their economic weight in terms of their share of world GDP, these countries have the greatest potential of all the emerging markets to compete with the West for global power. While O'Neill has moved on to a new category he calls growth markets – which includes the BRICs and Indonesia, Mexico, Korea and Turkey – he acknowledges that while their combined potential nominal GDP growth from 2010 to 2019 is US$16 trillion, at least three quarters of this is likely to come from the BRICs.[24]
2. The BRICs are also the emerging markets which have engaged the most intensively in the trade and financial aspects of globalization (as is suggested in Chapter 2), although some of them have set the terms of their engagement more than others.

One of the burning questions of our time is whether the BRICs will rule the planet. That is the question this book sets out to investigate. There are many ways BRICs could rule the world: by providing the engine of global economic growth; by getting other countries to make the political decisions they want them to; by providing the source of global knowledge and ideas. This book analyses the BRICs' trajectory in three dimensions – economic, political and intellectual – that are also the main dimensions of globalization. According to Giddens, globalization has five dimensions: the world capitalist economy, the nation state system, the world military order, the global division of labour (whereby industrial development results in the specialization of regions, industries, job tasks and skills) and culture.[25] This book will consider the global division of labour as a corollary of the world capitalist economy and the world military order as a corollary of the nation state system. Thus, the world capitalist economy (the economic), the nation state system (the political) and culture (the intellectual) are left as globalization's main dimensions. BRIC performance – and its sustainability – in each dimension will be examined.

The book's first part concentrates on what makes the BRICs' development experience special. Drawing on the experiences of the BRICs and South Korea, Chapter 1 puts forward five development models with different degrees and forms of interaction with the global economy. It emphasizes the experience of the BRICs' and South Korea in fine-tuning their development process within the constraints of globalization.

The second part of the book explores the BRICs' role in the globalization process. Are the BRICs becoming the engine of globalization from an economic, political and intellectual perspective, thereby allowing them to rule the world? Chapter 2 looks at the weight of emerging markets from a macroeconomic perspective. On the basis of their contribution to global GDP growth, trade and financial flows, the BRICs seem close to ruling the world from a macroeconomic perspective. Chapter 3 then discusses the implications of the economic ascent of the BRICs for global political leadership. Indeed, the BRICs are slowly laying a claim to global political power, largely on the basis of their economic ascent. Yet it is clear that major changes are required before they can achieve global political power. In order to achieve a global political landscape more in line with the new reality of BRIC economic might, not only do the World Bank and WTO need to undergo structural reforms, but the BRICs themselves must craft a common political and economic agenda. Finally, the new roles of the United States, Europe and the BRICs in a 'multipolar' global political economy are outlined.

However, because the BRICs' claim to global political power derives from their economic ascent, any threat to this supremacy annihilates their aspirations to global political leadership. The third part of the book highlights two such threats – domestic inequality and lack of innovation – which imply that the many forecasts of a new world order led by the BRICs might be premature. Chapter 4 explains that as long as the BRICs retain their high-inequality profiles, they cannot upgrade from emerging to developed countries. Chapter 5 contends that the BRICs' aspirations to long-term economic growth will remain mere aspirations unless they can become genuine innovators, which is not the case yet. Finally, a concluding chapter explains how, with the BRICs achieving a triangle of 'innovation-equality-development', their economic model may become sustainable.

1
BRICs: Beyond Developing?

The purpose of this chapter is to determine the factors behind the economic development of each one of the BRICs. Starting from a gross definition of development, as embodied by economic growth, the role of globalization in the economic growth of the four BRICs and South Korea will be examined. We outline five models of development, based on the degree of exposure to economic globalization and the degree of manipulation of globalization (i.e., a government's ability to shape the conditions of entry of foreign goods and companies into a country) to serve a national development strategy. It will be shown that the degree of manipulation of globalization by each BRIC, as opposed to its degree of exposure to globalization per se, has determined its economic growth performance. We then move on to a narrow definition of economic development, one predicated on the view that innovation capability is the main source of sustainable growth. In this perspective, globalization is mainly a means of providing a country with exposure to global knowledge, which can contribute to the building of domestic innovation capability. The extent and form of exposure to global knowledge in the BRICs is documented, and it is suggested that in all four BRICs, access to global knowledge in itself has not resulted in the creation of domestic innovation capability. The conclusion is that exposure to globalization has not been central to the BRICs' economic development, whether defined by growth or by innovation capability. Instead, we highlight the role of institutions in creating the conditions for growth and innovation in the BRICs.

The main schools of thought on economic development

Before starting the discussion, it might be useful to give the unfamiliar reader a brief background on the main economic approaches to development. For the sake of simplicity, this book distinguishes between two main competing paradigms, the neoliberal approach and the state-led approach.[1] According to the neoliberal approach, free markets ensure an efficient and just development process. They are efficient because they are driven by individuals, who are the best judges of how to allocate their resources, and they are just because they reward individuals on the basis of productivity. The main assumption is that firms will maximize wealth creation at the national level if government does not interfere with them. Hence, some key neoliberal policies, which have been packaged as the so-called Washington Consensus, are the privatization of state-owned industrial and financial firms, deregulation of finance and industry, liberalization of trade and investment and reduction in income taxes and welfare payments. Economic development will flourish if the forces of globalization are left unhindered and they are not managed by government. As noted by Chang, 'these policies, their advocates admitted, may temporarily create some problems, such as rising inequality, but ultimately they will make everyone better off by creation of a more dynamic and wealthier society'.[2] Outside the developing world, the US economy embodies the neoliberal model.

The main alternative model is one where the state is omnipresent in the economy. This was very much the dominant school of thought in the early days of economic development theory and policy (the 1960s and 1970s). It gave rise to policies which distorted free markets, among them import-substitution industrialization, a protectionist industrialization policy whereby barriers against industrial imports are erected by the state to protect new domestic industries and foster industrialization. It also gave rise to export promotion industrialization, whereby exports are subsidized to achieve industrialization. Both policies were applied across the developing world over the sixties and seventies. In the eighties, as the Thatcher and Reagan administrations took over, a global policy shift occurred: the discredited state-heavy model, which had dominated economic development policy circles, was replaced by the neoliberal model, which became the new mantra. Import substitution, viewed as heresy, was swiftly replaced by the Washington Consensus, described above.

In turn, by the end of the 1990s, the Washington Consensus was discredited as an economic development model in the face of multiple failures (although among developed countries, the United States continues to embody the neoliberal model). Although since then some alternatives have been put forward – including the Post-Washington Consensus, which puts institutional change at the centre of economic development policy – they were only variations on the neoliberal theme. Seemingly, the collapse of the neoliberal model left a policy void.

Or did it? The state-heavy ideology is now experiencing a revival in a mutated form. The economic success of China is such that it has some, like Stefan Halper, talking about a 'Beijing Consensus' of economic development policy (see Chapter 2).[3] As Dambisa Moyo puts it, in China there exists 'an economic model couched in capitalist thinking, laced with a hefty dollop of state intervention'[4] – that is, a combination of stringent rules and regulations and tightly managed macroeconomic policies.

The BRICs as a development model

Do these theoretical debates meet the test of reality? The experience of the BRICs can be used to support one theoretical approach or another. Yet possibly their greatest contribution to the developing world is the hope they give developing countries that development is not beyond reach. Developing countries are desperate to find out what lies behind the BRIC economic miracle, in the hope that they can replicate it. Of course, given that every country's development experience is context-specific in both time and space, it is naive to believe that such replication is possible. Yet this chapter outlines some lessons from the BRICs' common experience of development in the midst of globalization. Are the skyrocketing growth rates of the BRICs related to their economic opening, in what would be a validation of the neoliberal model of free markets? More precisely, what degree of exposure to the global economy has coincided with their skyrocketing growth rates? To assess this, one needs to look at the individual economic histories of the BRICs. In addition, their histories are contrasted with that of South Korea, a member of the NICs (newly industrialized countries), which were the BRICs of the eighties.[5] Comparing today's globalized BRICs and South Korea, which developed in pre-WTO days with a strong philosophy of economic self-sufficiency, provides a contrasting historical perspective.

In what sense have they made it?

As the world's investment bankers understand it, 'making it' to BRIC status simply means that a country is responsible for a significant share of world GDP and is displaying a strong economic growth performance. For now, let us ignore the limitations of economic growth as a yardstick for economic development and switch to a more valuable yardstick: the ability to innovate. The charts and tables below summarize GDP growth-based

indicators of economic development, globalization intensity and indigenous innovation intensity for the BRICs and South Korea. The summary
gives an initial sense of the interplay of the three variables.

Figure 1.1 confirms the BRICs' significance in terms of their share
of world GDP at PPP (see the Introduction), with their total share of 25
per cent being greater than the 19.7 per cent of the United States. Based
on Table 1.1, all the BRICs have sustained high rates of real economic
growth in the last ten years, but there are clearly various degrees of performance. China's extreme economic performance can be summarized
easily: China has maintained the fastest-growing economy worldwide
and is the clear outperformer among the BRICs, so much so that the
Economist recently forecast that the Chinese economy would be larger

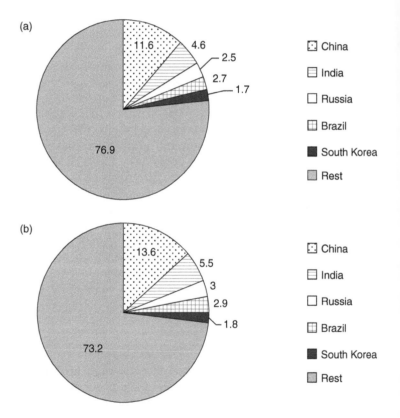

Figure 1.1 BRIC and South Korea share of world GDP at PPP, 2000(a) versus
2010(b)

Source: World Bank.

Table 1.1 BRIC and South Korea average annual real GDP growth rates, %, 1980–2011

	1980–90	1990–2000	2000–5	2006	2007	2008	2009	2010	2011 Forecast
Brazil	2.8	2.9	2.8	3.7	5.7	5.1	−0.2	7.5	3.8
China	10.3	10.4	9.6	11.6	13	9	8.7	10.3	9.5
India	5.8	6	6.9	9.8	9.3	7.3	7.4	10.4	7.8
Russia	NA	−4.7	6.2	7.4	8.1	5.6	−7.9	4.8	4.3
South Korea	9.4	5.84	4.6	5	5.1	2.3	0.2	6.1	4

Source: UNCTAD Handbook of Statistics (for 1980–2005); IMF, World Economic Outlook, January 2012 (for 2006–11).

in dollar terms than that of the United States by 2019.[6] However, the double-digit growth rates which prevailed between 1980 and 2007 (excluding 2000–5) have given way to high single-digit rates since the beginning of the global recession. It is interesting to contrast China's growth trajectory with that of South Korea, which shared skyrocketing growth rates with China in its earlier phase of development, as is clear from its 9.4 per cent growth average in the period 1980–90. Yet since 1990 Korea has experienced a normalization of its growth rate to a still impressive 4–5 per cent level. This opens up the question of when China will experience a similar normalization process, a question explored in more depth in this chapter's conclusion. India has grown significantly and more regularly, with a notable acceleration since 2006. As for Russia, after experiencing a severe crisis in the 1990s, it posted significant growth throughout the 2000 decade, powered by the oil and gas sectors. Yet the heightened role of these sectors was also responsible for a 7.9 per cent contraction in 2009, as commodities were hit by the global recession, which also affected Brazil, with GDP contracting by 0.2 per cent in 2009. Before 2009, Brazil had seen a significant rise in economic growth, starting from 2006, although it is the underperformer in terms of growth relative to the other BRICs.

Before proceeding to an in-depth analysis of each BRIC in turn, some general observations on the relationship between growth and openness in the BRICs can be made. It is a natural question to ask whether BRIC growth, which seemed to take off at the turn of the century, was related to the economic opening of the BRICs. After all, the emergence of these countries as economic powers did follow a period of reforms and opening.

Table 1.2   Indicators of globalization intensity, BRICs and South Korea

	Date	Brazil	China	India	South Korea	Russia
Merchandise exports as % of world total	2010	1.33	10.4	1.44	3.1	2.63
Trade as % of GDP	1990	16	**44**	23	59	55
	2008–10 average	23.8	**55.4**	47.7	**105.8**	**51.5**
Merchandise exports as % of GDP	1995	6.1	20.4	8.6	24.2	20.5
	2010	9.6	**26.8**	12.7	46	27
Average simple most-favoured nation (MFN) tariffs (%)	2010	13.7	**9.6**	13	12.1	9.5
Average trade weighted MFN tariffs (%)	2008	8.8	4.3	6	8.3	10.3
Stock of inward foreign direct investment (FDI) as % of GDP	2010	22.9	**9.9**	12	12.6	28.7

Source: WTO Secretariat, 2009; WTO Trade Profiles, October 2011; WTO Tariff Profiles, 2011; OECD Factbook 2010; UNCTAD World Investment Report 2011.

Yet the potential for a causal link between these two factors breaks down, as soon as one remembers that trade and foreign direct investment liberalization have been applied by the IMF and World Bank the world over as a recipe for development since the 1980s, resulting in a plethora of failed development stories.[7] Still, it is worth contrasting the BRICs' various degrees of economic growth with their various degrees of economic openness, which are displayed in Table 1.2. All the BRICs have expereinced significan growth in their export and import levels since the 1980s. But while foreign trade has reached more than 50 per cent of GDP in China and Russia, in Brazil and India it is closer to 30 per cent. Do China's economic outperformance and Brazil's relative underperformance in terms of economic growth have anything to do with the intensity of their exposure to globalization? Probably not. As suggested below, not just the intensity but the terms of each BRIC's engagement with globalization

Table 1.3 Indicators of indigenous innovation intensity, BRICs and South Korea, 2008

	Brazil	China	India	South Korea	Russia
Government R&D expenditure as % of GDP	1.09	1.54	0.71	3.37	1.03
Triadic patents per million population	0.36	0.39	0.14	43.93	0.45

Source: OECD Science, Technology and Industry Outlook 2010, OECD, Paris, 2010.

have determined their rate of economic growth. The contrasting experience of South Korea reinforces this hypothesis. South Korea was the outperformer among the NICs, despite its exposure to globalization being limited in the early stages of development.[8] Instead, South Korean policymakers were able to pick and choose the aspects of globalization which were seen to benefit their national development plan.

After examining South Korea as an outsider case, the four BRICs at the time of their economic opening are compared in terms of (1) their degree of exposure to globalization and (2) the degree of 'manipulation' of globalization exerted by their government; that is, its ability to shape the conditions of entry of foreign goods and companies. Each BRIC government has chosen a different degree of exposure to globalization, and each one has also manipulated globalization to a different extent. At one extreme, the Indian government has been the most reluctant 'globalizer', with low levels of exposure to globalization; its economic policy is founded on the goal of self-reliance. It has had the tightest grip on how much and how it opened up, thereby resembling the South Korean government the most in that respect. Like India's government, Brazil's has been a reluctant globalizer. Even today, Brazil has the lowest trade intensity indicators of all the BRICs, which is partly the result of industrial opposition to liberalization. However, unlike India's,in Brazil the government's reluctance has not been matched by an effort to manipulate the forces of globalization as it has in India. Once the Brazilian government decided to open up, it applied liberalization in a very orthodox manner, with no overt attempt to impose conditions on trade and foreign direct investment for the purposes of a national development strategy. Incidentally, Brazil happens to be the poorest economic growth performer among the BRICs, consistently registering the lowest growth rates from 1980 to 2008. Moving further down the spectrum of 'globalization reluctance', China, which has clearly been the economic outper-former, has been an enthusiastic and intense participant in international trade and foreign direct investment. Yet its government has practiced 'managed globalization'; that is, above all, the Chinese government has set the terms of its engagement with globalization by forcing foreign investors to fulfil local development requirements.

Finally, the Russian government is the most enthusiastic globalizer, resulting in Russia's high degree of integration, illustrated by its trade-to-GDP ratio above 50 per cent; but the government manages globali-zation when it comes to deciding and amending the terms of inward foreign direct investment. Yet, as explained below, Russia is in a cat-egory of its own among the BRICs. Its mixed economic performance has less to do with the terms of engagement with globalization, which are set by its government, than with the challenges posed by Russia's identity as a transition economy, which needs to rebuild an indigenous infrastructure for knowledge creation.

Obviously, it is very hazardous to draw implications from country case studies, as they do not lend themselves to generalization in the way that quantitative analysis derived from statistically significant samples does. Still, it is worth highlighting a crude observation from Table 1.4, where 1 is the lowest level and 4 the highest of a particular indicator: the top two BRICs in terms of economic growth – that is, China and India (at levels 4 and 3, respectively) – present a high degree of manipulation of globalization in common (at 3 and 4), although China has high expo-sure to globalization (3) in contrast with India's lower exposure (2). This confirms that in both cases, the government's ability to manipulate globalization was a contributing factor to high growth rates.

From growth to innovation and from openness to the globalization of knowledge

Even if one reduces economic development to the investment bankers' standard of success (i.e., economic growth), economic openness does not in itself produce miracles. The obvious evidence is the growth suc-cess of China's managed globalization relative to the mediocre growth performance of Brazil's textbook liberalization. Besides, if one starts from the assumption that ideas and innovation are the foundations of long-term growth, it is no longer the relationship between openness and growth that needs to be focused on but that between the globaliza-tion of knowledge and innovative capability. This book focuses on glo-balization as a conduit for developing countries to access the knowledge

Table 1.4 Five models of insertion into the global economy in early development

Country	South Korea[9]	India	Brazil	China	Russia
Model	'Selective' globalization: reluctant globalization, where South Korea picks and chooses aspects of globalization which advance national development strategy. Protect new industries through tariffs to give them time to absorb new technologies	Very reluctant globalization due to an economic policy founded on self-sufficiency.	Reluctant globalization given industrial opposition. Low trade intensity, but textbook application of orthodox liberalization to a commodity-based economy.	'Managed' globalization: enthusiastic globalization, but terms of foreign involvement are set by placing development/ technology transfer conditions.	'Managed' globalization: commodity-based economy requires high trade intensity, but the Kremlin is highly selective when it comes to inward FDI conditions.
Degree of exposure to globalization at time of opening, based on trade and FDI intensity (1 = low, 4 = high)	Low at time of opening (very high now)	2	1	3	4
Degree of manipulation of globalization at time of opening (1 = low, 4 = high)	Very high	4	2	3	1

(continued)

Table 1.4 Continued

Country	South Korea[9]	India	Brazil	China	Russia
Degree of economic growth performance	High-income economy and OECD member	3	1	4	2
State of indigenous innovation	One of the most 'inventive' nations in the world. Among top five nations in terms of the number of patents granted annually by the US Patent Office	Some islands of excellence such as pharmaceuticals and IT, but R&D infrastructure is weak.	Some islands of excellence: oil and gas, aeronautics, biofuels, agro-industry, mineral ores, paper and cellulose. Commodity curse: no incentive to innovate.	Seeks to become an innovator like South Korea, but so far innovations remain adaptive and marginal.	Same as Brazil. Specific problem is the rebuilding of Soviet S&T infrastructure.

that will help them develop. In turn, a country's ability to draw on global knowledge will be affected by trade, foreign investment and technology transfer – that is, by economic liberalization at large. Hence, this chapter looks at how each one of the BRICs liberalized and then draws implications for their access to global knowledge.

The relationship between the globalization of knowledge and domestic innovative capability is one which changes through time. To assess how the BRICs made it, one needs to go back to the days when the BRICs had a lot of catching up to do. In theory, when there is a big gap between a country's technological capability and the global technology frontier – that is, in sectors where a country has a lot to catch up on to achieve state-of-the-art technology – proactive efforts to acquire and use global knowledge should offer the greatest pay-off for a developing country, since using knowledge that already exists as opposed to trying to reinvent the wheel should yield more immediate returns. That is not to say that global knowledge is a complete alternative to local efforts: after all, assimilating global knowledge requires a minimal level of local technological capability to interpret information, select, buy and internalize technology. Still, one could make a strong argument in favour of emphasizing the assimilation of global knowledge in the early stages of development. Reinventing the wheel can come later. As the country starts to catch up, more emphasis can be placed on developing new knowledge to remain competitive; this is examined in Chapter 5. One could easily see this chapter as 'development, part 1', or 'how to join a select club of countries by using global knowledge', and Chapter 5 as 'development, part 2', or 'can the BRICs rule the world by developing their own innovations?' In reality, strict separation between these two theoretical phases of development, based on a global knowledge / local innovation divide, rarely works in practice, as is demonstrated by the BRICs' individual experiences.

Model 0: a path no longer available, or South Korea's 'selective' globalization

Before covering the development history of the BRICs, it is useful to briefly consider the development trajectory of South Korea, which belonged to one of the BRICs' predecessors, the NICs, South Korea's government was very selective of the aspects of globalization which it let in so as to allow indigenous knowledge to flourish. In a post-WTO world, where WTO membership and adherence to its rules are musts, the South Korean option is no longer available to aspiring BRICs; globalization now has to be adopted as a package, and exceptions are granted to developing countries only on a temporary basis. Still, it is worth reflecting on South Korea as a test case on how to encourage the development of indigenous knowledge through selective globalization. While South Korea stands for an extreme policy choice which is no longer applicable, extremes give the best available evidence on the effectiveness of particular development policies – in this case on a policy of indigenous knowledge promotion.

South Korea's development history is impressive. Back in the early 1960s, the average South Korean earned less than half of what the average Ghanaian citizen earned. Between 1960 and 2000, per capita income in South Korea grew 14 times in purchasing power terms. It is now a member of the Organisation for Economic Cooperation and Development (OECD), and its per capita income is equivalent to Portugal's. According to the great South Korean economist Ha-Joon Chang, 'it took the UK over two centuries (between the late eighteenth century and today) and the United States around one and a half centuries (the 1860s to the present day) to achieve the same result'.[10] As Chang notes, from a country whose main exports were such commodities as tungsten and fish, it has become a leading exporter of mobile phones and flat-screen televisions. South Korean policymakers must have done something right. Various interpretations of the South Korea miracle have been offered, some of which ascribe South Korea's development to its engagement with globalization. This is very tempting, given that South Korea is currently one of the most open economies in the world (Table 1.2 shows its impressive 105.8% share of trade in GDP), yet the fact that South Korea only became this open once it had built up its domestic industries is well documented. In Chang's words, Korea 'nurtured certain new industries, selected by the government in consultation with the private sector, through tariff protection, subsidies and other forms of government support until they "grew up" enough to withstand international competition'.[11] Protection was a means to allow new industries to absorb new technologies. Foreign exchange was used only for importing key machinery and industrial inputs. The government controlled foreign direct investment, too, by welcoming it only in certain sectors in line with the national development plan. As for trade, it was turned into the main means of achieving a development strategy; that is, exports of textiles and cheap electronics were promoted to earn the hard currencies required to pay for the advanced technologies and expensive machines necessary for the new protected industries. What industries were singled out? In 1973, the first steel mill and the first modern shipyard went into production. Today South Korea is the world's sixth largest steel producer. New firms were also set up in electronics, machinery and chemicals. Per capita income between 1972 and 1979 grew by more than five times in US dollar terms.

By 1982 Korea had managed to copy advanced products through reverse engineering. Yet according to Chang, 'it was still not sophisticated enough to come up with original ideas and to develop and own international patents, copyrights and trademarks. Today as suggested in Table 1.3, Korea is one of the most "inventive" nations in the world – it ranks among the top five nations in terms of the number of patents granted annually by the US Patent Office'.[12] Chang argues that South Korea achieved this status largely because it started its development process with lax intellectual property legislation, which allowed it to 'borrow' foreign technologies from more productive foreigners; that is, it encouraged reverse engineering and overlooked the pirating of patented products.

In other words, South Korea took what it wanted from globalization: it took foreign technologies and industrial inputs; it took advantage of the export component of the globalization by exporting textiles and cheap electronics, which generated foreign exchange for essential imports; it welcomed foreign direct investment in sectors which fitted with national development priorities. Yet it shut out the parts of globalization it considered detrimental to its development: imports of goods and services that competed with those of new Korean industries and foreign direct investment in sectors that were not those emphasized by the national development plan. Globalization was unbundled into those aspects that furthered national development and those that did not. Above all, globalization was manipulated as a means towards the goal of national development, which consisted in building competitive domestic industries with a capability for indigenous innovation.

Model 1: China, or 'managed' globalization

History of economic reform

China has been the world's fastest-growing major economy since 1980. To what extent is this related to China's trade and foreign direct investment (FDI) liberalization? China's embrace of reform was gradual: from 1978, reform measures were tested in isolated experiments confined to a particular location or industry, which would then be scaled up to the national level if successful. Hence, one can identify three stages in economic reform. Between 1978 and 1984, reform focused on rural areas and on early economic opening. Agricultural communes, which were large rural organizations run exclusively on the basis of socialist principles, were replaced with the household responsibility system, whereby individual farmers had to produce a set quota of goods for the state, but they could sell any food they produced beyond the quota on the free market at unregulated prices. The liberalization of the rural areas was very successful, resulting in an increase in the standard of living of the rural population, which benefited from the household responsibility system. At the same time as the rural sector was being reformed, China's first attempts at economic opening were made. In 1978 Hong Kong businesses were allowed to sign 'export-processing' contracts with Chinese firms in the Pearl River delta. A Hong Kong firm would ship an input, such as fabric, to a Chinese rural firm and have it sewn into a final product, such as shirts. Then four special economic zones (SEZs) were created in the coastal areas, where trade and foreign investment were liberalized for non-state firms. In the SEZs non-state enterprises, joint ventures and foreign firms were able to import world-class inputs nearly duty free and export to world markets. The result was an export boom based on labour-intensive growth. In contrast, outside the SEZs currency remained inconvertible, and many state enterprises were subject to rationing of imports.

Following the success of reform in the rural sector and SEZs, the second stage of reform occurred between 1985 and 1992. More coastal SEZs were created in the context of a 'coastal development strategy', resulting in a significant rise in foreign investment. Furthermore, an export promotion policy was applied outside the SEZs, in contrast with the high tariff and non-tariff protection against imports which had prevailed outside the SEZs until then. A partial system of rebates of value-added taxes for exports was begun in 1985 and expanded in the nineties. Banks provided preferential interest rates to exporters. Finally, the Chinese government decided that a more sweeping structural reform was in order; hence the third stage of reform, which began in 1992 (and was still underway in 2012). It was crowned by financial sector liberalization (see Chapter 2) and access to the WTO in 2001. By then, Deng Xiao Ping's 1992 pronouncement that capitalism was not just for capitalists had become a fact.

As China witnessed the gradual success of early stages of reform, its embrace of economic reform soon became enthusiastic. The enthusiasm had clearly become visible by the time China concluded its bilateral trade agreement with the United States (November 1999) with a view to obtain WTO membership, which it obtained two years later. China had to satisfy more stringent conditions for WTO membership than original members or even signatories to the 1994 Uruguay Round of trade negotiations. It had to agree to the establishment of a transitional product-specific safeguard mechanism for a 12-year period after accession, which allowed WTO members to access the mechanism if Chinese exports caused market disruption. China also accepted a cap of 8.3 per cent of the value of output on domestic support to agriculture, which was below the 10 per cent cap for developing countries. China ended up cutting tariff and non-tariff barriers significantly. In 1992, the unweighted mean tariff was 43 per cent, on a par with Brazil's, while 51 per cent of imports were subject to non-tariff barriers. Today, the simple average tariff applied by China on a most-favoured nation basis[13] is, at 9.6 per cent, not only the second lowest among the BRICs (see Table 1.2) but already close to its 'bound tariff' rate – the tariff ceiling which China agreed to upon signing its membership agreement.[14] This is important because the WTO holds countries only to this bound tariff, not to the actual tariff. If a country's bound tariff is much above its actual tariff, the country can raise its actual tariff towards bound levels. The fact that the Chinese actual tariff is already close to its bound tariff means there is no leeway for China to suddenly increase its tariff in the event of a crisis. Furthermore, only 10 per cent of Chinese tariff lines carry a tariff of more than 25 per cent. As a clear testimony to China's unequivocal opening, exports grew from 3.9 per cent of world exports in 2000 to 10.4 per cent in 2010. Trade represents 55.4 per cent of GDP, up from an already high 44 per cent in 1990. Merchandise exports represent 20.4 per cent of GDP.

Why did China set itself up for such a rough deal with WTO membership? In the answer lies the key to the relationship between globalization and China's growth. Chinese leaders used commitments undertaken in the WTO accession agreement as an excuse to accelerate domestic reforms. The demands of globalization were presented as an unavoidable, external constraint, one that had to shape the domestic economic agenda. It is in this indirect sense – that is, as a political tool for the legitimization of domestic economic reform – that globalization has had the greatest impact on Chinese growth. Whether trade liberalization as an economic process in itself is responsible for Chinese growth is something that will be debated forever. The indirect political channel is much harder to refute. In fact, the best evidence of a pre-commitment to liberalization on the part of the Chinese authorities is the fact that China had even begun to reduce its trade barriers from 1994, well before its accession: Naughton reports that the average nominal tariff was reduced from 43 per cent in 1992 to 17 per cent in 1999, when the breakthrough in WTO negotiations occurred. In the actual agreement, China agreed to lower average industrial tariffs to 9.4 per cent by

2005, a figure actually achieved in 2004.[15] Similarly, Srinivasan finds that in almost every commodity, China's market share had grown rapidly between 1978 and 2000, before accession.[16] In other words, WTO accession was only the institutionalization of China's already existing, clear-cut policy of liberalization.

Global knowledge

One of the main purposes of liberalization is to gain access to global knowledge. Indeed, the more a country has to catch up, the more value it will extract from already existing global knowledge. Hence, at the beginning of the Chinese development process, the acquisition of global knowledge was a central goal, as is suggested by the well-named 'market for technology' policy initiated in 1978. Economic liberalization represented a door to this global knowledge, whether through trade, FDI, technology licensing, copying and reverse engineering, print or the internet.

Here, let us focus on FDI, China's main source of global knowledge. As was the case in South Korea, in China globalization was manipulated towards a development and innovation goal. Yet the difference between South Korea's 'selective globalization' and China's 'managed globalization' was that China opened up to globalization in a much more comprehensive and enthusiastic way. In particular, while in South Korea incoming FDI was considerably less than 1 per cent of GDP during its periods of most rapid growth,[17] in China it exceeded 6 per cent of GDP in 1994 and averaged 4 per cent between 1996 and 2002. South Korea closed entire sectors to trade and FDI to allow domestic industry to blossom through protection, while China was more concerned with encouraging FDI in the sectors it prioritized and with dictating the terms of foreign involvement in these sectors by placing development or technology transfer conditions on it. One could say that South Korea put the onus on negative discrimination of FDI, while China practiced positive discrimination. Yet in both cases 'control' was the key word.

After an initial opening to FDI in the 1980s, the Chinese government soon succeeded in attracting it en masse; China became the largest recipient of FDI in the world in 1993. Up until 1992, China had largely confined incoming FDI to export manufacturing activities. In 1992 Deng Xiao Ping began selectively opening China's domestic market to foreign investors. China influenced the sectoral distribution of FDI flows by issuing guidelines to foreign investors, whereby inflows were categorized as 'prohibited', 'permitted' or 'encouraged' (the last category mainly involved the high-tech sector). Sectoral discrimination was one aspect of FDI policy. Yet regardless of the sector, the overall relationship between China and foreign direct investors became a clear case of quid pro quo from 1992, with access to the Chinese market at one end and a transfer of technology to China at the other. According to Srinivasan, 'the large market provide[d] effective leverage for technology transfer'.[18]

But success in attracting FDI does not equate to the successful transfer of technology. Hence, FDI access became conditional on the establishment of joint ventures. As late as 2000, joint ventures accounted for over 50 per cent of all foreign investment. While many projects failed to produce technology transfer on a massive scale, a potent example of the effectiveness of Chinese FDI policy in sourcing technology is the construction of the Three Gorges Dam in June 1996. For the left bank of the dam, foreign companies could win the first 12 of 14 equipment contracts, but Chinese companies had to be involved in building. For the last two equipment contracts, a Chinese company had to be the main player. Foreign companies had to design and manufacture the equipment jointly with Chinese partners. According to Yu,[19] it is through the learning process created by this model of collaboration that China's Harbin Electricity Power Station Equipment has become the largest player in the market.

Perhaps the greatest success stories of joint ventures from the perspective of technology transfer have occurred when the Chinese government negotiated local content and training requirements with the foreign joint-venture partners of Chinese firms. For instance, Alcatel, set up a joint venture with the Belgian Bell subsidiary of ITT in 1984. The purpose was to produce digital switches for telecoms. Because the foreign partner was not a technology leader, it was willing to agree to transfer technology and manufacture custom large-scale integrated chips used in telecoms in the Chinese facility. The joint venture enjoyed the patronage of the Ministry of Post and Telecom, which ensured the smooth running of business. In return, many Chinese engineers were trained at Shanghai Bell and were introduced to the technologies of digital telecom switches at that plant. This training was arguably critical to developing the expertise later used in the development of domestic telecoms equipment enterprises, including successful firms like Huawei. Similarly, Motorola developed an extensive training programme for the management of the thousand-largest Chinese state-owned enterprises. This helped them gain enough technological and managerial capability to eventually enable them to compete with Motorola products.[20]

However, the joint-venture model of technology transfer came to an end when China joined the WTO in 2001, at which point restrictions on wholly owned subsidiaries were lifted.[21] By 2008 nearly 80 per cent of all FDI consisted of wholly owned foreign subsidiaries. Thus, certain limitations must be borne in mind when celebrating China's joint-venture approach to technology transfer.

(1)   Only a country with the size and market power of China has sufficient bargaining power to impose a joint-venture investment and receive it, because the option of no market access at all is worse for a foreign investor than a joint-venture investment.

(2)   A developing country keen on WTO membership no longer has the same leeway to impose joint-venture requirements. Indeed, while the WTO's prohibition of trade-related investment measures does not include joint-venture requirements, article XVI of the General Agreement on Trade in Services prohibits WTO members from using requirements on the type of legal entity, including joint ventures. Given the increasing role of services in the global economy and the increasing role of emerging markets in providing these services, this is a serious concern.

(3)   The ability of joint ventures to spin off a technologically capable domestic industry is a contentious issue; there are as many cases of success as of failure.[22] In China itself, the joint-venture model of technology transfer was applied to the automobile sector with limited success. Honda and Toyota were obliged to establish joint ventures with the same Chinese manufacturer, allowing the latter to use the best of both systems to develop its own brand and production. Yet only Chery and Jeely have emerged as local brand manufacturers, and they produce only a tenth of the 2,000,000 passenger cars produced in China.

Beyond the debate on the role of joint ventures in technology transfer in general, the government succeeded in encouraging strong competition among foreign multinationals to bring their best technology when they locate in China. The fact that China's intellectual property protection is limited has not acted as a major deterrent. Zhao even finds that patents developed in China displayed uninterrupted growth between 1993 and 2000.[23] Besides, protection is improving gradually, as China now has more interest in strengthening protection as it becomes an innovator itself.

Multinationals are increasingly conducting research and development (R&D)[24] in China (Liu et al. estimate that China has around 300 multinational R&D centres).[25] This is partly the result of specific policies to attract multinational R&D centres. As a result, Liu et al. report a great deal of cooperation between foreign companies and Chinese universities and government research institutes, which should allow universities to become more informed about the global technology frontier and benefit from spillover effects. However, a sobering statistic is provided by the Commission for Science and Technology of Beijing, which finds that from 2001 to 2006, 94 per cent of the technology sold by 52 multinationals with R&D centres in Beijing was bought by their headquarters and other subsidiaries in China, implying that there was no leakage of knowledge outside the multinational. This not altogether surprising statistic illustrates that multinationals are predominantly closed knowledge systems that rely on an intracompany network that is a network within the firm. Given that this is a multinational competitive advantage, why would it allow that precious knowledge to leak? It takes a very astute negotiator, like the Chinese government, to ensure that the multinational finds a worthwhile benefit in creating an external knowledge network with Chinese institutions, outside the multinational firm. Again, this rings alarm bells: joint ventures may not be the most appropriate source of global knowledge for every emerging market.

For China, another more subtle means of access to global knowledge has been its diaspora. Indeed, according to Naughton, in the entire 1985–2005 period, Hong Kong, Taiwan, Macau and other tax havens (which are largely associated with Hong Kong, Taiwan and Macau funds) accounted for 60 per cent of total FDI in China;[26] hence, the Chinese government's decision to set up the first export-processing zones opposite Hong Kong and Taiwan. Multinationals from these countries first moved their labour-intensive operations to China, whose opening to foreign investment was a boon at a time when Hong Kong and Taiwan exporters wanted to escape increasing wages and costs at home, as capabilities in their home countries were becoming higher skilled. Gradually they started to move more technology-intensive operations to China, especially in the electronics industry. For instance, in the notebook computer industry, the production of monitors and motherboards was moved to China in 2002–3. In other words, Hong Kong and Taiwanese investors have turned China into an assembler of high-tech exports, although, as explained below, China's ability to assemble high-tech products does not mean that it has acquired significant technological capability in the process.

In summary, China's exposure to globalization has been anything but passive: the government adopted a strategy, which sourced the best global knowledge from abroad in the forms that were the most likely to build local capability. Perhaps the best illustration of the benefits of China's managed globalization model has to do with the aspect of globalization China decided to opt out of. China's choice not to liberalize the capital account was very judicious from an innovation perspective. Indeed, China's capital account, unlike Brazil's or Russia's, was not liberalized. This meant that in China investment was not diverted into portfolio inflows, as it was in Brazil or Russia. where portfolio flows never yielded any innovation dividend. Conversely, the decision by China not to allow portfolio inflows meant that productive investments with the potential for technology transfer and innovation flocked to China instead.

Model 2: Russia, or rebuilding the infrastructure for indigenous innovation

History of economic reform

Unlike China, whose gradualist approach to economic reform was a major success, Russia opted for a 'big bang' approach to reform with mixed results. A critical mass of market reforms was implemented in the winter of 1991–2, under the leadership of Deputy Prime Minister Yegor Gaidar and President Yeltsin. In the context of quasi-complete shortages and state bankruptcy, Gaidar emphasized the need for instant liberalization of prices (domestic, export and import), macroeconomic stabilization and privatization. The so-called big bang, launched in January 1992, was to be completed in one year. Radical price liberalization and balancing the consolidated state budget were its two pillars. Upon price liberalization, prices rose instantly by 250 per cent; shortages diminished gradually. Gaidar also focused on a few major cuts in the state budget. Price liberalization eliminated large price subsidies de facto, and military procurement was slashed by 85 per cent.

Upon first inspection, the overall reforms seemed successful. According to Aslund, Gaidar turned a budget deficit of 31 per cent of GDP in 1991 into a slight budget surplus on a cash basis of 0.9 per cent in Q1 1992.[27] However, macroeconomic imbalances, such as continuously spiralling inflation and collapsing output, remained unresolved. Indeed, between 1990 and 1995 GDP declined by roughly 50 per cent, and industrial output fell by over 50 per cent because of the paralyzing effect of heavy political lobbying: 'as early as spring 1992, the government came under strong pressure from various lobbies. The agrarian lobby was the most effective, and by summer of 1992 it had actually wiped out the success of stabilization in the early months of reform', according to Sergei Vasiliev, an adviser to Gaidar.[28]

As for privatization, it was a failure which set the tone of the Russian economy for years to come. Because high inflation had wiped out the savings of the Russian people, they could not afford to buy the privatized enterprises. Even if they did, they were faced with high interest rates and few funding sources to restructure the enterprises. As Stiglitz notes, 'not only did ownership have to change but so did management; and production had to be reoriented, from producing what firms were told to produce to producing what consumers wanted. This restructuring would, of course, require new investment, and in many cases job cuts. Job cuts help overall efficiency, of course, only if they result in workers moving from low-productivity jobs to high-productivity employment. Unfortunately, too little of this positive restructuring occurred'.[29]

In conclusion, until 1998 the macroeconomic results of reform were poor, mainly because of lasting high inflation and the opposition of lobbies to reform. Rent seeking prevailed, high inflation persisted until 1996 and the budget deficit averaged 9 per cent of GDP from 1993 to 1998. Between 1991 and 1998 the initial package of radical reforms served to ensure that the market economy survived but did little else. The financial crash of August 1998 functioned as a catharsis that cleansed the Russian economy. From 1999 to 2008 stability returned, as high oil prices, an initially weak currency and increasing domestic demand helped the economy grow.

Trade and FDI liberalization reform, which suffered from the same weaknesses as domestic reform, was conducted at the same time as domestic price liberalization. Before export prices were liberalized, at the time of the Soviet union, export contracts were signed by the state. When Gaidar attempted to liberalize export prices in early 1992, liberalization was delayed by a strong energy lobby. Because of the collapse of the Council for Mutual Economic Assistance, which was a trading bloc between Russia and other communist states, Russian exports of machinery declined, and primary goods became prominent among Russian exports, which explains why the government was paralyzed by the energy lobby. In the spring of 1992, the state price of oil was still 1 per cent of the world market price. Even in 1993 the average Russian oil price was only 8.3 per cent of the world market price. Managers of state companies acquired oil at fixed state prices and sold it abroad at the world market price, thereby creating a massive rent economy. As Joseph Stiglitz has said, 'instead of making money by creating new enterprises, managers got rich from a new form of the old entrepreneurship-exploiting mistaken government policies'.[30] The total export rents amounted to 30 per cent of GDP in 1992. As a result of the efforts of the energy lobby, President Yeltsin decided not to fully liberalize the energy sector.

Instead, by opting for a gradual hike in energy prices, he created one of the largest sources of rents in the world.

When it came to import prices, liberalization also had major repercussions. While the Soviet Union existed, state committees decided upon purchases of imported goods; there was always a shortage of consumer goods. When import prices were liberalized in 1993, the so-called shuttle trade flourished: thousands of individuals and small firms became importers of consumer goods from Poland and Turkey and from China and other East Asian countries. Import-penetration ratios increased to almost 50 per cent in some consumer goods industries.

As for FDI, the first joint ventures were allowed into Russia in 1987, with foreign ownership restricted to 49 per cent. But FDI was fully liberalized through the 1991 Foreign Direct Investment law, which stipulates non-discrimination between national and foreign investors and allows FDI in most sectors, with a cap on foreign ownership at 11 per cent of total capital for natural resources, 12 per cent for banking, 15 per cent for insurance, 25 per cent for aerospace and 25 per cent for electricity.

Ever since its economic revival in 1998, Russia has become increasingly integrated into global trade. Its share of world exports has grown rapidly, fostered by the Chinese commodity boom. It grew from 1.64 per cent in 2000 to 2.63 per cent in 2010. At 55 per cent of GDP, the share of trade in Russia's GDP is nearly as high as China's 55.4 per cent. After 15 years of struggle and reform, Russia was the last of the BRICs to enter the WTO (2011). This accomplishment symbolizes its determined effort to be recognized as a global trading power. Russia is also very open in terms of FDI, with an FDI-to-GDP share of 20.5 per cent, the highest among the BRICs. But the fact that the terms of investment can be modified from one day to the next by the Russian government has led to a high degree of caution on the part of potential foreign direct investors. To compensate for this the Russian government has established a US$10 billion FDI fund in order to bring in private equity groups and sovereign wealth funds to co-invest with the state. Yet, co-investment with the state is unlikely to make up for the volatality of the Russian government's decision-making, as BP, in its joint venture with TNK, found out to its detriment.[31] In that sense, government control over FDI is just as strong as it is in China; hence, the Russian government's control over the globalization process can also be qualified as managed globalization. Yet whether in Russia it is as geared towards goals of national development and innovation as in China is a different story.

Global knowledge

Russia has an important similarity with Brazil: with the exception of its defence-related industrial complex and a strong production base in non-electric machines and equipment, it is a commodity-based economy. It has the largest-known natural gas reserves in the world and the second-largest coal reserves. It is the world's second-largest oil producer and has the eighth-largest oil reserves. Domestically, its oil and gas industry alone is responsible for 10.2 per cent of gross value added. To a large extent, high revenues from oil have been enough to keep the economy afloat and increase wages without the government having to tackle structural reforms, which alone can increase productivity. To be sure, resource production will continue to be the bedrock of the economy, but even if the government chooses to continue building on this strength, future diversification has to be considered, even if only within the sector. Russia should support development of refineries to produce oil products and of smelters and processing facilities for metals and minerals.

As for diversification to other sectors, Russia also shares with Brazil the main challenge of creating a culture of innovation to help diversify its production structure. Notable during the reform period were the waning of machinery exports and the simultaneous boom in (1) oil and gas exports and (2) consumer imports. This period seems to mark the beginning of a regression in Russia's innovative capability, a deterioration that has often been blamed on trade and FDI liberalization, in so far as foreign influences have not acted as sources of global knowledge but have instead resulted in regression. Such analysis seems irrelevant, however, given that Russia was once itself at the innovation frontier; thus, access to global knowledge could never be a sufficient answer to Russia's current lack of domestic innovation. Russia's challenge is above all one of transition, a major aspect of which involves the restoration and reinvigoration of pre-existing domestic innovative capability.

On the face of it and unlike Brazil, all Russia needs to do is re-create a culture of innovation. The foundations of the Russian science and technology system were put in place in 1917. From 1922 to 1940, employment in the science and scientific-services sector grew from 35,000 to 362,000. There was intensive investment in R&D facilities and equipment to carry out research in the most important areas of science and technology. Hence, according to Gokhberg et al., 'in the years up to the 1980s, an extremely large R&D base was developed, greater, in absolute terms, than that of most of the industrially developed countries'.[32] In theory, then, the role of global knowledge in catalyzing innovation should be less critical: if the base for innovation was there, why not just revive it? It should be much easier and cheaper than to source it from abroad.

In reality, whether this is true depends on the extent of the rebuilding required and on the new requirements of a market economy. The basic foundations of the R&D system inherited from Soviet times clashed violently with the requirements of a market economy: according to Gokhberg et al., the old system was very large, centrally directed and government financed.[33] Hence, the R&D sector suffered a major crisis in the course of its own transition. To start with, the economic collapse which followed the early reform years meant that there was no money available to finance R&D. But when growth returned in 1999, it was not growth based on innovation, largely because there was an imbalance between resources devoted to research activities in public institutions and innovation performance. Yet research in public institutions has always been strong. What is going wrong then? Demand for R&D comes mostly from government. Why so? According to Gokhberg et al., 'investment in innovation is considered by private businesses to be more risky and less profitable than investment in mining and quarrying activities (especially natural gas and oil)'.[34] Such is the 'curse' of abundant natural resources. With 34 per cent of Russia's goods exports consisting of crude oil (1.2% of exports are high-tech products), where does the case for innovation lie?

More than access to global knowledge, a culture of innovation is what is missing in Russia. What good is importing state-of-the-art knowledge if there is no will to use it? It seems in this case that the rebuilding of a local innovative capacity and spirit does take precedence over the sourcing of external knowledge. Not that there is no role for external knowledge; the Russian government is right to promote its own Silicon Valley – namely, a technology hub at Skolkovo, near Moscow, in which Cisco and the Massachusetts Institute of Technology (MIT) have invested. MIT has committed itself to collaborate with Russian researchers in the creation of the Skolkovo Institute of Science and Technology, a three-year collaborative project whose purpose is to bring Russian scientists together with foreign peers. This type of project could be a catalyst of local innovation. Yet the rebuilding of local innovative capacity requires, first and foremost, the re-creation of links between the Russian innovation system's constituent parts, which have become disjointed. Isolated R&D by public research institutes has not done the trick. Networks connecting public and private research institutes and firms are needed to reinvigorate the capabilities of a country that was once a science and technology giant. Skolkovo may act as a catalyst, but these networks are key to re-creating a sustainable culture of innovation.

Model 3: Brazil: *dependencia* again, or a BRIC status on loan from China

History of economic reform

Brazil's integration into the world economy is the least intense of the BRICs: it has the lowest trade-to-GDP ratio of the BRICs (23.8%) and a low ratio of merchandise exports to the world total (1.33%). This is largely the result of a history of autarkic policies, which were put in place in the 1960s and provided the foundations of Brazilian industry. Brazil was one of the Latin American pioneers of import-substitution industrialization (discussed above). In the 1980s, when the neoliberal ideology replaced the state-heavy ideology, import substitution was viewed as heresy and swiftly replaced by the new creed of trade and FDI liberalization. This development, common in policy circles the world over in the 1980s, also occurred in Brazil. Yet here the old import-substituting industries, which were negatively affected by trade liberalization in the short term (especially the automotive industry), became a powerful and effective lobby group against trade liberalization. Overall, it is fair to say that industry has been relatively protected from global competition. This fact is reinforced by the level of Brazil's average simple MFN tariff, 13.7 per cent, the highest among the BRICs. In that context, it is remarkable that Brazil is much more FDI-intensive than it is trade-intensive, in so far as inward FDI (i.e., into Brazil) constitutes 22.9 per cent of GDP, well above China's 9.9 per cent. Recently, the strengthening of the Brazil-China relationship has de facto increased the exposure of Brazilian industry to Chinese competition via both trade and FDI, as is explained below.

In the early nineties, Brazil opted for trade and capital liberalization in the context of creeping inflation rates, which reached 2,447 per cent in 1993. According to Cassiolato and Vitorino, 'the idea was to enforce the integration of the Brazilian economy into the globalizing economy in order to guarantee price competition between national and international (tradable) products, and to ensure that internal prices would be stable'.[35] At the same time, foreign capital was brought in to finance the Brazilian balance of payments deficit. This resulted in an increase in short-term capital inflows, which were mostly speculative. Yet in the 1990s Brazil was also a major destination for FDI due both to the process of privatization that swept the country during this decade and to liberal FDI policies. Restrictions on the entry and operation of foreign companies in the information technology sector were lifted, financial flows were partially liberalized and a series of amendments to the constitution (mostly adopted in 1995 and 1996) did away with the distinction between national and foreign companies, as well as state monopolies in telecommunications, oil and gas. Overall the effects of trade and capital liberalization were less than impressive. While capital inflows did stabilize inflation, the 1993–8 period was characterized by currency overvaluation and very high interest rates, resulting in very low levels of economic growth. Despite the autarkic roots of Brazilian economic policy once the decision to liberalize was taken, policy makers made no attempt to 'manage' globalization in Chinese style or exercise sectoral selectivity in Korean style. While Brazil thus became a textbook example of orthodox, undiscriminating liberalization, it has less to show for it than China has to show for managed globalization. China's engagement with globalization was in fact more intense than Brazil's, and China succeeded in channelling global forces into a national development strategy in a way that Brazil did not.

The main achievement of Brazilian reforms has been to create the necessary conditions for a strengthening of the economic relationship between Brazil and China. Arguably, the current golden economic age Brazil is experiencing is related to its central role in the commodity boom opened up by China's increasing demand for resources. In short, the Brazil-China relationship has allowed Brazil to acquire BRIC status. Indeed, China now accounts for 15.2 per cent of Brazil's total exports, whereas the United States, which used to be Brazil's main partner, is now far behind at 9.5 per cent. Similarly, the boom of Chinese FDI into Brazil reflects China's central role in the Brazilian economy. In 2010 China accounted for about US$17 billion of Brazil's total FDI inflows of US$48.5 billion. In 2009 China became the largest importer of Brazilian products, and in 2010 the Chinese craze for Brazilian products continued, as exports to China increased by over 46 per cent relative to 2009, reaching US$31 billion.

But China is after commodities, not just any exports. Brazil has always been a big commodities exporter, but today it is the world's largest exporter of coffee, sugar, chicken, beef and orange juice; the second-largest grower of soybeans; and the third largest exporter of maize, all of which are increasingly in Chinese demand. Ironically, in the 1950s Celso Furtado and other economists from the United Nations Economic Commission for Latin America were among the first to blame underdevelopment on *dependencia*, the dependence of commodity-exporting developing countries on 'core' countries.[36] They argued that Brazil also suffered from a second type of dependency: reliance on commodities as the centre of economic development strategy..In particular, Raoul

Prebisch and Hans Singer even suggested that Latin America was suffering from a secular deterioration of its terms of trade due to the diminishing value of commodity exports relative to developed-country-manufactured imports.[37] It may seem that the liberalization of the 1990s has rewarded Brazil with a superficial BRIC status, but in reality Brazil is now dependant on a new core country for its commodity exports – mainly China.

Until 2007 Brazilian growth averaged 2.6 per cent a year – a long way from China and India's 8 per cent. Since 2008, however, Brazilian growth has picked up; it reached 7.5 per cent in 2010 despite the global recession. That fact could be revealing the real story behind Brazil's BRIC status: it could well be borrowed from Chinese growth. The privileged position of its special relationship with China has allowed Brazil to outperform other countries which do not benefit from this relationship and have sunk in the context of recession. Thanks to booming commodity exports driven by Chinese demand, Brazil records large trade surpluses and dollar reserves that approach US$300 billion. Brazil has been able to pay-off foreign creditors early and even become a heavy net creditor – to a large extent thanks to the inflow of Chinese dollars from the commodities boom. These benefits of Chinese dependency are not to be sneered at.

Yet dependency on China begs the question of how long Brazil can maintain its position among the BRICs as a high growth economy. This question is related to another: 'How sustainable is the commodity boom powered by China?' Some think that China's demand shift is permanent, that it is tied to the emergence of a sustainable middle class. But if there is a commodity bust and Brazil does not show that it can outlive the commodity boom and maintain high growth rates beyond it, today's Brazilian economy will be no different from the one prior to the 1990s that depended on natural resource exports. Hence, while Brazil's relationship with China appears to spur record growth, one has to ask whether it is leading to Brazil's de-industrialization. In that sense, the end of the Brazilian miracle could come from the so-called Dutch disease, whereby commodity exports inflate the value of a country's currency, which in turn undermines domestic industry. The recent find of 50 billion barrels of oil in the pre-salt deposits of the Santos basin, which is expected to boost the share of the oil industry in GDP from 10 to 25 per cent, is likely to aggravate this disease. In reality, the Dutch disease has already taken hold of Brazil: while the Brazilian real appreciated 108 per cent between early 2003 and the end of 2010, the share of manufactured exports in the Brazilian export mix fell from 55 to 44 per cent, while that of raw materials increased from 28 to 41 per cent. Brazil may have a trade surplus with China thanks to its commodity exports, but the 2010 trade balance in manufactured goods shows a record US$23.5 billion deficit, up from US$600 million in 2003, with imports of manufactured goods from China rising 60 per cent in 2010. No doubt the Brazilian central bank has introduced capital controls to weaken the currency,[38] yet this is not a long-term response to Brazil's double dependency on commodities and China.

Global knowledge

The most effective way for Brazil to overcome the limitations of dependency is to acquire innovative capability, first by accessing global knowledge and then by innovating by itself. Between 1990 and 1998 Brazilian government circles largely assumed that trade liberalization and encouragement of foreign investment would naturally result in innovation. According to Koeller and Cassiolato, the idea was 'that the process of trade liberalization would induce enterprises to innovate, as part of their struggle to survive'.[39] Put differently, a 'competition shock' would result from eliminating or reducing tariffs, eliminating subsidies and incentives and strengthening competition. The assumption was that competition would create pressure for new products and processes and would lower costs, hence stimulating innovation. In reality, liberalization had two results. It lowered the cost of imported capital goods and encouraged their substitution for existing domestically produced machinery and equipment; the coefficient of import penetration in machinery and electronic goods jumped from 29 per cent in 1993 to around 70 per cent in 1996. At the same time, subsidiaries of multinational corporations discontinued local engineering activities that they used to undertake in order to adapt or improve product and process technologies provided by their parent companies. According to Koeller and Cassiolato, 'as they could operate on the basis of imported parts and components, these firms reformulated their "adaptive engineering" strategies and discontinued domestic technological programmes that were justified in the more closed economy of the past'.[40] Another reason the innovation potential of FDI was not fully realized was that a large percentage of total FDI, motivated by the advantages afforded by the protected domestic market, involved little innovation, or else it was motivated by the goal of exploiting domestic natural resources in the context of privatization. Though Brazil could offer investors a large market as a bargaining chip, the pull of this particular market was not as great as that of the Chinese market. In the 1990s investors still perceived Brazil as a fairly risky bet despite its large market, especially in terms of macroeconomic stability.

At the same time, Brazil's government was not as skilled as China's at inducing a transfer of knowledge from investors. In the 1990s, in the auto and the oil exploration and production sectors, market access was made conditional on the fulfilment of trade-related investment measures, including requirements concerning the trade balance in the auto industry and national content in the auto and oil sectors. But the Brazilian government lacked bargaining power, because the pull of the Brazilian market was not the same as the pull of the Chinese market. This has, of course, changed since Brazil acquired BRIC status, and the government has used increased bargaining power to tighten the terms of foreign entry particularly in the oil sector, following the discovery of substantial oil reserves in the Santos basin. But if one goes back to the early years of liberalization – the ones that matter to the developing countries looking to emulate the BRICs – Brazil's liberalization story is the story of China's liberalization in reverse; that is, a story of sweeping trade and capital liberalization with few effective conditions. The Brazilian government, unlike the Chinese, did not set the terms of engagement with globalization; consequently, Brazil did not reap substantial innovation rewards in the post-liberalization period.

Interestingly, Brazil's few successful innovation sectors were largely a product of domestic R&D efforts undertaken in the pre-liberalization period, when Brazil practiced import-substitution industrialization and the state created innovation-intensive state-owned companies in some key sectors. These efforts produced Brazil's current islands of excellence: petroleum and gas, aeronautics, biofuels, agro-industry, mineral ores, paper and cellulose. Possibly as a reflection of this successful outcome, over the period 1999–2006, the Brazilian government put in place a specific innovation policy. The idea was that because liberalization had not produced an innovation dividend, the state had to make it happen domestically. Sectoral funds were created as incentives for R&D, with a view to rebuilding the capacity for promoting and financing R&D and innovation. These funds experienced some degree of success.

The most exciting prospects for Brazilian innovation policy are in the oil sector. Arguably the greatest event in recent Brazilian economic history, the discovery of oil in the Santos basin, could prompt local innovation excellence. Yet many fear that this discovery could create a 'resource curse' for Brazil, resulting in poor governance and corruption, as it has in Venezuela or Nigeria. As Harvard's Kenneth Rogoff puts it, 'it's a little bit like you've gotten rich, and how do you prevent your kids from being lazy?' But the oil could just as well create a new pole of domestic innovation and expertise. Indeed, because the exploitation of the Santos basin involves deep-water drilling beneath a layer of salt hundreds of kilometres from the coast, if Brazilian engineers can meet this challenge through domestic R&D, they can develop a niche in this particular type of extraction and sell their expertise to other markets with similar geology. This would allow Brazil to become a major oil services centre. Already the Federal University of Rio de Janeiro's engineering centre, Coppe, has built an 'ocean tank' that it says is the world's largest, to simulate wave patterns on oil platforms. Similarly, the state-owned oil company Petrobras has assembled computer power of about 190 teraflops, the largest capacity in Latin America, to process data on the layers of salt. The government is sending a clear message to foreign companies through its local content requirement: it limits the scope for foreign companies to develop deep-water drilling expertise in the Santos basin, as Petrobras is the sole operator of fields in the new discoveries, with a minimum 30 per cent stake in any project in the area. The message is 'lay off our oil resources'. Whether Petrobras will be able to maintain this 'monopoly' position, considering the masses of oil tankers, platforms and drilling rigs which will be required to extract the oil, is a question still to be answered.

Model 4: India, the reluctant globalizer

History of economic reform

India is the most globalization-phobic of the four BRIC economies. Its economic opening was reluctant and partial, in contrast with China's enthusiastic liberalization. Significant economic reform began only in 1991, after a macroeconomic and mainly fiscal collapse forced India to approach the International Monetary Fund (IMF) and World Bank. Before then, the economy had functioned on the basis of a system of Soviet-style planning, whose rationale disappeared together with the Soviet Union in 1991. Hence, the call for help; the IMF and World Bank were more than happy to extend financial assistance subject to India's fulfilling a set of economic reforms, including fiscal consolidation, devaluation of the rupee, market determination of exchange rates, trade and investment liberalization and financial sector reform. In India, unlike China, the reform process was not gradual and experimental; it was very much dictated by external financial institutions via the central government in a top-down approach. While the overall results of reform were significant, they were much less conclusive than in China, according to Saith; in the post-reform period labour productivity went up by 2.2 to 3.5 times (versus 2.5–2.9 times in China) and total factor productivity growth went up by 3.6 to 5 times (versus 8–14 times).[41] These figures are very meaningful given China and India's structural similarities before China embarked on reform in 1978; in 1950 China's per capita GDP at 1960 prices was US$65, and India's was US$62; in the labour force the share of agriculture was 77 per cent in China and 72 per cent in India; in China in 1952, the share of agriculture in total output was 48 per cent, in India in 1950, it was 51 per cent.

As for trade issues, India was invited to sign the General Agreement on Tariffs and Trade as a founding member in 1946. Yet ever since, it has fought for an 'exemption status' for developing countries, one that would allow them to stall their trade liberalization process on account of the special circumstances they face in having to catch up and industrialize. While India's post-1991 trade and investment regime invites foreign trade and investment on paper, the reality is that India is a reluctant liberalizer and one of the most protected economies in the developing world. Again, this is well illustrated by a comparison with China. While simple average bound tariffs in China are a modest 9.6 per cent, they are 13 per cent in India. The simple average of China's applied MFN tariffs is close to its bound rate, while India's is far below the bound rate. In fact, in line with its aversion to liberalization, India is resisting international pressures for it to lower its bound tariff levels. Only 10 per cent of Chinese tariff lines carry a tariff of more than 25 per cent, whereas more than 89 per cent of India's are above 50 per cent. More important, India is the top WTO user of anti-dumping measures,[42] which are the most protectionist measures in existence. An examination of WTO data shows that its usage of these measures shows no signs of a decrease. Between 1995 and 2006, India initiated 457 such measures, or 15 per cent of the world total of 3045. Between 1995 and 2010, it had initiated 637 out of 3853 measures – 16.5 per cent of the total.[43] Thus, India initiated 180 measures in the last 4 years versus 457 in the first 11 years of the WTO. The filings of the last 4 years amounted to 28 per cent of the total Indian anti-dumping complaints of the last 15 years, indicating no change in India's resort to anti-dumping.

The results of India's reluctant liberalization in terms of trade indicators are clear: India's share in world merchandise exports has risen only to 1.44 per cent in 2008 from 0.5 per cent in 1983, and its share of imports to 1.4 per cent from 0.7 per cent, making it only the world's

28th-largest exporter and 17th-largest importer. Even in commercial services, which would seem to be where India's comparative advantage lies, it has only a 2.7 per cent share of world exports and 2.7 per cent of world imports, making it the 10th-largest exporter and 12th-largest importer, while China, which is not even specialized in commercial services, has an export share of 3.2 per cent and an import share of 3.8 per cent. Measures of capital liberalization tell the same story. According to the UN Conference on Trade and Development's Global Investment Trends Monitor,[44] FDI inflows into India in 2010 were only US$23.7 billion (up from US$0.24 billion in 1990) versus more than US$100 billion going to China. In the first quarter of 2011, India attracted only US$3.4 billion in inflows, down 25 per cent from the first quarter of 2010. Perceptions of the Indian government's aversion to foreign direct investment and a less-than-enticing investment climate have prevented foreign penetration through FDI. The breakdown of flows by sector shows that the heavier the hand of the state in a particular sector (mining, energy, chemicals), the lower the foreign investment. That being said, the relative weight of FDI in the economy has grown significantly, so that inward FDI stock now represents 12 per cent of GDP. Also, at the beginning of 2012 there has been a genuine move towards greater capital liberalization, with two key measures taken by the government early in 2012: the Indian governmetn widened India's investor base by allowing foreign nationals, trusts and pension funds to invest directly in Indian equity markets while foreign single-brand retailers were permitted to own their Indian stores outright.

Global knowledge

India is a fascinating country for those interested in the relationship between innovation and exposure to globalization. Indeed, almost all Indian policies formulated from the mid-1960s were intended to influence either domestic generation or imports of technology or both, and that includes policies relating to industry, trade and investment. Indeed, innovation has been shaped by successive policy reforms to either regulate or liberalize the Indian economy and its sources of knowledge in particular. One can distinguish two policy phases. The goal of the first phase up to the 1980s was technological self-reliance under restrictive rules, which resulted in a streamlining of the procedure for approving foreign investment proposals. This pre-liberalization phase has had significant implications for the development of Indian innovation. The Foreign Investment Board was set up to deal with all cases involving foreign investment of less than 20 million rupees and within the 40 per cent equity limit. The government also made a list of industries where foreign collaboration was considered necessary and of those where technical collaboration could be permitted. Foreign collaboration was severely restricted, and FDI was allowed only in core industries where no alternative local technologies were available. As a result, there was a marked decline in reliance on foreign technology, with foreign collaborations during the early 1970s falling to levels less than half those approved in the early 1960s. At the same time, imports of capital goods were subjected to monitoring and regulation by the state.

The second policy phase, dating from 1980, took a more liberal approach to technology imports, with a radical intensification of the approach from 1991, according to Joseph and Abrol.[45] The switch to liberalization was prompted by the inability of protectionist, phase 1 policies to achieve higher growth rates of productivity and output. The centrepiece of the second phase was alliance building with foreign companies, much as China's early liberalization was focused on this goal through joint ventures. Indian firms were allowed to enter into collaboration with foreign firms of their own choice, with a view to increasing the take-up of imported technological know-how. Finally, like China, India has recently allowed foreign companies to set up R&D facilities in the country. That would seem to be the most direct channel for a transfer of knowledge, but here again that is not necessarily the case. As was noted in the case of China, without any specific policies to ensure that R&D internal to the multinationals spills over to the economy, there is no reason to believe that a transfer of global knowledge will take place.

In the meanwhile, liberalization coincided with a steady decline in government R&D expenditure as a proportion of GDP. After a high of 0.91 per cent was reached in 1987–8, there was a steady decline to 0.71 per cent by the mid-1990s. This is one reason why total factor productivity (TFP), which is the main source of long-term growth, was lower in the 1990s – that is, under liberalization – than in the 1980s. Arguably, another reason was that the mechanism whereby global companies were supposed to help fill the knowledge gap of backward local companies and trigger local innovative capability did not work. Hence, the companies that did best out of liberalization were (1) multinationals, which already had the top technologies and came mainly for market access; followed by (2) those domestic firms which had only a small technology gap with the multinationals.

However, the overall picture of stagnating domestic technology is qualified by the success of two sectors: software and information technology services and pharmaceuticals. In the 1990s, the former sector recorded an annual compound growth rate over 50 per cent. Software and services now account for over 20 per cent of merchandise exports. In this sector, even though top multinationals are competing with Indian firms, domestic firms continue to hold a leading position. Yet just as Brazil's sectoral islands of excellence are an inheritance from the days of state-led autarkic industrial policy, Indian excellence in information technology services is largely related to the government's promotion of domestic innovation through autarky in phase 1. Phase 1 policies prepared the industry to withstand global competition. The main achievement of the autarkic period had been to create an infrastructure base for science and technology, including research labs, higher education institutions and highly skilled human resources, which are obviously the key inputs for a skill-intensive sector like information technology. In that sense, the sector is very much indebted to the architects of the first phase of innovation policy.

India's second island of excellence, pharmaceuticals, owes its emergence to a more specific aspect of innovation policy: a weak intellectual property regime. This regime facilitated copying and reverse engineering and was designed to protect the nascent domestic industry. It abolished product patents on food, chemicals and drugs and reduced the life of patents from 14 to 5 years from the date of the sealing of the patent or 7 years from the date of filing, whichever came earlier. In particular, the lack of protection of process patents helped develop a strong indigenous pharmaceutical industry. Domestic firms were able to copy foreign products and produce them with slightly different processes, leading to 'marginal' adaptive innovations by Indian companies. By the time India extended process patents to pharmaceuticals (2005), it had developed a strong domestic industry that could compete with foreign firms. Hence, as regards both information technology and pharmaceuticals, one cannot attribute the development of these competitive industries to exposure to globalization in itself.

Finally, like China, India has sought to make use of its diaspora to source global knowledge by using special tax breaks to attract it back to India. Partly because it is, a much more recent phenomenon in India than in China this tactic has not yielded significant results as of 2012. Still, India's success in information technology services has been largely associated with linkages to its diaspora in the high-tech sectors of the United States and Europe.

The standard view is that development is likely to follow from an initial sourcing of global technology and a subsequent focus on local innovation yet India did it the other way around: it built the local capability first by blocking off the global supply of knowledge. This strategy had the advantage of applying liberalization to an already vibrant innovation system, one that had created a sound infrastructure science and technology base able to assimilate global knowledge relatively easily. Yet as India began to rely increasingly on global sources of knowledge, the domestic technology-generating effort stagnated, as measured by R&D expenditure at 0.71 per cent or by triadic patents per million population at 0.14, well behind China's 0.39. Still, excellence prevails in certain isolated sectors like information technology and pharmaceuticals. To a certain extent, it is as though the late access to global knowledge resulted in local innovators' growing lazy instead of combining their pre-existing local capability with the benefits of global knowledge. Is this a case of too much too late? It certainly contrasts with China's strategy of allowing global knowledge in from the early years of development yet with a close monitoring of its spillovers. Now China needs to make a transition to a system powered mainly by local innovation, while India still needs to learn to make the best of global knowledge for local innovation.

Conclusion: the role of institutions in overcoming global knowledge limitations

At least two conclusions can be drawn from the development trajectories of the four BRICs. First, exposure to globalization and global knowledge has the potential to catalyse economic transformation and development. While much global knowledge is protected by intellectual property rights, some is in the public domain; hence, policies of opening to global knowledge through trade, foreign direct investment, technology licensing and reverse engineering are helpful. Yet no country illustrates the fact that global exposure in itself does not ensure sustainable economic development better than China. This most enthusiastic globalizer among the BRICs may not continue to grow at the skyrocketing rates it has achieved recently. The lack of sustainability of the Chinese growth miracle is partly related to the limitations of a globalization-driven model of economic growth in stimulating the improvement of local innovation capability. Upon first inspection, the fact that machinery and electronics constitute 50 per cent of total Chinese exports seems to indicate that China has turned globalization to its advantage by becoming a high-technology exporter. In reality, subsidiaries of multinationals account for 88 per cent of high-tech exports. This fact suggests that China is merely the final assembler of high-tech goods, due to changes in the nature of production processes: just as the various parts of the manufacturing value chain have been sliced up and partly relocated to China for cost purposes, so, too, have the many services embedded in the high-technology value chain, leading to partial relocation to China. But the actual value added in China to these high-tech goods is limited, and the production process involved is often as labour intensive as the production process behind the garments and toys that were the hall-marks of China's early growth miracle. For instance, Chinese subsidiaries complete the most routine modules in integrated-circuit design, so that they function as an assembly point. While evolving from assembler of labour-intensive products to assembler of high-tech goods might constitute an apparent 'upgrade', China will become a sustainable economic power only when it has the technological capability to create as opposed to assemble. In that sense, the high trade-to-GDP ratio of China and even its high share of high-tech exports to total exports have done little to ensure the sustainability of the Chinese growth miracle. According to Naughton, who wrote in 2007, 'the root of China's comparative advantage is still in labour-intensive manufacturing, where the highly elastic supply of cheap semi-skilled labour will continue to work to China's benefit for at least a decade'.[46]

The notion that China can get away with cheap, semi-skilled specialization for much longer is highly doubtful. It is more likely that China, will need to focus on indigenous innovation and its institutional prerequisites, in order to continue growing (even if it ends up only at high single digits). Labour-intensive manufacturing can only be a source of growth for so long. The number of those between 15 and 24 years of age entering the Chinese workforce had already peaked in 2005 at 227 million and is likely to fall to 150 million by 2024 – a circumstance that in 2010 and 2011 resulted in double-digit increases in China's cost of labour.[47] The ageing population described in the introduction is one of the major constraints on a labour-intensive strategy. As it happens, China, which used global knowledge effectively as a development trigger, is itself well aware of the need to move on to a strategy focused on indigenous innovation. It is nowhere near where it wants to be in this respect; that is, on a par with South Korea and other high-income Asian countries, if not with the United States (see Table 1.3). South Korea is responsible for 43.9 triadic patents per million population, but China is responsible only for 0.39. Reaching Korean levels is a tall order.

Given that even South Korea itself has to work out a means of sustaining its own growth miracle at the current advanced stage of its development, the scale of the effort still required by China becomes all the more obvious, and it makes all the more sense for it to get a head start on its effort to build an indigenous innovation capability. Once China reaches the development level of South Korea, it may have further challenges to face. Eichengreen, Park and Shin show that the growth rate of fast-growing economies starts to slow by at least 2 percentage points as per capita income reaches about US$17,000 a year in 2005 international prices.[48] While China is expected to reach this level by 2015, South Korea surpassed it long ago – and sure enough, its annual growth rate has more than halved, from 10 per cent in the last 40 years to 4 to 5 per cent.

It can be argued that this slowdown is related to innovation bottlenecks, at least partly. While South Korea's record on patents is impressive (especially relative to China's), South Korea nonetheless faces an innovation challenge of its own. Its large industrial conglomerates were experts at improving imported technologies, including the high technology of touch-screen smartphones, but South Korea still lacks the start-ups and venture-capital firms that are an essential component of innovation. To some extent, the large conglomerates have not allowed such firms to emerge, as they have snapped up the most talented entrepreneurs and kept them in-house, thereby preventing them from spreading innovation by setting up their own shop. Furthermore, a major imbalance is emerging between competitive conglomerates and small firms. The latter spend only about half as much on R&D as large conglomerates per unit of sales. Since most of these small firms are involved in services, South Korea presents a dual economy of competitive manufacturers and uncompetitive services. No doubt China, as it seeks to complete the transition from an economy dominated by manufacturing to one dominated by services with higher added value, will be keen to avoid such an outcome. Overall, the lessons learned from the challenges faced by South Korea's high-income economy are all the more reason for China to kick-start its indigenous innovation effort as early as possible.

A second conclusion is that economic reform (including domestic reforms and trade and FDI liberalization) is only as effective as the reformers implementing it. Hence, institutions are the ultimate determinants of success. Here again, one can learn a lot from China. Saith argues that China's development can be traced to a system of 'mass mobilization that relied on massive inputs of human labour'.[49] Rural collectives and the household responsibility system can be seen as institutions which worked as engines of accumulation by ensuring an integration of agriculture and rural industry. Rural industrialization occurred within the collectives, which were based on using a skilled rural workforce that was competitive in unit costs. Saith believes that this labour-intensive mass mobilization system triggered the Chinese economic miracle. Playing a role similar to that of the collectives in domestic reform, the SEZs were the domestic institutions that made FDI liberalization work, yet it was the WTO, a global institution, that gave the Chinese leadership the legitimacy to impose reform.

But what lies behind the neutral terminology of 'institutions'? Institutions do not exist in a void. Who did the mobilizing, and how was it done? As Saith rightly notes, 'in India, the institutional framework specifies the context and constraints for policy formulation; in China, the institutional framework is itself a prime target variable, an object of policy'. The collectives, the SEZs and the WTO were institutions used by the state to fulfil China's development strategy. The role of China's authoritarian state in buttressing institutions conducive to growth cannot be ignored, and here the question of the apparent trade-off between economic growth and political freedom immediately raises its head.

There need not be a trade-off if one considers the sources of growth in a long-term perspective: economic growth itself suffers if the labour-intensive miracle of mass accumulation, which is orchestrated by the authoritarian state, does not evolve into an innovation-intensive miracle led by entrepreneurial individuals. There is a point where the state's main input into the development process is precisely to let other institutions take the lead in the creation of growth. Continued economic growth requires innovation and a new institution as the source of innovation; namely, Chinese entrepreneurs. To be effective innovators, entrepreneurs cannot be manipulated by the state. Just imagine Apple's Steve Jobs being told what to do by President Obama. Hence, the great irony for the Chinese government is that its legitimacy is based on the continued delivery of high growth rates, but it will only be able to continue delivering these rates if it gives into democratization. China's 2006–20 National Programme for the Development of Science and Technology represents an acknowledgement by the Chinese government that China needs a new engine of growth in the form of innovation. That is a step in the right direction, but until the government acknowledges that innovation requires entrepreneurs that are free to think, it will only be able to extend a growth built on marginal adaptation of Western technology and only for so long. Consequently, institutions and the political system need to change over the course of the development process, which is divided into two phases of economic transformation. In the first, the state plays a strong part in sourcing global knowledge and mobilizing the drivers of economic transformation. Then the state must step back to let individual creativity and innovation sustain economic transformation from below. This theory is developed in Chapter 5.

2
BRICs and Global Economic Power

A key idea in this book is that emerging markets are changing the face of the global economy but that their ability to dominate in non-economic spheres is more uncertain. This chapter focuses on the central dimensions of their economic domination; namely, their growing contributions to global economic growth, inflation, trade and finance. This data-heavy chapter aims at giving a sense of the overall size and forms of the emerging markets' engagement with the global economy and thereby provide the foundation for a deeper analysis in later chapters of the sustainability of the BRIC miracle.

Emerging markets to the rescue: economic growth

Despite growing criticism of it, the most widely used measure of a country's economic wealth remains GDP. By extension, the most obvious measure of the emerging markets' contribution to the global economy is their contribution to world GDP. After first examining the former contribution, the chapter swiftly turns to the emerging markets' contribution to the growth of world GDP per se, as it is a better indicator of which countries will dominate world GDP in the future, as opposed to today. According to Kose and Prasad, in 2008–9 emerging markets[1] as a whole accounted for almost 40 per cent of world GDP at PPP.[2] As was explained in the Introduction, increases in the shares of emerging markets are much greater when using PPP exchanges rates than when using market exchange rates, yet the trend of rising emerging market contribution to world GDP is undeniable, regardless of which metric is utilized. Among the emerging markets, as was also noted, the BRICs all together account for approximately 25 per cent of world GDP at PPP. Kose and Prasad focus on Brazil, China and India; they exclude Russian data, which they consider too patchy. They find that the 'BICs' account for 22.6 per cent of world GDP at PPP in 2009, up from 15.1 per cent in the period 1986–2009 and from 9 per cent in the period 1973–85. The BIC share's quasi-doubling between 1973 and 2009 is particularly striking, as is the fact that the BICs have now overtaken the EU-15 countries, which are, according to them, responsible for only 22 per cent of world GDP, and account for a share of world GDP quasi-equivalent to that of the United States (24%). The bulk of the growth in the BICs' contribution can be explained by China's and India's growing contributions. Kose and Prasad find that China's share of world GDP increased from 3.2 per cent during the period 1960–72 to 9.8 per cent during the period 1986–2009, while India's share rose from 4.4 to 5.6 per cent.

Behind these shares of world GDP at this point in time, there is a radical transformation occurring, one best captured by individual shares of world GDP growth. During the 1986–2009 period, emerging markets contributed around 40 per cent of world growth, up from 26 per cent in the 1973–85 period, just as the share of advanced economies[3] fell to about 57 per cent from 70 per cent in the earlier period.[4] Once again, focusing on the BICs, their contribution rose from 10.9 per cent to 22.2 per cent.

Having looked at the emerging markets' quantitative contribution to the world growth aggregate, the qualitative drivers of emerging market growth must be examined from a macroeconomic perspective, through a composition of emerging markets' growth contribution through the so-called Keynesian expenditure approach, which singles out contributions to final demand from consumption, investment and exports. This approach will give an understanding of what fuels emerging market growth and by extension, what increasingly fuels global growth. The BRICs' average contribution to world GDP growth over the period 1986–2007 was 1.37 per cent at PPP, largely powered by BIC exports, whose average contribution to world export growth reached 0.92 per cent, and BIC investment, whose average contribution to world investment growth reached 0.83 per cent. In contrast, the average contribution of BIC consumption to world consumption growth over this period was only 0.36 per cent. These data are strong confirmation (not that it was needed) that export and investment intensity are important characteristics of emerging market growth. The implications of this growth model are the focus of the rest of this book, which will reflect on the scope for change towards consumption-driven growth and on its benefits for the sustainability of the emerging market miracle.

Another macroeconomic approach which can yield greater insight into the nature of emerging market growth is the so-called output approach, which separates the contributions to output of each economic sector. It is striking that among emerging markets the share of agriculture has fallen significantly, but it still accounts for about 12 per cent of output, as opposed to 2 per cent in the advanced economies. The share of industry, has risen to 34 per cent of GDP in 1986–2000 from 29.7 per cent in 1973–85. Across emerging markets, industrial output has grown slightly faster than service sector output in the last two decades (the Indian services boom notwithstanding). Overall, while the aggregate phenomenon of impressive emerging market growth projects the image of modern economies ready to graduate to developed country status, the reality of emerging markets remains to a large extent that of developing countries. This has already been shown to be the case with reference to an output structure which still has a significant agricultural component. Beyond that, there are other dimensions in which emerging markets remain developing countries – inequality (see Chapter 4) and innovation (see Chapter 5).

The good comes with the bad: inflation

On the flip side of global growth, emerging markets have frequently hit the headlines as engines fuelling global inflation. Brazil, Russia, India and China post average annual inflation rates between 5 and 10 per cent. Arguably, Brazil and India are most at risk of overheating. The *Economist*'s 'overheating index', which ranks 27 emerging markets on the basis of inflation, GDP growth, unemployment, credit growth, real interest rates and the current account balance, puts Brazil in second-highest place, with 83 out of a maximum overheating of 100 (primarily due to risks of a credit bubble and tight labour markets), and India in fourth place, at 82 (primarily due to its negative real interest rates). China is much lower down the line, at 58 (14th place), and Russia even lower, at 42 (20th place), both thanks to spare capacity and in China thanks to more aggressive monetary policy tightening.

At the same time, Eurozone inflation rose to 3 per cent in November 2011 from a trough of –0.7 per cent in July 2009, and US inflation peaked at 3.9 per cent in September 2011 from a trough of –2.1 per cent. It is easy to argue that emerging markets, BRICs above all, are exporting their inflation. Yet this is only one half of the story.

Global inflation results from a combination of two factors: low interest rates in the United States and rigid exchange rates in emerging markets. In the aftermath of the subprime crisis, as the US Federal Reserve reduced interest rates, emerging markets with currencies tied to the US dollar were forced to run a loose monetary policy, irrespective of domestic inflationary pressures. This was especially true where currencies were most closely tied: Asian and Middle Eastern countries. Low domestic interest rates in emerging markets resulted in a rise in domestic demand, a rise in the demand for commodities and hence a rise in commodity prices, which culminated in emerging market inflation. Beyond the effect of loose US monetary policy on emerging market demand, another external driver behind emerging market inflation was that developed countries were (a) suffering from much lower growth rates relative to emerging markets and (b) suppressing domestic investment through record-low interest rates and hence returns. This combination resulted in a flow of surplus funds out of the developed economies. In turn, this surplus was recycled into speculation on commodities, which generated higher global commodity prices or investment into high return emerging market assets, causing asset bubbles and inflation in these countries.

An aspect of emerging market inflation that is not 'imported' from the developed countries has to do with the long-term rise in food prices (documented in greater detail in Chapter 4). While the food price rise involves some global factors in terms of speculation on so-called soft commodities, it is essentially structural, the result of a shift in the pattern of emerging market demand for food. In that sense, it is particularly problematic. Instead of higher food prices being imported from the developed countries just as loose monetary policy is, the opposite is occurring: emerging markets' growing demand for food has led to rising commodity prices, which spill over into high import prices for the non-emerging world. Hence, emerging markets are contributing to global inflation. At the same time, higher food prices also have serious domestic repercussions in those markets. As Chapter 4 explains, food price inflation has significant social implications that could threaten the emerging market economic miracle.

According to Morgan Stanley, these domestic and external forces, taken together, have left only 20 per cent of emerging markets – namely, Mexico, Chile, Colombia, the Czech Republic, Malaysia, South Africa, Thailand, Turkey, the UAE, Peru and Taiwan[5] – with no inflation worries. Solving the global inflation problem requires the cooperation of the United States and the emerging markets since, as already noted, global inflation has been partly generated by loose US monetary policy and pegged emerging market exchange rates. Fixing the problem requires change in both the policy and the exchange rate management. In June 2010 China abandoned the informal US dollar peg it had adopted in mid-2008, as did Kuwait; speculation has increased that Hong Kong, frustrated with its continued US dollar peg, might instead peg its currency to a basket of currencies, just like Singapore. But even if official pegs are abandoned, the problem, albeit slightly rephrased, will remain unchanged in essence. Once having switched to flexible exchange rates, how much appreciation will emerging markets be willing to tolerate?

Were emerging markets to decide to let their currencies appreciate against the dollar, they would still, despite skyrocketing growth rates, lack a key source of power in the world: the US Federal Reserve sets global monetary policy; they don't. This is arguably their greatest weakness in an otherwise impressive rise as a global economic force. This power asymmetry has implications beyond the political biases of UN Security Council representation or World Bank voting structures. It constrains emerging markets' ability to control their own monetary policy, which is by definition partly set by the Fed.

The fact is that if the Fed decides not to tighten monetary policy for some time, as seems to be the case, by default the onus is on emerging markets to let their currencies appreciate to solve their domestic inflation problems. China should be first among them to move, given that it has accumulated the highest value of foreign exchange reserves among emerging markets. While the export benefits of undervalued exchange rates cannot be denied, appreciation has real benefits in the fight against inflation.[6] In 2011 China let the renminbi appreciate by 4.3 per cent; much of this appreciation, recorded in the year's first ten months, coincided with the period when the inflation rate was highest. Not that exchange rate appreciation is sufficient to stall Chinese inflation: 2011's appreciation of 4.3 per cent pales in comparison with the 35 per cent rise in the annual average OPEC basket oil price relative to the 2010 annual average. Also, there is a limit to the extent of appreciation that the exporter lobbies, which tend to be strong in emerging markets, will tolerate. Still, emerging market leaders have undeniably seen exchange rate appreciation in a more positive light at the height of inflationary pressure.

This is no reason for the Fed to sit on its laurels and let the emerging markets stem the global inflation tide instead of itself tightening US interest rates, which it seems disinclined to do unless it comes to believe that US inflation has become entrenched and structural, as opposed to just being a temporary, imported phenomenon (currently, it seems that high unemployment is its main concern). In any case, central banks are not supposed to change domestic interest rates in response to such a temporary shock as imported inflation. Yet the cost of Fed inaction is far from insignificant. Letting the emerging markets sort out their inflation problems by themselves is not ideal. In order to combat domestic inflation, emerging markets have been tightening fiscal policy after a period of stimulus spending; such tightening has negative repercussions on developed economies relying on external demand from emerging markets. That is, emerging market inflation indirectly takes a toll on developed countries in the form of foregone economic growth. Failure to tackle a key cause of emerging market inflation – that is, ultraloose US monetary policy – could become equally detrimental to developed countries with sclerotic growth rates. Without cooperation between developed and emerging markets, globalization could become a mere mechanism for the contagion of economic ills and global inflation its prime symptom.

Emerging markets to the rescue: trade

Apart from growth and inflation, probably the most powerful embodiment of the ascent of emerging markets is their growing share of global trade. A good measure of it is the acceleration of emerging market export growth. According to Kose and Prasad, 'during the period 1960–72, the average growth rate of exports of emerging markets was lower than that of the advanced economies, but since the mid-1980s it has been more than twice higher than that of the advanced economies' exports'.[7] Emerging markets' export growth accounted for the lion's share of global export growth during the period between 1986 and 2009.

But it is not just a case of growth of emerging market exports in general. More specifically, a rising share of emerging market exports is destined for other emerging markets. Thus, in the words of Halper, 'the integration of developing nations with the global economy may not presage integration with the West'.[8] According to Kose and Prasad, the share of intra-emerging market trade in emerging markets' total trade increased nearly fivefold over the last five decades, from less than 9 per cent in 1960 to slightly more than 42 per cent in 2008.[9] During this period, the share of emerging markets' trade with advanced economies declined from 83 to 50 per cent. The role of the United States and Europe as final markets for emerging market exports has declined significantly. Put otherwise, the emerging markets are less and less dependent on advanced economies as an outlet for their products.

Table 2.1 Chinese trade with other BRICs, 2001 and 2009, US$ billions

	China exports 2001	China exports 2009	China imports 2001	China imports 2009
India	2	29	2	14
Russia	3	17	8	21
Brazil	1.5	14	2.5	28

Source: World Bank.

A look at the export patterns of the BICs in particular makes this feature remarkably clear. As noted by Halper, in each BIC 'the collective share of trade with South America, Africa, the Middle East, Russia and Asia is greater than with North America and Europe'.[10] In 2007 Brazilian merchandise exports amounted to US$158 billion; only 47 per cent of these exports were destined for North America and Europe. Indian exports amounted to US$146 billion, 38.3 per cent of which were similarly destined. Chinese exports amounted to US$1217 billion, with 43.3 per cent similarly destined.[11]

These figures mask one peculiarity of emerging market trade: its concentration. In particular, intra-BRIC trade, though greatly intensified, consists primarily of BRI trade with China. In other words, China is at the centre of BRIC integration. According to UBS research, China accounts for 12 per cent of trade among the BRICs, while Brazil, India and Russia devote only 3 per cent of their resources to such trade. This percentage share has not increased in the last decade.[12]

The heavy weight of China in BRIC trade can be seen from Table 2.1, especially in comparison with the weight of the second-greatest trade power among the BRICs – India – which is visible in Table 2.2. In fact, growing trade between China and India is one of the most salient developments in BRIC trade in recent years. China is now India's largest trade partner, which can be ascribed largely to a high volume

Table 2.2 Indian trade with other BRICs, 2001 and 2009, US$ billions

	India exports 2001	India exports 2009	India imports 2001	India imports 2009
China	1	12	2	31
Russia	1	1	1	4
Brazil	0.25	3	0.5	3.8

Source: World Bank.

of Indian imports of Chinese manufacturing products and, to a much lesser extent, to Indian services exports. Beyond the growing integration of China and India, China overtook the United States as Brazil's biggest trade partner last year, with Brazil mainly exporting commodities to China. Finally, Asia's economic growth, along with the push within Russia to develop trade ties outside its traditional partners in Europe, have turned China into Russia's largest trade partner, ahead of Germany, with Russia exporting commodities to China en masse. On one level, China's domination of BRIC trade flows illustrates the fact that there is only one economic superpower among the BRICs, which turns the BRICs into a legitimizing vehicle for Chinese ambitions. That being said, it is no surprise that China is at the heart of the BRIC trade: its internal trade dominance only reflects its increased weight within global trade. China is, after all, the world's largest exporter – during the period 1995–2007 China's market share in global exports almost tripled, from 4 to 11.8 per cent – and the most rapidly growing importer. Quantitatively, it is a given that China is in a different league from the rest of the BRICs. More problematic are the qualitative biases of China-BRI trade. To a large extent China is exporting its higher-tech manufacturing products to the BRI and arguably locking those nations into the production of commodity exports to China. (Brazil in particular comes to mind here, although recent agreements in the aircraft industry, which give Brazil's Embraer access to the Chinese market, are a sign that Brazilian policymakers are starting to hold their own in negotiations with China.) While China can be expected to look after its own interests alone, it is up to the BRI to ensure that their industrial policies do not allow the above trade specialization to become entrenched. Only by doing so are the BRI likely to become more nearly equal partners with China in the BRIC grouping.

Emerging markets to the rescue: finance

Measuring global financial integration

One simple way of assessing the emerging markets' absolute level of integration into global financial markets is to calculate the sum of their gross international financial assets and liabilities. Between 1986 and 2009 the gross stock of assets and liabilities of emerging markets rose rapidly; the total stood at nearly 20 trillion at the end of 2007, compared with about 165 trillion for the advanced economies.[13] Assets and liabilities can be divided into foreign direct investment, equity, debt and other categories. Looking further into the liabilities, one is struck by the fact that the share of debt in gross foreign liabilities of advanced economies remains dominant. The emerging markets' share of debt has fallen steeply, from about 80 per cent in 1985 to below 40 per cent in 2007, with substantial increases in the shares of FDI and portfolio equity making up the difference. This fall contrasts with the growing indebtedness of the Eurozone countries. The days when the emerging markets were at risk of a debt crisis seem long gone.

More interesting, perhaps, is the extent of financial integration across emerging and advanced markets. While financial flows among advanced economies still constitute the main driving force behind expanding global financial flows, the volume of flows between advanced and emerging markets has significantly increased over the past two decades. For example, Emerging Asian liabilities from a US origin constituted 4.8 per cent of Emerging Asia's GDP in 2004, and they jumped to 8.3 per cent in 2007; in the same years Emerging Asian liabilities from a Euro area origin jumped from 2.5 per cent of the Euro area's GDP to 5.5 per cent (the rise is less pronounced on the asset side). Yet intraregional flows have been on the rise for the past decade, especially in the Euro area and among emerging Asian markets. The sustained pace of intraregional financial integration in emerging Asia is indicated by the rapid increase – from 22 per cent (2004) to 38 per cent (2007) in its share of intraregional holdings of foreign assets (the same trend is observable in the case of foreign liabilities, with a lesser rise from 17.3 to 20.4 per cent). The trend, slightly similar to the rise in intra-BRIC trade noted in the previous section, confirms the notion that while emerging markets are growing contributors to the world economy, they are at least as concerned with increasing their linkages among themselves as with increasing their linkages with the rest of the world. In contrast, the share of intraregional Euro area holdings of foreign assets was already very high by 2004, at 62.7 per cent, but it remained largely stable in 2007, at 61 per cent (the same trend is observable in foreign liabilities, with a small rise from 62.9 to 63.2 per cent).

The next M&A power

A more specific aspect of emerging markets' integration into global finance can be observed in the form of their increasing share of global merger and acquisition (M&A) activity. M&A falls within the foreign direct investment subset of gross financial assets, which itself represents a growing share of emerging market liabilities, as noted above. Hence the role of emerging markets, in inward and outward foreign direct investment trendsis first considered with a focus on BRICs, then M&A is examined in particular.

Regarding inward FDI (i.e., FDI into emerging markets), the UN Conference on Trade and Development, in its *World Investment Report 2010*, noted that for the first time ever, developing and transition economies were absorbing half of global FDI inflows.[14] Within this grouping, the BRICs stood out quite clearly. In UNCTAD's global ranking of the largest FDI recipients, two of the BRICs were ranked among the six largest foreign investment recipients in the world in 2009, while the rest were developed countries and Hong Kong, which came fourth, at US$48 billion. China came second (after the United States), at US$95 billion, and Russia came sixth, at US$39 billion. Not far behind, India was the eighth-largest recipient (US$35 billion), and Brazil came 13th (US$26 billion). If the BRIC grouping is indicative of anything, it is indicative of market size, and one of the drivers of inward FDI is precisely market size; hence, the strong presence of the BRICs on the list of top FDI recipients.

In contrast, outward FDI has little to do with market size, and larger outflows are arguably more indicative of the fact that a country has already reached a certain level of development. In general, FDI outflows from developing and transition economies, having risen significantly, account for a quarter of global outflows. Here again, the BRICs are doing particularly well. In UNCTAD's global ranking of investment outflows for 2009, China and Russia were among the top 20 investors in the world, with China in sixth position,[15] (US$48 billion in outflows)[16] and Russia in seventh (US$47 billion; see Tables 2.3–2.5). The top destinations of Chinese outward investment were Australia and the United States, but Nigeria, Iran, Brazil, Kazakhstan and other emerging markets also figured prominently, with a notable intensification of investment in 2010 towards Brazil and South America in general. As one would expect, the top sector is energy and power, followed by metals and then finance and real estate. Finally, the Chinese have expanded outward investment in transportation.

Outward investments from India and Brazil have also made their mark on global investment flows. The BRICs' outward investment in 2008 reached US$147 billion, or nearly 9 per cent of world outflows, compared with less than 1 per cent in 2000.

Table 2.3   Top host countries for Chinese outward investment, 2006–10

Country	Total, US$ billions
Australia	34
USA	28.1
Nigeria	15.4
Iran	15.1
Brazil	14.9
Kazakhstan	11.1

Source: Heritage Foundation Dataset, China's Outward Investment: Non-Bond Transactions over US$100 million (2006–10).

Table 2.4   Chinese outward investment per host region, 2006–10, US$ billions

Region	Western Hemisphere	West Asia	Sub-Saharan Africa	Arab world	Europe	Australia	East Asia	USA
US$ billions	61.7	45.2	43.7	37.1	34.8	34	31.6	28.1

Source: Heritage Foundation Dataset, China's Outward Investment: Non-Bond Transactions over US$100 million (2006–10).

Table 2.5   Sector patterns of Chinese outward investment, 2006–10

Sector	Non-bond investment, US$ billions
Energy and power	102.2
Metals	60.8
Finance and real estate	39.2
Transport	7.3
All other	6
Total	215.9

Source: Heritage Foundation Dataset, China's Outward Investment: Non-Bond Transactions over US$100 million (2006–10).

A large part of the rise in outward foreign direct investment by emerging markets was fuelled by the recent rise in M&A activity by emerging markets; the two main modes of FDI entry are M&A and 'greenfield investment'; that is, the opening of a new wholly owned subsidiary. This increasing contribution of emerging markets to M&A is particularly significant: in the 1980s there was no greater symbol of the monopoly of developed countries over global finance than the million dollar M&A deals negotiated by the Wall Street investment banks; M&A was where the 'big bucks' were being made. It is no coincidence that Gordon Gekko, the hero of the cult movie *Wall Street*, was a Wall Street M&A guru. Even during the second half of 2006, the value of M&As attributed to emerging market acquirers of developed market target companies amounted only to 23 per cent of that attributed to developed market acquirers of emerging market target companies. Today, this share stands at 47 per cent; that is to say, the gap between emerging and developed market acquirers has nearly closed. Among the BRICs, according to UNCTAD, between 2000 and 2009 Indian firms finalized 812 deals abroad, Chinese firms finalized 450, Brazilian firms 190 and Russian firms 436, with some among these deals valued at more than US$1 billion.[17]

China, above all, has become an M&A power to contend with. Between 60 and 70 per cent of total Chinese outward FDI volume can be attributed to M&A deals. The total value of China's outbound M&A deals has risen impressively from US$1.6 billion in 2000 to US$55.4 billion in 2010, with a peak in 2008 at US$70.3 billion. Of course, the 2010 figure compares with global M&A deals totalling US$2.4 trillion, implying that Chinese deals represent only 2.3 per cent of global deal value (see Tables 2.6 and 2.7). Still, according to the Asia Society, if China follows the typical pattern of an emerging economy, it will spend between US$1 and 2 trillion in outward direct investment by 2020.[18] Given that much of this FDI is likely to occur through M&A, the next Gordon Gekko could well be Chinese.

Money supply and sovereign wealth funds

Finally, another illustration of emerging markets' integration in global finance is their increasing hold on money supply. In 2008 the broad money supply growth of emerging markets increased on average almost 20 per cent, accounting for a staggering three-fifths of global monetary total expansion while also adding to global inflation pressures.[19]

In 2008 emerging markets were also sitting on 75 per cent of global foreign exchange reserves, which summarizes well the position of strength of emerging markets vis-à-vis the sleepy US giant. How did the emerging markets end up accumulating so many foreign exchange reserves? Part of the answer is that the United States has become the world's

Table 2.6   China's outbound M&A value

	2000	2001	2002	2003	2004	2005	2006	2007	2008	2009	2010
Value, US$ billions	1.6	2.9	4	3.4	3.8	9.2	15	29.4	70.3	40.6	55.4

Source: Dealogic.

Table 2.7   China's outbound M&A value per sector, US$ billions

	2006	2007	2008	2009	2010
Materials	0.8	3.6	18.1	10.3	15.3
Energy and power	9.2	1.4	10.1	20.9	26
Industrials	2.1	0.6	1.5	2.1	6
Financials	2	21.7	6.3	3.6	4.8

Source: Dealogic.

largest debtor nation and is in an uneasy relationship with its creditors. With a US current account deficit of 7 per cent of GDP, a significant number of countries with matching current account surpluses (in particular China, with its 10% of GDP surplus) have become big holders of dollar reserves, since as global trade imbalances have grown, so have global capital inflows into the emerging markets. As the Bank for International Settlements notes, net capital flows to 23 large emerging market economies amounted to about US$1 billion a year in the 1980s, helping their FX reserves to rise by about US$11.5 billion.[20] In the 1990s capital flows strengthened, and their reserves grew by US$62 billion a year. These trends continued in the noughties, so that in 2007 alone, total capital inflows amounted to US$1440 billion, net capital inflows amounted to US$439 billion and reserves grew by nearly US$1 trillion. Half the growth in emerging market foreign exchange reserves could be traced to the growing surpluses in the current account of the balance of payments (see Table 2.8).

Emerging markets, particularly in Asia, partly invested those reserves by financing a significant portion of the US federal debt. But in the noughties, with dollar reserves on such a massive scale, Asian emerging markets started to realize that mere investment in US Treasuries was not the most profitable strategy, and they began to feel the need to diversify into real estate, equities, emerging market assets and even private equity, all of which offered higher returns. Not that the United States is in too much trouble: the bulk of Asian FX reserve investments remains in US Treasuries. Still, it became clear that if they were going to diversify

Table 2.8   SWF assets to foreign currency exchange ratio, end 2010

	Total SWF (US$ billions)	Reserves	SWF assets to foreign currency exchange ratio (%)
China	826	3045	27.1
Abu Dhabi	698.3	45	1552
Saudi Arabia	472.5	466	101.4
USA	58.8	143	41.1
Singapore	404.5	243	161.6
Russia	142.5	525	27.1
Norway	571.5	45.117	1267
Bahrain	9.1	3.474	261.9
Kuwait	202.8	19.63	1033
Kazakhstan	38.6	19.974	190
India		310	

Source: Sovereign Wealth Fund Institute.

into assets more exotic than Treasuries, Asian emerging markets needed institutions to administer their reserves. Asian sovereign wealth funds (SWFs), which are independent state agencies, were created to do so. Other SWFs already existing in the United Arab Emirates had invested the benefits of the commodity boom. The purpose of those commodity funds was to ensure that when commodity prices fell, government and private spending could be sustained; that of the Asian FX reserve funds is to provide sustainable investments for future generations. The total assets held by commodity and non-commodity funds together was estimated at US$3.8 trillion at the end of 2009 and had grown to US$4.4 trillion by June 2011, according to the Sovereign Wealth Fund Institute.[21] They invested US$22.9 billion in FDI in 2009 – 15 per cent more than in 2008, despite the backdrop of global recession.[22] These investments were increasingly directed towards Asia instead of their previous focus on developed countries, and towards primary resources and industries instead of finance, with a view to avoid sectors vulnerable to the crisis.

The largest SWF, Abu Dhabi Investment Authority, was created in 1976 to invest oil trade surpluses; it is now estimated at US$627 billion. Norway's Government Pension Fund, which has invested much of the country's North Sea oil riches, is worth US$571.5 billion. The Kuwait Investment Authority, the oldest SWF, is worth US$296 billion, and the Sovereign Wealth Fund Institute estimates that Saudi Arabia's holdings are worth US$477.8 billion. Other oil and gas producers with funds include Russia, Qatar, Libya and Brunei (see Table 2.9).

These commodity funds account for almost two-thirds of the total, but Asian funds investing foreign exchange reserves have been growing faster. With only US$1200 billion of assets at the end of 2007, they have doubled in size in three years and will rise to account for half the SWF total by 2015, according to International Financial Services London. Much of this growth is expected to come from Asian countries, whose share of official currency reserves has risen from a third of the global total to two-thirds over the past decade. Singapore's two SWFs are among the ten largest; they are jointly worth almost US$400 billion. One of the newest funds is China Investment Corporation, whose US$332.4 billion of assets is expected to grow sharply. China's foreign exchange reserves rose to US$3045 billion in 2010. As for the other BRICs, Russia also has a well-endowed SWF, at US$142.5 billion, but India and Brazil have so far kept a low profile in the world of SWFs. Every so often there is speculation that India will create an SWF to channel its heavy US$310 billion reserves, but so far it has not come to pass. Brazil created its own fund in 2008, specifically with a view

Table 2.9   Largest SWFs, June 2011

	Assets under management, $US billions	Country	Inception year	Source
Abu Dhabi Investment Authority	627	Abu Dhabi	1976	Commodity
Government Pension Fund-Global	571.5	Norway	1960	Commodity
SAMA Foreign Holdings	472.5	Saudi Arabia	n/a	Commodity
SAFE Investment Company	347.1	China	n/a	Non-commodity
China Investment Corporation	332.4	China	2007	Non-commodity
Kuwait Investment Authority	296	Kuwait	1953	Commodity
Hong Kong Monetary Authority Investment Portfolio	292.3	China (HK)	1993	Non-commodity
Government of Singapore Investment Corporation	247.5	Singapore	1981	Non-commodity
National Social Security Fund	146.5	China	2000	Non-commodity
Temasek Holdings	157	Singapore	1974	Non-commodity
National Welfare Fund	142.5	Russia	2008	Commodity
Qatar Investment Authority	85	Qatar	2005	Commodity
Australian Future Fund	49	Australia	2004	Non-commodity
Libyan Investment Authority	70	Libya	2006	Oil
International Petroleum Investment Company	58	Abu Dhabi	1984	Oil
Others	509.3			
Total	4415.8			

Source: SWF Institute.

to recycling the oil revenues from the new discoveries made off the Santos basin. This fund should grow significantly in the years to come from the current US$11.3 billion.

The objection raised against SWFs is an obvious one: that while in theory independent from the state, they are in fact vehicles of government policy. Each time the China Investment Corporation proposes to acquire a US company, one can imagine the frowning members of the US Committee on Foreign Investment (CFIUS) wondering whether the company is involved in a 'strategic interest' – strategic sectors include telecoms and the defence industry – that clashes with the suspected political agenda of the China Investment Corporation. In reality, the strategic interest argument is often just a veiled protectionist excuse on the part of the United States (see Chapter 3). Hence, the best approach for SWFs with their eyes on US assets is discretion: the approval in 2010 by the CFIUS of China Investment Corporation's acquisition of a 15 per cent stake in Chesapeake Energy, a developer of power projects, suggests that the CFIUS is likely to be more open to SWF acquisitions of US assets when they involve minority shares.

What SWFs, especially the China Investment Corporation, seem to stand for is the different way that emerging markets do business: they are very much guided by the state so that, the boundary between the two is blurred. US state and corporate sectors may object to this unorthodox approach to capitalism, but the fact is that the SWFs have access to the capital that the world lusts after, and they run business hand in hand with the state, whether they acknowledge it or not. In fact, the hand of the state extends beyond the SWFs; for instance, much of Chinese and Russian outward investment is undertaken by state-owned companies (see Chapter 5). Similarly, in Brazil and India, where there are no proper SWFs, the economy is dominated by national champions, which, having benefited from significant state support, are therefore subject to the state's influence. Beyond their contributions to growth, inflation, trade and finance, that is the real contribution of the emerging markets to the world: an alternative state-driven approach to the economy and an alternative approach to development, which will be explored in Chapter 6.

Conclusion

This chapter has examined the many aspects of the rise of emerging markets in the global economy. Whether growth, inflation, trade or finance is examined, one cannot but acknowledge that these markets have become an economic force to be reckoned with. Yet while a strong economy is, in itself, an increasingly important source of global power, one must still ask whether the emerging markets have succeeded in matching this new economic might with global political power. This is the subject of the next chapter.

3
BRICs and Global Political Power

The ascent of the emerging markets cannot be dissociated from the global financial crisis. Although it preceded the global financial crisis, the latter certainly contributed to the weakening of Western economic power, which opened up a space for emerging markets to drive the world economy. The financial crisis helped raise questions as to the foundations of economic and political globalization and placed new actors at its centre. Not only did the emerging markets become the heroes of the post-crisis world, but also the state, a dominant force in emerging markets, made a major comeback in the context of a collapsing private sector – before, some might add, collapsing itself.

After some introductory remarks on the global financial crisis, this chapter will examine the various symptoms of a revival of the state as the regulator of globalization. Its most salient and pernicious manifestation has been the rise of new forms of insidious protectionism; among these forms, emphasis is laid on the failure of the Doha round of trade talks, the proliferation of environmental standards on emerging market imports and of preferential trade agreements based on discrimination, the protectionist discourse of world leaders and the calls for restrictions on the activity of sovereign wealth funds. This crisis of a model of political globalization driven by a select few players within the developed countries is then examined. Finally, the results of the questioning prompted by the financial crisis are considered. It is suggested that while the financial crisis has prompted a reflection on the need to correct global political imbalances, it is unlikely that significant change in this area will come to pass, for reasons which have to do with emerging markets themselves: (1) they lack a common agenda, and (2) they would be reluctant to carry forward any such agenda, even if it were to exist.

The main schools of thought on power in international relations theory

Given that the financial crisis has raised questions as to the role of the state and the sources of global political power, some background on the theoretical debates on power from an international relations perspective might be useful. With the advent of the BRICs, the main issue tackled by international relations theories becomes how to reconcile conflicting interests between the BRICs and developed countries. There are four main schools of thought which addresses this question: realism, liberalism, a combination of these two, and constructivism.

According to the realist school, in the global political system dominant countries either supply public goods and permit others to free-ride or they punish free riders. As noted by Kenneth Shadlen, 'the realists focus on the distribution of resources as the determinant of countries' strategies and the underlying power differentials among countries'.[1] For them, power results from the material resources that actors have at their disposal. If we examine the place of the BRICs in realist theory, the implications are obvious: given that developed countries have more resources and power, their interests prevail in the international political economy if the BRICs come into conflict with them. In several of its chapters. this book suggests that, based on the realists' own criteria – resources and economic might – the BRICs do not have what it takes to rock the boat of international political economy in their favour; hence, the international political economy will continue to reflect the interests of the more developed countries.

The BRICS' ascent can also be examined from the perspective of the main competing paradigm in international relations (i.e., liberalism). In contrast with the realists, who view states and their resources as the foundation of a conflictual global political system, the liberals emphasize cooperation through global institutions as a means of reconciling the diverging interests of states, including the BRICs and the developed countries. For the liberals, BRICs and developed countries share an interest in the creation of institutions, albeit for different reasons. As noted by Shadlen,[2] developed countries, which are largely the ones who write the global rules, may go so far as to create rules that fail to reflect the underlying distribution of power (which is still slightly biased towards developed countries, at least in dollar terms) and are even biased towards BRIC interests, in order to secure their compliance and thereby reduce costs of monitoring the global political economy. Developed countries are willing to accept institutions that provide procedures and rules, even if they constrain the exercise of their own resources, because they reduce transaction costs involved in securing information, monitoring activities and enforcing compliance. The value of institutions is that they increase predictability.

As for the BRICs, they also favour institutions because institutions reduce their vulnerability in the international system and provide stability. Even if the BRICs do not make the rules, as Shadlen argues, 'bad rules that are universally acknowledged are better than no rules',[3] according to the liberals. On balance, the fact that developed countries will tolerate rules that fail to reflect the current distribution of resources allows the BRICs to exert a significant degree of influence on global political outcomes.

Apart from the realists, who focus on states, and liberals, who focus on institutions, a third school of thought, which combines complementary aspects of realism and liberalism, states that institutions change the relationship between states. This is the point made by the illustrious political economist Joseph Nye. In a book he co-authored with Robert O. Keohane[4] in the 1970s, Nye presented institutions as logical extensions of power politics between developed countries. Keohane and Nye coined the term 'complex interdependence', whereby interstate reliance is strong enough to change the nature of the relationships between states and their strategies. In particular, it is often in the self-interest of states to pursue non-military strategies towards one another. Yet Keohane and Nye highlight that it must be in the self-interest of states to form and maintain institutions and that states will go against institutional rules if they consider it necessary. Hence, theirs is ultimately a realist theory, where states drive the global political system.

Nye later developed the idea of 'soft co-optive power', whereby a state will encounter less resistance if it can make its power seem legitimate in the eyes of others. He viewed soft power as a useful alternative to the increasingly costly exercise of hard power. In the 1990s he started to take the position that the United States would be best able to exercise dominance through soft power. In *The Future of Power*[5] (2011) he revisits the debate on a supposedly waning US supremacy, which he denies. He emphasizes the country's capacity to constantly renew itself largely due to a well-educated labour force (a point also highlighted in this book). Conversely, he does not believe in China's capacity to challenge America's position as 'the dominant power in the world' over the long-term. He criticizes those who regard China's economic transformation as heralding a smooth transition to major political change: 'a China that cannot control flows of migration, environmental effects in the global climate and violent and internal conflict poses severe problems. Politics sometimes has a way of confounding economic projections'. This volume presents China's future collapse as primarily rooted in economic weaknesses; Nye uses a political lens to come to the same conclusion. Overall, his focus on soft power and institutions (touched upon later in this chapter) is an interesting complement to this book's primarily realist focus on economic resources.

Finally, a fourth approach to power in international relations is the constructivist perspective. According to Kenneth Shadlen, 'constructivists focus on the importance of ideas in sustaining cooperation between states, as well as the emergence of norms and the role of experts in generating common visions of the world'.[6] If the realists focus on states and the liberals on institutions, the constructivists put ideas themselves at the centre of the global political economy. Their theories[7] find an echo in this book's analysis, which suggests that one of the two roots of BRIC decline is the absence of ideas in the form of innovation (see Chapter 5); the other being inequality. But in this book the absence of innovation seems to matter mainly because it prevents the sustainability of economic growth and dominance. In the sense that ideas serve as an input into economic resources, the constructivist perspective can be seen as being framed by the realist one. Overall, then, the approach to power which this book adopts is a cross between realist theories (Chapters 1 and 2), liberal theories (the rest of this chapter) and constructivist theories (Chapter 5), with a realist focus in the main.

The great catalyst: a financial crisis

Which of these theories were supported by the reality of the global financial crisis, which began in August 2007? This crisis began on a high, as all collapses do. An acceleration in the rate of growth of US housing prices and easy loan conditions had encouraged high-risk borrowers to assume difficult mortgages in the expectation that they would be able to quickly refinance at more favourable terms through the so-called subprime market. However, once housing prices started to drop moderately in many parts of the United States (2006–7), refinancing became more difficult. Defaults and foreclosures increased dramatically as house prices failed to increase as expected, and mortgage rates were reset higher. The key element in the spread of the subprime crisis across the financial system was the process of securitization. Many lenders had passed mortgage payment rights and related credit and default risk to third-party investors, including banks, via mortgage-backed securities and collateralized debt obligations. When the value of underlying mortgage assets declined, there were no takers. What followed is well known: from a subprime crisis the US financial sector went into a liquidity and a solvency crisis, resulting in a generalized freeze in lending that had major implications for real economic activity, well beyond financial sector activity alone.

After funding insolvent emerging market governments (in the so-called lost decade of the 1980s), Wall Street created easy money for US subprime borrowers, this time resulting in its own disarray. The fact that the financial crisis had its epicentre in the United States and not the emerging markets had huge symbolic power: it was the United States' very own debt crisis. There have been other developed country financial crises in recent years – not least the savings and loan crisis of the 1980s and the long-term capital management crisis in the late 1990s – but nothing with the same capacity to damage economic activity. This financial crisis and its consequent downturn brought US federal debt[8] from 32 per cent of GDP in 2001 to 67 per cent of GDP in 2009.[9] While optimists like to point out that the United States spent less than 5 per cent of the 2010 budget on net interest payments, which means that debt servicing has not crowded out other spending too much, its fiscal position remains alarming. US federal debt as a percentage of GDP is above Brazil's 61 per cent, India's 53 per cent, China's 18.9 per cent (as with many other Chinese numbers, this figure might be seriously misstated) and Russia's 8.7 per cent.[10]

Not that the emerging markets were spared by the US meltdown. While their exclusion from the crème de la crème of securitized financial products allowed them to at least weather the subprime part of the financial storm, they were affected by global credit contraction. There was much talk of a decoupling of emerging markets from the developed economies in the early days of the meltdown, so that the emerging markets were viewed as immune, but facts disproved this view. To be sure, emerging markets, certainly the BRICs, were partly protected by their stronger position at the start of this crisis. In historical perspective, they benefited this time around from a sizeable reserve cushion and a favourable external balance. That being said, net flows to the emerging markets, according to the Institute for International Finance, fell to US$466 billion in 2008, down from US$929 billion in 2007. Emerging markets still needed to borrow whether the developed world was struggling or not. With foreign sources of emerging market financing drying up, the most important consideration in the outlook for emerging markets became their capacity to self-finance through export revenues. Unfortunately, many of the exports of the major emerging markets were still skewed towards the same moribund developed world, whose import demand contracted dramatically in the context of slower global growth. China was a case in point: despite the fact that intra-Asian trading partners are assuming increasing importance as a Chinese export destination (22.8% of Chinese exports went to the NICs and 4.6% to Association of South East Asian Nations countries in 2006),[11] China is the prime example of an emerging market that still needs developed country export markets. Beyond export market diversification, it has not yet achieved the even more crucial transformation of transition to an economy relying primarily on domestic demand, which would be the best way for it to lessen its external vulnerability.

Still, compared with the West and its unexpected woes, emerging markets came out of the crisis as big winners. Economists and policymakers started wondering what the particular features of their economic and political systems were that allowed them to be more resilient than the West. One answer that was given was the heightened role of their states in regulating globalization.

Questioning economic globalization: bringing back the state?

Following the crisis, a debate emerged on whether globalization would go into retreat. This is not the place to engage in full-scaled discussion of the arguments in favour of and against this assertion. More interesting is the extent to which the state, as the manager of globalization, was seen as a solution to the crisis. In the early days following the financial crisis, a consensus seemed to emerge that, while globalization would prevail going forward, it would have to be constrained by state regulation. Indeed, in a March 2010 presentation to the London School of Economics entitled 'After the Crisis: Industrial Policy and Developmental State', Robert Wade noted that 'the recession has induced some scepticism on Western mainstream policy prescriptions for "more market and less state"' or that 'the financial crisis has shaken confidence in the "free market" model'. In his presentation, he explained the pre-crisis orthodoxy of free markets and the post-crisis consensus on the need for a growing role of the state in the economy.[12] The means of state regulation seemed to become the main subject of discussion; the experiences of the

BRICs, outlined in Chapter 1, started to attract much Western attention in this respect. Some, like Philip Stephens, argue that a lot of water has passed under the bridge since then. For Stephens, while initially it was expected that 'popular fury with the bankers would translate into renewed faith in the efficacy of the state', the final verdict of the public was that 'the crisis came to be seen as one of public borrowing and debt as well as of bankers' greed'.[13]

The fiscal and public sector crisis of the Eurozone (and to some extent the USA) has certainly raised questions as to the financial capability of the state in regulating the economy, as has been noted by Lawrence Summers.[14] Yet this crisis has not damaged the main conclusion from its early stage, which was focused on the private sector; namely, that self-regulation of markets led to disaster; hence, a greater role for the state is required in managing markets. It seems to be the case that the fiscal crisis has only highlighted the importance of finding the most effective means of state regulation Stephens's view that 'talk of "responsible" capitalism, of rebalancing economies and constraining the rewards of the super-rich, falls short of anything resembling a grand plan'[15] has merit: the search for the most effective means of state regulation has not ended, nor has it become irrelevant. The rise of the Tea Party movement and the centre-right in general does not mark the end of that search or question its importance, especially if one considers the countervailing rise of the BRICs, which was associated with the heavy hand of the state. More problematic, however, is the fact that the one way in which the state has effectively demonstrated its revival since the crisis is through the escalation of a new type of protectionism.

A protectionist revival

Many pundits forecast the acceleration of old forms of protectionism in the aftermath of the crisis, but it failed to happen. The IMF estimates that the volume of international trade in goods and services contracted by 11.9 per cent in 2009, but crisis-related protectionism has been remarkably restrained compared with the protectionism coinciding with the Great Depression. In the 1930s protectionism was synonymous with an upfront declaration of trade war, with tariff hikes, blanket quotas and foreign exchange controls. This time around, as Erixon and Sally note, 'multilateral trade rules, international policy cooperation and market-led globalization have provided defences against a headlong descent into 1930s-style protectionism'.[16] The WTO notes in its 2009 update on trade measures that new protectionist measures have affected only

1 per cent of global trade in goods; services have not been affected.[17] However, the WTO focuses on import and export tariffs, quotas and licenses and trade remedies; it ignores new forms of non-border protectionism. Among them are standards, preferential trading agreements, public procurement ('buy national') restrictions, limitations on foreign investment, financial mercantilism (i.e., home government pressures on banks to lend at home at the expense of foreign lending), monetary mercantilism (i.e., through the manipulation of exchange rates) and tight immigration policies, all of which are gradually spreading. Hence, the discrepancy between WTO data and the data from Global Trade Alert, which is published by the UK think-tank Centre for Economic Policy research and includes new forms of protectionism; the latter paints a more alarming picture and counts at least 297 trade-discriminatory measures from November 2008 to November 2009.[18]

What exactly is a trade-discriminatory measure? It is a measure which violates the non-discriminatory principle of multilateral trade liberalization. The latter holds that every WTO member must treat every other WTO member as its 'most favoured nation'. For instance, if the USA has an applied tariff of 5 per cent on some electronic equipment, that tariff must apply to exports from all WTO members: the USA cannot impose a 5 per cent tariff on some countries and a 10 per cent tariff on others for the same electronic equipment (if it did, it would not be treating the others as most favoured). Yet many forms of discrimination persist.

New protectionism (1): the Doha debacle

Perhaps the lightest and most passive manifestation of protectionism is the stalling of multilateral trade negotiations, which is summarized by the World Trade Organization's failure to complete the Doha round of negotiations, which began in 2001. The Doha round of global trade talks, which was supposed to be the 'development round' because it was meant to secure the liberalization of agricultural markets which is key for the developing countries, was suspended on 23 July 2006. This failure was put down to the fact that the G6 (Australia, Brazil, India, Japan, the EU and the USA) could not agree on cutting subsidies to farming and lowering tariffs on agriculture. Since then, there have been multiple attempts to revive the talks, none of them successful. In June 2008 the WTO trade ministers managed "convergence" on 18 of the 20 topics set before them by Pascal Lamy, the WTO's director general. But they disagreed on the 19th, a 'special safeguard mechanism', which is a device for protecting farmers in developing countries against surges in imports. The USA wanted the trigger for this mechanism to be set high; India and China wanted it low. According to the *Economist*, both developing countries also 'wanted to be able to jack tariffs up above existing ceilings, not merely those set in a Doha deal'.

It is interesting to examine the interpretation of the *Economist*: it does not lay the blame on China and India. Instead, it argues that 'as these countries are becoming aware of their increased bargaining power, they are coming up against a world political system illustrated by the WTO as a global institution, which refuses to be updated. Rich countries no longer call the shots, as they did in the WTO's predecessor, the General Agreement on Tariffs and Trade (GATT). China and India, infuriating though they may be, are as powerful as America and the EU'. This judgment might be qualified somewhat: China and India now have the power to torpedo WTO talks, but that is only a negative power – to block agreement. They are powerful enough that they do not need to sign an agreement drafted to suit developed country needs, but they do not have the positive power to shape the agreement to better reflect their own needs (see more on this below). The latter power is the only one that can lead to a constructive globalization.

Arguably, as the Economist continues, 'if the US put up resistance because it refused to acknowledge change, it has its share of responsibility in the Doha failure, and not a small one. Especially as the breaking point of the special safeguard for farmers against surging imports truly is a mountain to India, with its 200 million farmers, while it is a molehill to America's one million farmers'. Ultimately it is only partially appropriate to blame the Doha debacle on the US' inability to adapt to a new world order when emerging markets themselves find it difficult to agree on the shape this order should take. While Peter Mandelson, Joseph Stiglitz and some others believe that there is hope for progress on a Doha development trade round, scepticism abounds that the United States has changed its stance or that emerging markets have become committed to a more constructive globalization agenda. Both requirements are central to the completion of the round. In that sense the stalling of the Doha round is the inevitable and natural reflection of the lack of direction of the global political economy.

New protectionism (2): standards

While the United States and emerging markets continue to waver, a new, more insidious form of protectionism has emerged: standards. For instance, technical and food safety standards have been used as controls on imports, with an acceleration of technical barriers to trade noted by the WTO in 2008/9.[19] The underlying problem with these measures is that they conflict with the fundamental principle of trade non-discrimination in trade.

The greatest standards-based protectionist weapon could be environmental standards. While emerging markets are still seldom subject to stringent environmental standards, their contribution to world pollution is expected to increase significantly, in line with their growing contribution to global growth. The International Energy Agency estimates that in 2030 emissions from non-OECD countries will exceed those from OECD countries by 77 per cent.[20] Hence, it will become more and more tempting for developed countries to use emerging markets as the victims of trade wars on the basis of environmental excuses. European green subsidies in favour of domestic renewable energy providers already discriminate against emerging market producers. The European Union Renewable Energy directive specifies that to qualify for the excise tax exemption which applies to European biofuels producers, a biofuels-producing entity entering the union must have a 35 per cent saving on greenhouse gas emissions. Effectively, this policy discriminates in favour of French and Spanish producers of rapeseed oil at the expense of East Asian competition. Similarly, the EU's recent energy efficiency directive mentions reduced energy imports as one of its main economic benefits. Finally, as emissions trading schemes in the EU and the United States impose significant costs on domestic energy-intensive sectors, they increase the pressure on the European Parliament to impose tariffs on cheaper, carbon-intensive imports not subject to regulation elsewhere. The European Union is already heading in that direction, as is clear from its decision to charge any airline flying into the EU for its carbon pollution from 1 January 2012. While the United States has been particularly vocal in criticizing the plan and has threatened to take retaliatory measures, China, Russia and Brazil have also joined the United States in this criticism.[21]

Europe is not the only power engaging in new forms of protectionism. In 2011, when China was reprimanded by the WTO for its export restrictions on zinc, coke and other raw materials, China invoked the conservation of exhaustible natural resources as an excuse. Yet as the *Financial Times* was quick to point out, 'had this been the motive for China's actions, quotas on production, rather than exports, would have been the solution'.[22] While the WTO's ruling against China should hold some degree of dissuasive power for emerging markets thinking about using the same methods, one cannot rule out that some emerging countries may still want to resort to export restrictions, given the back-drop of rising global competition for natural resources.

New protectionism (3): preferential trading agreements

Also symptomatic of an unacknowledged yet mounting protection-ism, preferential trading agreements have increasingly been resorted to as a favoured alternative to multilateral liberalization. The unre-solved Doha round has coincided with the emergence of smaller trade pacts. These agreements end up being highly politicized outcomes, which heighten the role of the two states under consideration in the political bargaining of bilateral economic preferences. Since the Doha round was launched (2001), over 100 preferential trading deals have come into force, lowering tariffs for some members of the WTO but not others. The United States is pushing for these 'coalitions of the willing', while some emerging markets are criticizing them. Especially when it comes to the conclusion of an agreement on trade in services, the United States supports the concept of a 'plurilateral agreement', involving a subset of WTO members that would agree to open their markets only to each other. In December 2011, Bolivia, Venezuela, Nicaragua, Cuba and Ecuador protested that 'it is essential to preserve multilateralism without the inclusion of a plurilateral initiative'.[23] Preferential deals do violate the central non-discriminatory principle of multilateral trade liberalization as, defined above. Worse still, as the illustrious economist Jagdish Bhagwati points out in *Termites in the Trading System* (2008), by playing special favourites with its trading partners, a country can dupe itself into paying more for its imports. Its consumers may switch from a low-cost supplier to a more expensive one only because the new supplier can sell its goods duty free and the other cannot. Consumers pay less, but the Treasury is deprived of tariff revenue. Thus, discriminatory trade deals do not hurt just those countries left out of the preferential agreement. Baghwati con-cludes that preferential agreements have re-created the situation of the 1930s, when world trade was undermined by discriminatory practices. Whereas overt protectionism applied in those days, ironically the United States and others now present preferential trade agreements as a trade-enhancing addition to multilateral trade liberalization. Yet it has been suggested that one of the stumbling blocks in the Doha round was precisely 'preference erosion'; in particular, some African and Caribbean countries did not want to see the EU expand its banana market, because in so doing it would have eroded the value of their pre-existing privileges. In that sense, discriminatory trade deals are clearly competing with multilateral trade liberalization.

New protectionism (4): the political rhetoric of 'buy national' restrictions

While coming short of raising tariffs and blanket quotas, the hard protectionist talk by US President Obama after the crisis was another manifestation of state stalling of economic globalization. On 16 June 2008, when he was only a presidential candidate, Obama gave a speech in Flint, Michigan, that contained a clear protectionist message:

> Allowing subsidized and unfairly traded products to flood our markets is not free trade and it's not fair to the people of Michigan. We cannot stand by while countries manipulate currencies to promote exports, creating huge imbalances in the global economy. We cannot let foreign regulatory policies exclude American products. We cannot let enforcement of existing trade agreements take a backseat to the negotiation of new ones. Put simply, we need tougher negotiators on our side of the table – to strike bargains that are good for Main Street. (http://www.youtube.com/watch?v=HMKMQvE63xA)

Obama was playing the protectionist card to attract the vote of the labour constituency, which often resorts to blaming international trade for job losses. At the time, many of his supporters argued that he was using general protectionist rhetoric without specific action points on the precise shape of a North American Free trade Area renegotiation, precisely because this was merely an electoral ploy, one on which he would not deliver.

Yet once Obama was elected president, one of the first outcomes was a US$800 billion stimulus package, which contained a clause pressing the use of American materials in public works. While Obama asked for a statement within the Buy American clause, which implied that the clause would not violate world trade agreements, and amounted to a relative watering down of the clause compared to its initial draft, he did not reject it altogether. How exactly buying American is compatible with multilateral trade commitments is not clear. True, the United States can get its Buy American way by excluding China and India among other developing countries from US procurement, while still complying with WTO procurement rules, given that these countries have not signed the optional WTO procurement code yet. Yet as US economist Jagdish Bhagwati has pointed out, 'these nations can also retaliate in

WTO-consistent ways'. In fact, China did so by including a Buy Chinese clause in its fiscal stimulus.[24] Furthermore, it is worth remembering that the WTO holds countries only to the 'bound tariffs' – the tariff ceilings they have agreed to. As their bound tariffs are above their actual tariffs, China and India can raise actual tariffs towards bound levels without being inconsistent with WTO rules. (This applies more to India than China, as India has a bound tariff of 32.6% and an actual one of 5.6%, versus 10% and 9.9%, respectively, for China.)

But what is the point of remaining consistent with WTO law while waging a protectionist war in practice? The very mention of a Buy American concept sends a protectionist signal to the world, and no amount of watering down by Obama can undo the damage it does. Obama's protectionist talk before the election combined with his implicit endorsement of the Buy American clause at a time of crisis are regrettable, as they have contributed to spreading a self-defeating tit-for-tat philosophy of trade. The State of the Union address he delivered on 24 January 2012 also had strong protectionist overtones, including proposal for a tax on foreign corporate earnings and for a tax credit to cover moving expenses for companies bringing jobs back to the US.

New protectionism (5): limitations on foreign investment

Another manifestation of US government protectionism is its complaints against Chinese investments, which supposedly threaten national security or create unfair competition. The Committee on Foreign Investment in the United States (CFIUS) has on these grounds rejected multiple Chinese investments, including Huawei's investment in 3Leaf Systems.[25] In May 2010 Huawei acquired certain assets of this near-bankrupt firm for US$2 million. The assets purchased were intellectual property rights, including patents. Huawei did not file a notice with CFIUS with respect to this purchase prior to completing the transaction. After learning in December 2010 that CFIUS was looking into the transaction, Huawei suddenly filed its notice. In mid-February 2011 CFIUS notified Huawei that it would not approve the notice. For days it appeared that Huawei would not relent. Then, on February 24, the Chinese company announced that it had decided to accept the recommendation of CFIUS to withdraw its application and would either sell off the patents or abandon the intellectual property altogether. After agreeing to ongoing oversight of its US operations by CFIUS, in October 2011 Huawei complained that it was 'high time' the United States justified more clearly the nature of its 'unsubstantiated' national security concerns around Huawei's investments.[26] Yet CFIUS' investigation is still ongoing. Also in 2010, CFIUS blocked investments by Northwest Non-Ferrous International in Firstgold, a U.S. mining company, and by Tangshan Caofeidian Investment Corporation in Emcore, a US manufacturer of fibre optic equipment.

New protectionism (6): financial and monetary mercantilism

The US government is particularly concerned about another form of what it views as unfair competition from Chinese companies, the provision of cheap credit by Chinese banks to Chinese state-owned enterprises, which it often describes as 'financial mercantilism'. The United States categorizes financial mercantilism as a non-tariff trade barrier – a veiled form of dumping. It is fast becoming a key subject of diplomatic friction in the annual US-China Strategic and Economic Dialogue (see http://iip-digital.usembassy.gov/st/english/texttrans/2011/05/20110505191406s u0.2003072.html#axzz1LwGvVtVr), which brings together 20 ministerial-level officials from each country. At the same time, it is probably the most difficult distortion for the Chinese political leadership to remove, for the simple reason that the banks which lend to the state-owned sector are themselves state-run and will always favour the safest credits, which are by definition state-owned enterprises. This allocation is far from optimal. Chinese small and medium-sized enterprises and private exporters are at a disadvantage in the pursuit of credit, whereas they should be at the helm of the economy, especially in the domain of innovation, where significant credit is required. It can be argued that the Chinese government is threatening its own economy's future by concentrating credit allocation in the state-owned sector. However, US pressure, acting through the threat of a countervailing antidumping measure, may change this somewhat.

Beyond the United States, French President Sarkozy has been clear on the extent and form of his protectionist agenda. He has unambiguously said that Europeans should not be afraid of the word protection. When he took on the EU presidency in July 2008, he argued that one of the things Europeans expected from the EU was for it to shield them from globalization's negative effects. In the run-up to the Doha talks, he said to the TV channel France 3 that the WTO head, Pascal Lamy, 'wants to make us accept a deal under which Europe would commit to cutting farm output by 20% and reduce farm exports by 10%. That would be 100,000 jobs lost, I won't let it happen'.

Also in 2008, Sarkozy started to bemoan the strength of the euro, saying that France was the victim of 'monetary dumping' from the United

States, China and Japan, whose currencies, he said, were undervalued. In an obvious escalation of protectionist talk across both sides of the Atlantic, his thoughts were soon echoed by US Secretary of State Timothy Geithner, who stated on 22 January 2009 that China manipulated its currency; he thereby broke with the diplomatic non-involvement in Chinese economic policy of the prior administration (George W. Bush). He saw the yuan's undervaluation as a deliberate policy to maintain a vast trade surplus that contributed to a US unemployment rate of 10 per cent. In September 2011 the Democrat-controlled Senate voted 63–35 to pass a bill entitled Currency Reform for Fair Trade Act of 2011 (5.328), which allows the United States to put duties on goods from countries with undervalued currencies, China being the main target. While the US Treasury is delaying the final ruling as Democratic lawmakers try to overcome Republican opposition to the bill, the issue of monetary dumping has become central to US economic policy (see http:www.bbc.co.uk/news/business-15161840).

In sum, Joseph Stiglitz notes that 'the world is waking up to the way exchange rates can be used in self-promotion at the expense of others'.[27] Here again, it is not just developed countries playing the protectionist card; the BRICs also know how to play it. For instance, to stem exchange rate appreciation, emerging markets have implemented capital controls (notably Brazil),[28] capital gains taxes, exchange rate interventions and lowered interest rates. At the same time China has qualified the US' quantitative easing as an artificial means of lowering the dollar as it promotes investment by lowering interest rates, resulting in a lower exchange rate. The Americans and the Chinese may have two different views of the world, but they have one point in common: their states assert themselves by manipulating the terms of their integration into the global economy.

New protectionism (7): tight immigration policies

The final manifestation of the new protectionism has to do with the immigration of skilled labour. In order to address the concerns of the unemployed, the United States passed a law in 2010 that increased the fee for H-1B and L-1 visas – which are used by companies to transfer staff employed in 'specialty occupations' to the United States – to US$2000, up from US$320.[29] For the H-1B visa the regulations define a 'specialty occupation' as one requiring theoretical and practical application of a body of highly specialized knowledge in a field of human endeavour including but not limited to architecture, engineering, mathematics, physical sciences, social sciences, biotechnology, medicine and health, education, law, accounting, business specialties, theology and the arts, with a bachelor's degree or its equivalent as a minimum requirement. For the L-1 visa employees must either be managers or executives or work in areas of 'specialized knowledge'. In a sense this is more than protectionism; this is an industrial policy which protects the US's high-skilled industries. An obvious victim of this rise in visa costs is the Indian IT outsourcing industry, which is estimated to suffer an increase in its US visa costs in the range of US$200–250 million a year. Even in the low-skilled labour segment, constraints to immigration are also rising. Britain's new coalition government has promised to reduce the number of immigrants in general from hundreds of thousands a year to tens of thousands. Anti-immigration parties have made breakthroughs in the Netherlands and Sweden, while the US's Tea Party movement has increased pressure to limit illegal immigration from Mexico. Human flows were always the least developed aspect of globalization, but the current anti-immigration backlash is arguably the most resonant measure of the state's control over globalization.

Restrictions on sovereign wealth funds

In addition to their protectionist behaviour, developed countries attempted to slow down injections of liquidity by emerging market sovereign wealth funds in the midst of the crisis. As was explained in Chapter 2, emerging markets recycle large dollar reserves into funds. At the beginning of the financial meltdown, when many of the US and European commercial and investment banks had taken large hits to their balance sheets over the subprime crisis because of bad investments, the capital infusions from SWFs enabled them to strengthen their balance sheets (not that it made a difference in the end, given the eventual collapse of a number of them). Between the fourth quarter of 2007 and the fourth quarter of 2008, SWFs poured about US$55 billion into US and European financial institutions. Yet the deployment of these funds in the United States and parts of Europe was not to everyone's taste. Concerns were widespread. Critics said that they were opaque, and they allocated investments on a political rather than commercial basis. Funds were urged to become more transparent and use external managers to allocate investments in line with publicly stated strategies. Most of them complied.

The above objections seemed to be putting off the funds when the crisis was at its worst. Gao Xiqing, the president of China Investment Corporation (CIC), China's sovereign wealth fund, said in June 2008 that he was disappointed that CIC's attempts at investing outside China sometimes ran into political opposition. He concluded that 'fortunately there are more than 200 countries in the world. And fortunately there are many countries who are happy with us'.[30]

The threat pronounced by Gao Xiquing was quite real, in so far as SWFs have recently displayed a preference for investment alternatives which do not involve pumping capital into collapsing developed economies. They have been increasingly active in the purchase of emerging market assets, often outside the banking sector. They are likely to continue buying more assets from emerging nations and selling US equities and especially bonds, considering the declining appeal of holding assets from a country whose debt has now been downgraded by the credit agency Standard and Poor's. With the US investment climate for SWFs becoming poorer, the SWFs from emerging markets are likely to look for alternatives, and that could do much damage to the US economy.

In 2008 Steven Schwarzman, chief executive of Blackstone, wrote in a Financial Times article, 'sixty years ago, we conducted a painful, expensive and accidental experiment called the Great Depression, with the Smoot Hawley tariffs to teach us the value of free trade. Let us not subject ourselves to another painful lesson in the value of direct investment and the free flow of capital by driving SWFs away'.[31] While history is easily forgotten, one cannot but wonder whether there was not an element of hubris in the behaviour of developed countries as they refused the much-needed injections of emerging market capital. It takes getting used to a world upside down. But the reality of 2012 is much different from that of 2008, and the US sovereign debt ratings have now been downgraded. Since beggars are not in a position to be choosers, the United States should consider itself lucky to attract SWF investments.

The above anecdotes on emerging market SWFs coming to the rescue of US banking giants illustrate one fact: the main actors in globalization and their roles have changed. As a process, globalization needs to be powered by someone, and those who created the concept – the United States and Europe – are no longer the main makers of the economic globalization process; they are in the throws of a major debt crisis, whose resolution is their overriding concern. In contrast, as noted by Nandan Nilekani, the former chief executive of Infosys, 'the transition of both India and China from rural economies to service and manufacturing powerhouses has moved the locus of global growth [to these economies]'.[32] With India and China becoming key makers of globalization, they should have a new role in shaping its current concept.

A developed-centric world: the politics of globalization as we know it

Beyond the recognized changes in economic globalization, this section looks into the politics of globalization. Current global politics are heavily skewed towards developed countries' interests. The first point to be acknowledged in any discussion of globalization is that economic globalization does not exist in the sense of a flat, non-hierarchical process of trade and capital flows between equal states. What does exist is polarization, whereby economic poles (some more developed than others) exchange trade and capital, in the larger context of a political hierarchy of states. The extent of existing hierarchical relationships within globalization is clear from an examination of the so-called global governance institutions, such as the IMF and World Bank, which are meant to manage globalization. Some basic facts will show the hierarchical nature of these institutions.

At the IMF, European countries have 32 per cent of the votes, while the BRICs have 11.5 per cent (see Table 3.1).

At the World Bank, developed countries control 60 per cent of voting shares, as its system is based on the principle of one dollar, one vote. Furthermore, the United States has a de facto veto. There is no need to elaborate further on the World Bank/IMF's unequal power structures; the above facts speak volumes. At the United Nations, while it is true that China and Russia have veto power in the Security Council, France, the United Kingdom and the United States have the veto as well, which means that the BRICs will find it difficult to enforce their views if they are opposed by any of the three developed countries on the council. The BRICs do, however, have the ability to block developed country views.

Table 3.1 IMF voting share, % of total

	IMF quota share, % of total[33]
Middle East and North Africa	7.5
Latin America and the Caribbean	5.9
European Union	32
Developing Asia	4.1
Other advanced economies	15.8
USA	17.7
BRICs and South Africa	11.5

Source: IMF.

The case of the WTO is more complex. Its structure is based on one country, one vote, and no single country has a veto. Given the large number of developing countries, they would seem to have an advantage in this set-up. WTO principles of unweighted voting (one country, one vote) and consensus-based voting create the widespread perception that WTO rules are emerging market–friendly. As has been argued by the previous head of the WTO, Michael Moore,

> the WTO system is built upon the rule of law and respect for the sovereign equality of nations. Ultimately, it is an open, rules-based multilateral trading system, based on democratic values. It is the most democratic international body in existence today. ... No one is forced to sign our agreements. Each and every one of the WTO's rules is negotiated by member governments and agreed by consensus. ... Because no decision is taken unless all member governments agree, effectively every country – from the largest to the smallest – has the power of veto.

Yet even at the WTO, the pragmatics of realpolitik contradict the rules of voting. Behind the facade of democratic rules lies the power politics of agenda setting. As suggested by Chang, 'all important negotiations were held in the so-called Green Rooms at Geneva 1998, Seattle 1999, Doha 2001 and Cancun 2003, on a "by-invitation only" basis'.[34] What is the problem with this approach? It can result only in the domination of the developed country agenda, while the participation of the developing countries remains procedural. In a personal communication with me, Robert Wade, a professor at the London School of Economics, even claimed that at Doha, a green room was carefully selected by the French Deputy Director General, Paul-Henri Ravier, on the grounds that it was not too large. Only 23 countries could be squeezed in to attend the drafting sessions there. Those not invited were reportedly thrown out. As Chang puts it, 'international trade negotiations are a lopsided affair; like a war where some people fight with pistols while others engage in aerial bombardment'.[35]

Similarly, as Aileen Kwa (2003) points out in 'Power Politics in the WTO', a study prepared for the non-governmental organization (NGO) Focus on the Global South, far from being rules-based, it is the organization's very lack of formalized internal structures that helps to serve the interests of the powerful.[36] In support of Kwa's argument, Wade notes that in the manufacture of the global consensus by which the WTO operates, silence is taken for agreement. Bullying, arm-twisting and bribery can be useful tactics in producing closed lips. With no formal provisions surrounding the drafting of documents, agendas can legitimately be stitched up by a select few, behind the closed doors of the famous Green Room, and presented as a *fait accompli*. No rules govern the conduct of meetings – allowing Charlene Barshefsky, US Trade Representative, both to chair the talks and lead the American negotiating team at the 1999 WTO conclave in Seattle, for example. The talents of WTO head Michael Moore would find an obvious home here. Read against the grain, Moore's book, *A World without Walls* (2003), confirms Kwa's findings of an institutionalized regime of intimidation, marginalization and outright coercion to ensure that the Quad countries (US, EU, Japan and Canada) get what they want.[37]

In sum, emerging markets are effectively, if not in principle, second-class citizens in global institutions. But more than the governance of the World Bank or WTO, it is the US's approach to global governance that is of central importance in this debate, as the Bank and WTO often take their cues from US policy, given that the United States is their primary source of finance. On this subject, Robert Wade's thesis is that globalization is an international framework of market rules to promote US interests.[38] While his thesis has often been labelled a conspiracy theory, many agree with his statement that 'globalization is never free of political power; so far, it has been a tool for developed countries, and mainly the US, to reinforce geopolitical dominance over other states'.[39] A good example of this is the way in which the United States offers trade deals to strategic allies as a reward for fighting the war on drugs or stabilizing the Middle East. An illustration of this thesis is provided by Limao.[40] He creates a model where the main motive for a country to provide trade preferences is to pay for cooperation in a non-trade issue that is under the control of its partner, and he applies this model to the USA. His model captures the numerous unilateral preference programmes where the United States provides market access and requires in exchange that its partners comply with conditions on intellectual property, environment, labour standards, drugs or terrorism. He also models the interaction of a unilateral programme with multilateral trade liberalization. He shows that such preferential trading agreements can cause a stumbling block to multilateral trade liberalization for the relatively larger countries, since they have a preference for an agreement which allows them to exchange access to the US goods market for compliance with the non-trade conditions. That incentive is obvious in the case of the United States: it consists in the ability to reinforce US geopolitical dominance.

Ironically, the sidelining of emerging markets and the protectionist policies of the leaders of developed countries are symptoms of the success that emerging markets, mainly the BRICs, have had in tackling economic development. As Jean Pisani-Ferry contends,[41] the developed countries launched their globalization project with a view to enlarge their own markets. In that perspective they roped the BRICs into this project, but now that the BRICs have lowered their tariffs, opened their markets and allowed foreign investment, the developed countries are complaining that the BRICs stole their jobs in the textile and low-skill activities. Yet since the BRICs achieved development with decades of policy efforts, which created competitive exports and multinational corporations, the developed countries are in no position to complain.

While Pisani-Ferry is right to point out that globalization was never meant to reach its completion in the form of the BRICs sitting at the global table, more and more of the world's wealth is being created there. That is not an invention or a concept; it is an unavoidable fact. It was easy in the 1980s for the developed world to promote globalization primarily as the integration of developed country economies, all the while keeping emerging markets at the periphery of the process, but this is no longer possible. Chapter 2 illustrated how important the BRICs' role in the world economy has become, whether one looks at money supply, global finance, or global growth and inflation. Hence, developed country leaders have had to acknowledge that globalization is no longer a developed country club. They cannot have globalization *and* protect themselves against the emerging markets. That is a contradiction in terms.

Even before the global financial crisis, US external and domestic debt had reached such levels that the United States had to place significant pressure on Asian countries to revalue their currencies and to continue to hold US assets, despite higher returns elsewhere and despite the appealing alternative of holding the euro as a reserve currency instead of the US dollar. Note that at the end of December 2011, China held 39.6 per cent of foreign holdings of US Treasuries; Japan, 34.1 per cent; Brazil 7.3 per cent; Russia 3.2 per cent; Hong Kong 3.9 per cent; and Taiwan 5.2 per cent (see http://www.ustreas.gov/tic/mfh.txt). O'Neill suggests that if China were to buy fewer US Treasuries, it would not be a disaster for the United States as long as it increased its savings rate, which has gone from 0.6 per cent of income to around 5 per cent since late 2008.[42] He notes that an improved US trade balance and the consequent reduced need for overseas finance would balance a reduction in Chinese purchases of US Treasuries.

Robert Wade offers a contrasting view: in his view if Asian countries were to stop funding the US fiscal deficit, the dollar could crash fast. This would inflict significant costs on the US economy, as foreign holdings of US Treasuries, the vast majority of which are in Asian hands, now constitute one third of total Treasury-issued debt. Not that China would ever engage in a sudden pull-out of Treasuries, which would put the United States at risk. Yet the threat that it might is nothing if not a tremendous bargaining chip for China. The Chinese government has frequently mentioned its long-term plan to diversify its dollar-denominated reserves in Treasuries – now valued at US$3 trillion – to a broader portfolio of investments with a higher yield, most likely managed through one of its sovereign wealth funds. In June 2011 Standard Chartered suggested that in the first four months of 2011, China's foreign exchange reserves expanded by US$200 billion, with three-quarters of the new inflow invested in non–US dollar assets, possibly indicating a turning point in foreign reserve diversification.[43] China's official holdings of US Treasuries were supposedly reduced by around 10 per cent between July 2009 and June 2010, but a simultaneous US$54 billion rise in the UK's holdings suggested that Beijing could be making purchases of US Treasuries through London instead. Finally, the fact that China was more than happy to publicize data on its declining holdings of Treasuries is a measure of its interest in keeping the threat of a pull-out alive. Yet even if US consumers are saving more than they used to and thus reducing US dependence on Asian purchases of Treasuries, this is a long-term process. The United States would do well to manage the risks of a pull-out scenario, whose trigger is largely in the hands of China, by sharing some global political space with the emerging markets, which it has come to depend upon. To some extent, the subversion of the US agenda by the BRICs at the Doha round of WTO trade talks shows that this is a fait accompli anyway.

Additional formal changes in the approach of the West towards global governance are required. A key requirement is reform of the unequal structure of the World Bank, IMF, WTO and other international financial institutions; this will be a long-term project (see Buira[44] and Wade[45] in particular). As was noted above, at the IMF, European countries have 32 per cent of the votes, while the BRICs have 11.5 per cent. Considering that the BRICs account for 25 per cent of the world economy in PPP terms and Europe for 20.4 per cent, this can only be described as an aberration. Conversely, the World Bank reforms introduced in April 2010, whereby the share of low- and middle-income countries on the governing board increased from 44 to 47 per cent, are a step in the right direction but still insufficient. Similarly, the fact that the World Bank's chief economist, Justin Lin, and the adviser to the IMF's managing director, Zhu Min, are Chinese is an encouraging sign. Yet the most pro–emerging market measure of all would be to remove the US's veto power at the World Bank and IMF by cutting its share of the vote to less than 15 per cent. That reform remains a pipe dream, as it would require US consent.

The absence of a BRIC common agenda

Whether or not the global political context is supportive of the BRICs' ascent, they are already a force to be reckoned with. In terms of economic growth and in the number of military and paramilitary forces they can deploy, they are rivalled only by the forces of the United States, Egypt, Indonesia, Pakistan and Turkey. Together they have nearly 5 million men and women under arms.[46] Furthermore, the BRICs have been trying to increase their global visibility. Just as the United States retired its space shuttle fleet (July 2011), China's success in launching men into space with a view to the completion of a future space station by 2020[47] is a clear attempt to display its political importance.[48] Yet, among all the attempts by China to increase its political visibility, the ascent of the Chinese navy is particularly striking. As the US Office of Naval Intelligence notes, 'over the past decade, the Chinese Navy has embarked on a modernization program with the goal of being the preeminent regional power in East Asia. By acquiring some of the world's most impressive naval technologies from abroad while simultaneously building advanced indigenous submarines, combatants, and naval aircraft, China is positioning itself to play a growing role in regional and trans-regional affairs'.[49] Interestingly, the naval office adds that 'this modernization effort partly aims to ensure access to trade routes and economic resources throughout the region', in a way very reminiscent of the behaviour of the US hegemon. This is definitely a case of China seeking to control the seas around its coastline so that it cannot be challenged by the United States in this maritime zone, so much so that China is often accused of implementing its very own Monroe doctrine in East Asia. This process has coincided with clashes with Japan over disputed islands in the East China Sea and with Vietnam over boundaries in the South China Sea, clashes involving substantial wealth and strategic importance. In 2010 Chinese vessels clashed with Vietnamese and Filipino boats off the coasts of Vietnam and the Philippines on multiple occasions.

In 2010 Vietnam reopened the Cam Ranh Bay naval and air base to foreign ships in an obvious attempt to counter China's growing assertiveness in the South China Sea. The base had been closed to foreign ships since 2002, after the departure of the Russians, who had been using it as a spying station. The Vietnamese government had said that it would never open the base to foreign powers again, but clearly the Chinese threat has forced a geopolitical rethink on its part. The United States and Russia seem keenest to take advantage of the renewed opportunity to use the base. It is quite a historical irony that Vietnam's two old enemies are coming together to counter the Chinese.

In June 2011 Vietnam conducted a naval exercise in the South China Sea; China condemned it. As Vietnam called on other nations to help resolve the dispute, the Chinese foreign ministry spokesman was quick to state that 'we hope that countries that are not parties to the South China Sea dispute truly respect the efforts of the countries concerned to resolve their disputes through consultation'. In other words, back off. The US government's statements were reserved; it merely mentioned that the United States was troubled by the tensions. Congress has been pressuring the White House to take a harder line, however. James Webb, a Democratic senator, spearheaded a unanimous Senate resolution condemning China's use of force and called for a multilateral solution to the issue. US Secretary of State Clinton encouraged talks on a code of conduct in the area. Overall there is little question that the US government actively desires closer contacts with Vietnam with a view to countering China, as suggested by the five days in April 2012 which the US and Vietnam navies spent jointly practising navigation, medicine and driving skills in the Vietnamese port of Danang.

A recent indication of China's geostrategic plans was its placing a new antiship missile, Dongfeng 21D, on operational status at the end of 2010; with the missile China now presents a real check to US military power in the region.[50] Also, while for many years the Chinese navy was focused on Taiwan, recently its focus has switched to 'far-sea operations', to ensure the protection of Chinese energy imports and maritime trade.

Yet while these actions have raised China's political profile in so far as they have increased its ability to threaten other countries, they have not yet increased its power to influence global governance positively. The power that comes from a check or threat is the power of dissuasion; it is not the same as the power of persuasion. Jonas Parello-Plesner and Parag Khann argue that while Beijing attempts to secure long-term access to economic resources, it is inevitably drawn away from its non-interventionist foreign policy into becoming a global policeman and intervening in other countries' domestic disputes.[51] That assertion is the subject of heated debate; this is not the place to engage in it.[52] However, as the above actions suggest, if policing there is to be, so far it seems based primarily on threat rather than constructive dialogue. The examples chosen by Parello-Plesner and Khann confirm this supposition; they note that 'the absence of credible government in Somalia has forced China to contribute more heavily to antipiracy operations in the Gulf of Aden' – by definition a threat. They further note that 'China is still reluctant to vote in favor of interventions such as in Syria' – precisely the sort of positive, constructive actions that are missing. China apart, the BRICs have not been able to exert leadership through persuasion either, because (1) they are divided, and (2) even if they were not, it is not clear what they would want to persuade the world of. The annual BRIC summits, which bring together their leaders (South Africa was also invited to the April 2011 summit), have not changed things in the least. Their achievements so far mainly amount to a flurry of business deals among the BRICs' national champion firms.

Perhaps the greatest challenge for the BRICs is ensuring a successful transition from the power to block global agreements to a positive power to shape agreements in a way that reflects BRIC interests. Why have the BRICs been lacking in positive power?

For one thing, they are plagued by divisions, on both political and economic levels. In general, there is more suspicion than unity between them. The divisions between Russia and China are a case in point. Russia likes to be seen as one of the BRICs, yet it stands in opposition to the US-led North Atlantic Treaty Organization (NATO), more as a result of history than anything else. Similarly, the fact that China despises Russia as a pure commodity exporter leaves scope for Russia eventually to grow tired of China's contempt and possibly switch economic allegiance to the West. Worse still, the animosity between China and India is well known. China is the most vocal opponent of India's permanent membership in the UN Security Council. More important, given China's strong ties with Pakistan, India is still concerned that war could break out with China. In June 2011, when Pakistan suggested that China could be offered a naval base at its south-western port of Gwadar, India certainly became inclined to cultivate friendship more with the United States than with China.

BRIC division was clear in March 2010, when Brazil opposed the fourth round of UN sanctions on Iran until the very last minute, while

Russia consistently use in favour and China eventually supported the sanctions. Brazil ultimately voted in favour of the sanctions (supposedly because 'there is a tradition of carrying out Security Council resolutions', according to the then Brazilian President Lula da Silva), but this vote was probably related to China's change of heart, as the latter decided to vote in favour after being strongly against. In fact, China's volte-face is the best embodiment of the 'each BRIC for himself approach'. While Beijing had long been the strongest advocate of a no-sanctions approach towards Iran, the United States appears to have managed to convince China to vote in favour of the sanctions, albeit at a high price: (1) Beijing watered down the sanctions to be adopted by the Security Council to ensure they did not restrain China from expanding its already massive economic ties with Iran; (2) Beijing won undertakings from Washington to exempt Chinese companies from any unilateral US sanctions to punish third-country trading partners with the Islamic Republic; (3) the Chinese newspaper *Global Times* claimed that China had secured US agreement that in any follow-on sanctions adopted by the United States and its European partners, China's considerable interests in Iranian energy, trade and financial sectors would be protected (note that verification of this claim has not been provided). The impact of US and EU follow-on sanctions would undoubtedly have been more important than that of UN sanctions. Clearly demonstrating BRIC divisions, China showed no concern to present a common political front with Brazil and Russia; its only concern was furthering its economic interests in Iran. Noteworthy, too, in this episode is the ease with which the United States was able to divide the BRICs on the basis of economic arguments. The US ability to divide the BRICs reflects the simple fact that the BRICs' rise has come on the back of economic might; if political arguments threaten their economic interests, they seem quite happy to forget about any political considerations.

In 2011, the BRICs have shown unanimity in voting against UN intervention in Libya. Yet again, it was a negative vote of non-intervention, not a constructive action. That is not to say that the political implications of non-intervention are not real. If Russia and China had used their veto instead of abstaining, the BRICs (India and Brazil are not permanent members) would have overruled the West's global political agenda, which in itself attests to their status as a global political force. They chose to abstain this time, but if they were to decide to use their veto, the global political economy would take on a very different appearance.

As it happens, there has already been an important example of what can happen when the BRICs unite, at least in numbers. Graziano da Silva, a Brazilian candidate, was elected to head the Food and Agriculture Organization in June 2011. He received 92 votes, largely from the developing world; 88 votes, largely from the developed world were against him. The political repercussions of this mathematical advantage are yet to be seen, but this could be a chance for a BRIC official to advance a common agenda, especially on the issue of food inflation, a severe problem for all the BRICs. Time will tell. Finally, an equally important test was the UN resolution on Syria. Russia made it clear that it would veto intervention this time, and China was also likely to veto; Brazil and India were lukewarm to the idea of intervention. But probably because the expectation of a veto was so high this time, the West, not taking any chances, avoided the intervention vote. Here again, however, the outcome was one of destruction of the Western agenda, not one of construction.

Even on substantive economic issues, the BRICs lack a common agenda. A prime example is the absence of a common BRIC position at the Doha WTO meeting. On first inspection the failure of the Doha discussions could seem to be a BRIC victory. The fact that failure was partly due to the inability of China, India and the United States to agree on protection levels for the special safeguard mechanism for farmers might be seen as a success from a power perspective. In the days of the WTO's predecessor, GATT, the United States would have spoken its word, and 'Chindia' would have had to give in. In this interpretation the Doha impasse is a symbol of a world where emerging markets are throwing their weight around. In reality, one cannot understate the role of the division between Brazil and China/India in the Doha impasse. Brazil, unlike India, was willing to compromise on non-farm sector protection. Even before the Doha talks, Brazil had made it clear that it was willing to sacrifice some of the protections of its manufacturing sector in order to secure agricultural access in the developed world, something India and China could not reconcile themselves to. In particular, Brazil had come close to an agreement with the European Union that would have given Brazil access to the EU's ethanol market in exchange for concessions on Brazilian barriers to manufactured goods, which Brazil's private sector seemed willing to accept.

Another illustration of the lack of a common BRIC economic platform is the following. There was much talk in the second half of the noughties that the BRICs might use a reserve currency other than the dollar. Yet China which was too exposed to the dollar through its investments in US Treasuries, quickly vetoed the idea, long before the Greek debt crisis ruled out the euro as an alternative reserve currency (assuming it remains a currency at all). However, given the euro crisis, it might be time to turn emerging market currencies themselves into reserve currencies. This process could be a platform to foster integration of emerging market currencies. Yet using these as reserve currencies requires a framework to facilitate the introduction of new currencies, one whereby central banks make measured allocations to them. So far the BRICs show signs of limited momentum towards this goal.

On the other hand, there was a slow rise in the issuance of Chinese renminbi-denominated corporate bonds in 2010–11, with a Russian bank, VTB, issuing such bonds, after McDonald's and Caterpillar. The latest company to join the bandwagon is Unilever, which issued 300 million renminbi in such bonds in March 2011. Multinationals and banks have done the same, mostly to gain the approval of Chinese authorities; the more foreign private sector players issue the bonds, the greater the credibility of the renminbi in the offshore market. Still, this is a corporate development, and it does not require the common framework that a new reserve currency would.

At the same time, by allowing domestic companies to move renminbi offshore for investment purposes since January 2010, China has gradually tried to turn the renminbi into a global currency for trade. Conversely, in December 2011 the Chinese securities regulator announced that renminbi held offshore could be used to buy equities within China,[53] which also contributes to turning the renminbi into a global currency, this time for investment. Still, foreign funds only account for 1 per cent of total market value in China, and one cannot draw the implication from these two reforms that China has abandoned controls on the movement of capital. Far from it.[54]

It will be a matter of great interest to see whether the renminbi takes off as a trading currency in the other BRICs. Economists at HSBC expect that at least half of China's trade flows with emerging markets could be settled in renminbi within three to five years, from less than 3 per cent in 2012.[55] They could well be right: in January 2011 alone, the Bank of China's total renminbi trade settlements amounted to 40 billion renminbi, a quarter of the total it handled in all of 2010. Yet one's amazement at this fact is a measure of how far the BRICs have to go before they use the renminbi as a currency for trade, let alone a new reserve currency, especially as it is not openly traded on the capital markets!

On the economic front, there are many more examples of division that exclude a common BRIC agenda. Brazil and India pressuring China to revalue the renminbi,[56] much to the US's delight, comes to mind instantly, but the list goes on. One of the most interesting developments concerns Brazil's plans to place restrictions on all new farmland investment from foreign sovereign funds; this is an obvious move towards food security in the context of booming food prices and an attempt to stall China's move to snap up Brazilian land.[57] Similarly, the Brazilian government's local content requirements in the oil industry also serve to avert a Chinese takeover of its prized oil resources. Petrobras is the sole operator of fields in the massive new oil discovery area off the coast of Rio de Janeiro; it has a minimum 30 per cent stake in any project there. This is a turnaround relative to previous policy, which stipulated that any company could bid for an oil block on an equal footing. The government has set-up a 100 per cent government-controlled company that has veto power over investment decisions in each block.[58] A final source of tensions between Brazil and China is tied to the Brazilian government's unseating of Roger Agnelli, the chief executive of the iron ore producer Vale, reportedly because he was exporting too many products to China instead of keeping them at home and investing in the domestic steel, shipbuilding and fertilizer industries.[59] All of these examples show that there is no solidarity or common BRIC agenda when it comes to asserting industrial policies, which are often at odds with each other.

Thus, the limits of BRIC solidarity are clear. No one is about to be blinded by BRIC political power, for the simple reason that there is no such thing as a BRIC block. Naturally, the United States and Europe play up these divisions, especially as a pressure point on China, so much so that BRI are now poised to exploit their position between China and the USA. Consequently, the development of a multipolar world, a world where BRICs will be one player among many, seems to be on the cards. A historical comparison with the fall of the Roman Empire offers a frightening parallel, in that it coincided with the ascent of the Visigoths and Goths. Unable to replicate the Pax Romana, they instead presided over a fracturing of European territories into weak kingdoms. The rise of the BRICs in the context of US and European decline could easily replicate this model, with the vacuum left by the declining US hegemon not being filled by a BRIC block with a strong new direction.

The next two chapters suggest that even of the BRICs were to agree on a common political agenda through some form of cohesion, the sustainability of this power would be threatened by inequality and by their lack of weight in the realm of ideas. Ideas – in the form of culture, science and innovation particularly – are still dominated by the West; this is likely to remain the case for a long time. Because ideas are the key to sustainable power, the conclusion reached is that the BRICs are far from 'ruling the world'.

4
Limit No. 1: BRICs and Inequality

Imagine for a second that you were poor in the BRICs. You can neither improve your lot through economic opportunities – you lack the assets, the land and the education to seize them – nor make policy more pro-poor – policy is shaped by a coalition of politicians and the economic elite. Your economic prospects are bleak, and politically speaking, you are effectively disenfranchised. What is left to you? The streets. Whether you take to them or not depends on how frustrated you are and how visible the enrichment of other classes is. With the BRIC 'economic miracle' under threat, frustration and visible enrichment are both reaching high levels in the BRICs. This chapter investigates the reasons for this situation.

As was suggested in the previous chapter, the scope for a new world order in which the BRICs would increase their global political power is limited, first, by the developed countries' opposition and, second, by the BRICs' own reluctance to embrace a common agenda. Yet even if enhanced BRIC political power had more momentum, there is reason to think it would soon collapse, not so much for political as for economic reasons. Since the BRICs' claim to political power is founded on economic weight, it would fall with the collapse of the economic miracle.

As it happens, there are two reasons for believing that the days of the economic miracle are numbered. First, domestic inequality in the BRICs, through which the incomes of the people at the top have risen much faster than those of the rest, threatens the economic miracle's sustainability. Second, the absence of genuine innovation capability leaves the BRICs with no engine of long-term economic growth. By investigating the implications of domestic inequality for economic growth in the four BRICs, this chapter examines the first threat, beginning with a theoretical discussion of the links between inequality and growth and then moving onto its application to the BRICs.

Reinventing Marx or can inequality become sexy again?

Heated debates on the subject of inequality ceased to be trendy long ago. Niall Ferguson's assertion about China's outbreaks of rural protest that 'only a fevered imagination could build a revolutionary scenario on these slender foundations'[1] implies that the days when inequality sparked revolutionary fervour are long gone. It is as if he were saying, 'how could you be so naive as to believe that rural discontent could spark a major social uprising'? After all, the mere mention of inequality instantly calls to mind Marx's belief that workers' intolerance of inequality would result in the overthrow of capitalism. Since Marx was proven wrong, it is only natural to dispose of his main concept, Ferguson seems to imply. Yet just as the collapse of civilizations is unpredictable as Ferguson admits, so is the decline of an economic powerhouse like the BRICs. Hence it makes no sense to rule out inequality as a central factor in the BRICs' economic decline, any more than it makes sense to rule out any other trigger. Kenneth Rogoff's view that 'inequality is the big wildcard in the next decade of global growth'[2] underlines why the unequal BRICs are in a vulnerable position. Rogoff focuses specifically on the fact that domestic inequality in developed countries, especially the United States, has returned to levels last seen a century ago. He notes that 'the status quo has to be vulnerable. Instability can express itself anywhere. It was just over four decades ago that urban riots and mass demonstrations rocked the developed world, ultimately catalyzing far-reaching social and political reforms'. Similarly, George Packer demonstrates the eroding consequences of US inequality on power and democracy in an article in *Foreign Affairs*.[3] Yet we suggest that inequality also looks to be the wild card in the next decade of BRIC growth (and by extension global growth). While the United States returns to previous inequality peaks, the BRICs are discovering for the first time the pain that comes from achieving a long period of record growth without due attention to income distribution. Until now, they had inequality without growth or with short bouts of growth.

If inequality is indeed about to become sexy again, it is important to understand its main features. Its first characteristic is that it is multidimensional. Instead of merely being experienced through income disparity, it is increasingly taking on forms such as differentiated access to basic services, infrastructure and knowledge. Access to knowledge is particularly relevant to this analysis given the focus on innovation, which builds on existing knowledge, as the driver of long-term growth. Race, gender, ethnicity and geography are also discrimination criteria; they determine people's access to income, basic services, infrastructure and knowledge. These different bases of discrimination are more or less accentuated in the different BRICs; geography, perhaps the most common one, is a direct consequence of the BRICs' development process, which has created local pockets of export-oriented economic dynamism in all four countries.

Inequality is multidimensional in that it can refer to opportunity or outcomes. Opportunity, which refers to the life chances of individuals, is based on a multiplicity of economic, political and social factors. One of the best measures of opportunity is access to education, as it is the central means of self-improvement; but access to land, health, knowledge and financing matter too. In contrast, outcomes can be measured through income, wages, the intersectoral differential between wages and productivity, or patterns of employment, which are mainly divided between formal and informal employment. Inequality of opportunity may be more important than inequality of outcomes, although the data on the former are unfortunately much harder to get, which leads to the use of outcome inequality data as a complement. Two individuals with the same opportunity may end up with different incomes, based on who is the more ambitious or hard-working; that seems like a fair outcome. More problematic is the situation where two individuals, with the same ambition and work ethic, end up with different incomes because they did not have the same opportunity. In that situation the cases where inequality reflects differences in individuals' efforts, such as education and type of work must be distinguished, from those where individuals are not responsible for differences in circumstances, such as family background. To understand inequality, one must identify the mechanism through which differences in opportunity emerge despite individual effort.

As far as income inequality is concerned, it is worth differentiating between relative and absolute measures of inequality. The difference is exemplified by Ravallion: 'consider an economy with just two households with incomes: $1,000 and $10,000. If both incomes double in size then relative inequality, which is about ratios, will remain the same;

the richer household is still ten times richer. But absolute inequality, which is about the absolute difference in their incomes, has doubled from $9,000 to $18,000. Relative inequality is unchanged but absolute inequality has risen sharply'.[4] Interest lies both in changes in relative inequality and in changes in the income ratio of the richest to the poorest segments of the population. As a macroeconomic summary measure of relative inequality outcomes in the dimension of income, this book uses the Gini index of inequality throughout. It is a coefficient that varies between 0, which reflects complete equality, and 100, which indicates complete inequality (such that one person accounts for all the national income or consumption, the others account for none). One of its advantages is that it can be used to compare income distributions across several countries as well as to compare income distribution within one country over time. It is also widely available. consumption, the others account for none). One of its advantages is that it can be used to compare income distributions across several countries as well as to compare income distribution within one country over time. It is also widely available.

The Gini index has some downsides, however, because the total Gini of a society is not equal to the sum of the Ginis for its subgroups, an alternative measure of income inequality, called the Theil measure, is preferable if the focus is on differences in inequality across subgroups. Furthermore, information on the relative Gini index misses out on other important information. First, it gives only a snapshot of income distribution at a point in time and reveals little about intergenerational mobility across income groups; thus, complementing information gathered from the relative Gini with information on mobility in the BRICs is important. Russia, for instance, displays a relatively low Gini, but income mobility remains a significant concern. Second, as Ravallion notes, 'perceptions that "inequality is rising" may well relate more to absolute than relative inequality. Observers such as citizens and non-governmental organizations working in developing countries can easily see the rising absolute gap in living standards between selected poor people and selected "rich" people. The fact that the proportionate gap may well be unchanged is less evident to the naked eye, if only because this requires knowledge of the overall mean'.[5] Given this book's particular concern with the role of inequality in fomenting political instability, the 'visibility' of inequality becomes highly important and highlights the importance of absolute inequality. Another criticism arises in considering an unequal society where the relative Gini is above 50 but where the poverty line[6] – the level of income below which people are considered poor – is much higher than US$1.50 a day. Inequality between people is of less concern where they all make a decent income than in a society where the poverty line is at US$1.50 a day. In other words, it is where poverty and inequality are combined that inequality is especially problematic. Hence, in our BRIC cases, we make a point of combining poverty and inequality data.

Theoretical links between inequality and growth

The central question this chapter raises is whether inequality can emerge as a threat to the growth miracle of the BRICs. To examine this question, the mechanisms through which inequality can affect growth at the theoretical level first need to be identified. Some arguments posit that inequality is good for growth; some are based on the premise that rich people's propensity to save is higher than that of poor people (see Bourguignon),[7] and others on the existence of a trade-off between equality and efficiency (see Mirrlees).[8]

Yet Mick Moore and Howard White noted that the, 'the intellectual paradigm has shifted in the noughties towards the idea that there is an intrinsic and positive connection between income equality and economic growth. The *World Development Report 2000/1* [the World Development Report is a key publication of the World Bank, which sets the tone of global development policy recommendations] argues that better income distribution is good for economic growth; hence, redistribution reduces poverty both by redirecting resources to the poor and by promoting growth'.[9] A good summary of why inequality can threaten the sustainability of growth is provided by Bardhan; as he notes, 'barriers faced by the poor in land and capital markets and in skill acquisition and in coping with risks sharply reduce a society's potential for productive investment, innovation and human resource development'.[10] Indeed, the point is that inequality is a killer of potential. Implicitly it reduces potential output, which is the highest level of output an economy could produce if all its resources were employed, even though it may not have immediate repercussions on real economic growth.

According to the World Bank, there are three main arguments supporting the hypothesis that inequality is bad for growth. The first, a political economy argument, is based on the idea that in unequal societies, the demand for fiscal redistribution financed by distortionary taxa-

ion is higher. Since fiscal redistribution increases the tax burden on capitalists and reduces their propensity to invest, it is bad for growth.

The second argument, related to the existence of credit constraints, starts from the premise that growth increases as investment in human capital increases. However, credit constraints prevent poorer individuals from investing in education, which means that inequality decreases growth prospects by reducing the number of individuals who are able to invest in human capital.

The third argument is the one to be emphasized by this book. Called the socio-political instability approach, it was spearheaded by Alesina and Perotti.[11] In an econometric analysis of 71 countries, they examined two questions: (1) Does income inequality increase political instability? (2) Does political instability reduce investment? They found that both answers were yes. The more unequal a society, the more likely it is to express social discontent through social unrest; hence; it is politically unstable, in the sense that it displays a higher probability of coups, revolutions, mass violence and policy uncertainty and is more of a threat to property rights. In turn, political instability has an adverse effect on investment, as it discourages accumulation and growth because of current disruptions and future uncertainty.

Nothing illustrates Alesina and Perotti's argument better than the comparison between the development trajectories of the newly industrializing economies (NIEs) and Latin America after the Second World War. In 1960 both the NIEs and Latin America had similar levels of GDP per capita. Since then, the two regional economies started to diverge, with the NIEs posting higher growth and political stability than Latin America. It can be argued that the land reforms which swept across the NIEs in the post-war period created the foundations of a more equal society, resulting in greater political stability and growth than in Latin America, where there were no such land reforms. Equally noteworthy is the fact that the development trajectory of the NIEs, which combines growth with low inequality, also contrasts starkly with the 'growth only' trajectory of the BRICs. In 2009, South Korea's Gini index was an impressive 32, while China's was 40.8.[12]

Finally, one should add a fourth link between inequality and growth, one that is particularly important in view of the overall thesis: if it can be shown that inequality is bad for innovation, it must be bad for growth, given that innovation is the engine of long-term growth. Intuitively, inequality would seem to have a high opportunity cost in terms of lost human capital and hence innovation. Yet it is hard to claim that inequality is systematically bad for innovation:

there are many examples of national systems of innovation which thrive despite large and enduring structural inequalities (Israel comes to mind). Whether they are reaching their full potential is another question, which the concluding chapter will examine (see its final section, "The Perverse Political Economy of Innovation in Cases of Economic Inequality"). At this point, what can be said with certainty is that inequality is likely to constrain the evolution of the system of innovation towards a particular profile of innovation. Indeed, since inequality means that learning capabilities are concentrated outside the low-income segment of the population, the supply of innovation is monopolized by the wealthy, as they have privileged access to existing knowledge – the main raw material of innovation. At the same time, the type of innovation produced is geared towards the demands of the middle- to upper-class segments, who are the main consumers of innovative products. Innovation is *by* the rich *for* the rich; the poor are excluded from the entire process, which ends up exacerbating yet another form of inequality: access to the production and consumption of innovation.

As is often the case, the empirical evidence from econometric analyses on the effects of inequality on growth is inconclusive. Some findings support the existence of a positive relationship, whereby more inequality increases growth (see Li and Zou[13] or Forbes[14]), or even no relationship (see Barro[15] or Lopez[16]).

Yet given that the theoretical literature which posits that inequality decreases growth seems more compelling, a close look at the evidence supporting the existence of a negative relationship is warranted. Alesina and Rodrick[17] and Perotti[18] find that more inequality leads to lower growth. In a related albeit slightly different investigation, Easterly and Rebelo[19] find that income redistribution is likely to have a positive impact on growth. Above all, the most conclusive evidence relates to the fact that asset inequality, more than income inequality per se, can have a negative impact on growth. Deininger and Squire[20] find that high inequality in land distribution has a significant negative effect on future growth. More generally, Birdsall and Londoño[21] find that the initial distribution of assets has a strong relationship with growth. These findings confirm this volume's focus on inequality of opportunity, which is primarily revealed by unequal access to assets. Hence we follow-up the above theoretical discussion with are individual case studies of inequality in the four BRICs, with particular focus on inequality of opportunity.

BRICs and the dangerous cocktail of inequality and inflation

Waking the dormant dragon of inequality: the critical catalysts

An important question regarding the role of inequality in BRIC sustainability is why inequality presents a threat *now*. Since the economic miracle occurred in conditions of inequality, some might even argue that inequality was good for the BRICs' growth.

In the case of China, sociologist Martin King Whyte argues that economic inequality lacks the power to mobilize the Chinese in a way that would endanger economic growth. Based on his research, the Chinese have a 'quasi-American' belief that individual effort enables people to get ahead and that there is no need to create a socially optimal outcome to rectify the outcome of individual efforts.[22] King's findings are based on the first systematic nationwide sample survey of popular Chinese attitudes towards inequality trends and distributive injustice issues. He finds that 'to be sure, most respondents felt that the gap in incomes nationwide was too large, and they objected to some other aspects of current inequalities, such as laying off state factory workers and systemic discrimination faced by urban migrants. However, the prevailing view is that, despite some unjust features and practices, overall patterns of inequality in China today are fair enough to enable ordinary citizens to get ahead and prosper based on hard work, talent and training'.[23] One still has to ask, what would the Chinese think specifically of inequality due to bad luck – that is, circumstances – as opposed to low effort? According to Yingqiang and Eriksson,[24] this type represents the bulk of Chinese inequality. Furthermore, in response to the position of whether the pattern of Chinese citizen responses to his questions indicates a potential source of future political instability, King claims that the answer is 'a resounding no', although he hastens to add 'for the time of the survey' (2004).[25] Yet this qualification is crucial to interpreting King's results. One of the main explanations King offers for the lack of anger against injustice is borrowed from the first phase of the 'tunnel effect'[26] described by development economists Hirschman and Rotschild, who compare perceptions of inequality in a developing society to a lane of drivers in a tunnel. If one lane starts to move after an irritatingly long time, drivers in the other lanes will be relieved rather than angry because they believe that their turn is next. This is the basic logic behind overall Chinese tolerance of inequality at the beginning of the process of development. However, Hirschman and Rotschild describe a second phase in 'tunnel psychology', one ignored by King. In this phase, if only the first lane continues to move for a long time, the sentiment of anger takes over in the other lanes. In other words, as the process of development continues, if only the few continue to benefit, social discontent arises. Many see China as having reached this second stage. While King's analysis might offer strong support to the reasoning of the first stage because it describes Chinese perceptions in 2004 (i.e., only a few years into China's experience of double-digit, export-driven growth), a number of facts examined in this chapter lead to the belief that the Chinese masses have started to lose their tolerance for a growth process that has not trickled down to them in the way they expected it to by now.

Still, the question remains as to why inequality should suddenly become an issue for societies which have lived with it for so long. As a rule, something specific causes inequality to become a threat to a society. This notion is related to the question of what causes the fall of civilizations in general. As Niall Ferguson argues, civilizations 'can appear to operate quite stably for some time, apparently in equilibrium, in reality constantly adapting. But there comes a moment when they 'go critical'. A slight perturbation can set off a 'phase transition' from a benign equilibrium to a crisis – a single grain of sand causes an apparently stable sandcastle to fall in on itself'.[27] One might add that the sandcastle usually has been unstable for some time, as has inequality in the BRICs. Just as civilizations seem to fall under the impulse of a slight perturbation (the Roman Empire's collapse under the impulse of the barbarian invaders of the early fifth century comes to mind), the BRIC sandcastles could easily appear to collapse due to a single grain of sand called inflation. In reality, though, the instability of inequality always makes these sandcastles vulnerable. As is shown below, inequality is a dormant threat, one that wreaks havoc on economic stability when it is activated by a strong catalyst – such as food or house price inflation.

One potential grain of sand could be the unprecedented inflationary pressures which the BRICs are faced with and which could force the poor into political action. Indeed, while BRIC inflation came off its peak in the last quarter of 2011, the structural forces behind BRIC inflation, especially food inflation, will exert upside pressures in the long-term, as is shown below. With Brazilian average annual inflation still at a disappointing 6.6 per cent versus a 4.5 per cent official target,[34] Chinese inflation at 4.2 per cent versus a 4 per cent target, Indian inflation at 9.4 per cent (India does not have a target per se), one can only

Table 4.1 BRIC inflation and growth, %

Country	Brazil	Russia	India	China
2010 average inflation	5.9	8.8	12.4	3.3
2011 average inflation[28]	6.6	8.7	9.6	5.5
Interest rate	11[29]	8[30]	8.5[31]	6.56[32]
2011 real GDP growth[33]	3.2	4.1	7.5	9.4

Source: Author's calculations based on Bloomberg.

be surprised that the Tunisian democratic revolution has not spread to all of these countries (while Russian inflation is now lower than the 7% target at 6.8%, inflation has also been above target for much of the year and is likely to return above target). Crucially, real interest rates, which are adjusted for inflation, are still very low or negative in many of the BRICs, as can be seen in Table 4.1.

So far, high inflation levels are largely the result of food price inflation in the BRICs; in China in particular, the average annual food price inflation is 13.4 per cent; in India it is 9 per cent. Food price inflation is not a short-term phenomenon. In an article called 'Rising Prices on the Menu', the IMF notes that 'policymakers – particularly in emerging and developing economies – will likely have to continue confronting the challenges posed by food prices that are both higher and more volatile than the world has been used to'.[35] The clear implication is that the present rise in food inflation is a secular phenomenon: 'since the turn of the century, food prices have been rising steadily – except for declines during the global financial crisis in late 2008 and early 2009 – and this suggests that these increases are a trend and don't just reflect temporary factors'. The IMF explains that the changing diets of consumers in emerging markets are the most important explanation for rising food prices, which they see as irreversible. As they get richer, these consumers are eating more high-protein foods: meat, dairy products, edible oils, fruits and vegetables, and seafood. Hence, more crops are used for animal feed, resulting in emerging and developing economies accounting for about three-quarters of the total growth in global demand for major crops since the early 2000s.[36] Ironically, this implies that food inflation is once again a by-product of the development process itself.

It is particularly problematic in the context of emerging markets. To start with, emerging market populations spend a much higher proportion of their income on food. Hence, when international food prices suddenly increase, the result is higher domestic inflation overall, as imported inflation passes into domestic inflation. If international food prices then stabilize, these 'first round effects' fade. But if food price increases affect domestic consumers' expectations of future inflation, then 'second-round effects' occur, and they are more serious. When people expect food to continue to go up in price, they begin to demand higher wages, leading to increased 'core' inflation – that is, non-food inflation. For instance, partly as a result of food inflation, Indian non-food manufacturing inflation, which amounts to core inflation, rose from –2.4 per cent in July 2009 to 6.1 per cent in February 2011 – hence, the Reserve Bank of India's decision to engage in aggressive interest rate tightening.

Unfortunately, risks of a pass-through from rising food prices to core inflation are higher for emerging economies. First, as noted above, the share of expenditure allocated to food in emerging markets is much larger than that in developed markets; the cost shares of raw food are also larger. Hence, food price spikes are more likely to unhinge inflation expectations and trigger increases in wage demands. Second, monetary policy credibility in emerging economies remains low despite recent improvements, implying that economic actors will be less confident that their central bank will succeed in containing inflation pressures than they would be in developed countries; consequently, they will be more likely to adjust their medium-term inflation expectations upwards.

The structural upward shift in food prices could be the straw that broke the BRIC camel's back, since inflationary pressures on unequal BRIC economies increase the likelihood in these countries of political instability. And an emerging market with an unequal income distribution, where the poor consume a greater share of their income on food, is especially likely to respond to food inflation with political instability, which poses a risk to growth and development at large. Yet it is important to grasp that while food price inflation may act as a catalyst, inequality is the root problem causing the development process to backtrack. Hence, policymakers must ensure that inequality is kept in check, especially as it seems that they will have little control over food inflation, a structural phenomenon. While many BRIC central bankers will still be tempted to resort to monetary policy instruments to control inflation, they are unlikely to succeed, as inflation's causes are to a large extent secular changes in patterns of food demand. Addressing inequality might be a more difficult, long-term goal, but it will at least provide a sustainable solution. The best way for policymakers to mitigate the effects of the structural rise in food prices is to reduce the vulnerability of the poor in the first place by attacking inequality. The alternative is significant political instability, as is clear from the cases of North Africa and the Middle East.

Unrest has already begun in India, Russia and China. In democratic India inflation has been above 9 per cent for nearly two years and is the highest on the Asian continent. The government of Manmohan Singh has been under threat, as he has been accused of privileging growth at all costs, thereby creating overheating and inflation, which penalizes the poor. According to the *New York Times*, in 2011 India experienced the biggest protests it has seen in nearly two decades.[37] They were led by an activist, Anna Hazare, who was on a hunger strike against corruption and high inflation; he galvanized the middle class and the young in particular. It came as no surprise that in December 2011 the cabinet approved a multibillion-dollar food subsidy bill. It guaranteed extremely cheap grains to the poor, as it sought to cover 75 per cent of the rural population and 50 per cent of the urban population.[38] Ahead of the state elections of 2012, it was clearly an attempt by the ruling party to boost its popularity. Also noteworthy was the fact that the government preferred to soothe the population's inflation concerns than to set up the anticorruption agency required by Hazare, especially in the run-up to the elections. While the food subsidy legislation still has to be approved by Parliament (the legislation is with the Parliamentary Standing Committee and would be voted on in the monsoon session of Parliament), it is already a good measure of the ruling party's concerns about political unrest and of its re-election ambitions. Russia also saw the rumblings of social unrest, as 100,000 people supported a protest movement in central Moscow on 24 December 2011. However, they were motivated more by anger against corruption and the lack of democracy evident in fraudulent Parliamentary elections than by concerns over inflation or inequality. As in India, there was significant participation of the middle classes in the protest.

In China students rioted specifically over food inflation, in a country where food accounts for 30 per cent of average household spending. Even beyond the role of food, there are structural reasons, in the form of supply shortages, indicating that Chinese inflation is likely to remain a significant problem in the years to come. Its population of 15- to 24-year-olds is shrinking about twice as fast as Japan's, which is already well known for its ageing population.[39] Because of the resulting scarcity, Chinese labour is gaining increased bargaining power, which has encouraged strikes and protests. A good example is the strike organized in the last week of 2011 at an LG Display factory in eastern China by 8000 workers who complained about the insufficiency of their year-end bonuses in the face of rising living costs.[40] As of early 2012, management had offered to double year-end bonuses but had not met workers' demands to have their bonuses tripled or quadrupled.

With official 'incidents' (strikes, protests and riots) reaching 180,000 in 2010, or twice as many as five years ago,[41] the Chinese government is concerned about the impact of inflation on democratization. Witness the rise in spending on internal public security to 549 billion renminbi (US$84 billion) in 2010, which for the first time overtook national defence spending of 533.4 billion renminbi.[42] The government has been making efforts to contain inflation through supply-boosting measures and subsidies to low-income workers and has engaged in aggressive interest rate tightening since October 2010.[43] But the People's Bank of China is still the puppet of the National Development and Reform Commission, which effectively shows more concern with the legitimacy afforded by record growth rates than with taming inflation. Recent increases in the minimum wage also testify to the inconsistencies of a government not focused entirely on inflation.

At least part of the solution to the inflation problem lies in letting the renminbi appreciate more significantly than it has so far. In June 2010 the exchange rate was allowed to appreciate, and the renminbi had appreciated by 7.5 per cent against the dollar by the end of 2011, in the space of one and a half years.[44] If the government is too slow to adopt this solution for fear of strangling growth, the discontent caused by inflation may prove to be a major source of political instability. A survey by Morgan Stanley found that Chinese consumers are among the most perturbed in Asia by the current bout of inflation.[45]

Alternatively, if food prices do not galvanize the poor into action, inaccessible house prices combined with inequality could do so. While house prices have come off their highs in most BRICs, especially China, they remain well out of reach for the poor. For a poor person, the vision of a growing share of affluent people making enormous profit margins from housing market speculation while the poor have no roofs over their heads is arguably just as frustrating as a lack of access to food. Access to food and housing are both defined as basic needs; when access to them becomes a privilege, it is likely to spark unrest. In India, house price indices suggest that prices in Chennai, Mumbai, Delhi and Kolkata more than doubled between 2007 and 2011.[46] This is also the case in such non-metropolitan cities as Bhopal and Lucknow. Similarly, while the annual growth in China's property prices has slowed from 12.8 per cent in April 2010 to 2.2 per cent in November 2011, prices displayed a fivefold increase in the last decade.[47] In 2011 a property tax on second homes, limits on home purchases and increases in down payment requirements were some of the government measures enacted to cool house prices. Even if these measures prove effective, they will be a case of too little too late, at least from a social point of view. In a country where a typical 1000-square-foot Beijing apartment costs about 80 times the average annual income of a Beijing resident, it is hard to see how public resentment against spiralling house prices could become more intense anyway.[48] In Brazil, too, while residential property prices in Rio de Janeiro and São Paulo have stabilized since September 2011, prices in Rio de Janeiro rose by 99 per cent between February 2008 and January 2011 and in São Paulo by 81 per cent, according to the Fipe economic research institute's newly launched index called FipeZap, Indice de Precos de Imoveis Anunciados.[49] Similarly, in Russia the average price of Moscow residential real estate increased more than fivefold between 2003 and August 2011,[50] after mortgages first became available in 2003 (the state gave people the homes they occupied after the collapse of the Soviet Union). Following the global financial crisis, demand for real estate has shot up, as the slump is allowing people to buy real property on the cheap. Given that eight out of ten Russians say they want to move, there is a significant housing shortfall in Russia, and it is boosting prices.

It is not just that high food and house prices in conditions of inequality have the potential to spark social tension and thereby threaten growth in the BRICs. Inequality in itself could threaten the BRIC growth miracle, even without political unrest, by simply causing BRIC financial markets to crash.[51] Recent interpretations of the causes of the US financial crisis highlight the role of inequality in the subprime disaster as a crucial factor; one look at the similarities between what happened in the United States before the financial crisis and what is now happening in the BRICs is chilling. Piketty and Saez have shown that in 2007 the share of total income going to the richest 1 per cent of Americans reached a peak unseen since 1928. They also found that during the period 2002–7 the inflation-adjusted income of the top 1 per cent of households grew more than ten times faster than that of the bottom 90 per cent of households.[52] Piketty and Saez showed that increased inequality caused households to borrow excessively to maintain their consuming power.[53] They believe that the combination of inequality and the credit boom sparked economic disaster. When home prices began to decline in 2006, the unsustainability of credit-fuelled consumption became evident, with the repercussions that we all know about.

If one considers the property bubbles which have developed in the BRICs and the credit booms which have fuelled these bubbles,[54] the similarity with the US situation becomes striking. While the Chinese government has introduced credit quotas in banks, informal sector loans made by trusts are providing an easy alternative for the private sector to continue fuelling the credit boom. In Brazil the IMF suggests that there has been a nearly 100 per cent rise in private credit since 2007; after hitting a low in 2010, the Brazilian arm of the credit rating agency Serasa Experian reports that defaults have started to rise since May 2011.[55] In India even the State Bank of India, the country's largest, is plagued by the provision of bad loans.[56] Maybe the BRICs have something to learn about the dangers of inequality from the US and maybe it is worth reducing inequality after all.

Inequality in the BRICs

While Brazil is one of the countries with the worst distribution of income in the world, India and Russia are among those with the largest percentage of the population living below the poverty line, at 28.6 and 30.9 per cent, respectively, in the mid-2000s. Both India and Brazil have made improvements to lessen inequality, measured in terms of the Gini index, with Brazil the real outperformer. According to the CIA World Factbook, it reduced its index value from 60.7 in 1998 to 53.9 in 2009; India's index fell from 37.8 (1997) to 36.8 (2004); China's increased from 40 (2001) to 41.5 (2007); Russia's also increased from 39.9 (2001) to 42.2 (2009).[57] One source of income disparity common to all four BRICs is geographical. In a sense, one could argue that this is an inevitable impact of development, in the form of the initial emergence of localized nuclei of high performance. In other words, development has to start somewhere, and to begin with, that somewhere will be the more developed areas. The challenge is to create linkages between these nuclei and the rest of the economy as soon as possible so as to diffuse the process of development. Yet practically 60 per cent of the total GDP of Brazil still originates in the states of the South-east. The Chinese economic development model also favours the coastal provinces. As for Russia, high incomes are focused geographically around Moscow. A second side effect of the process of development is the appearance of another fault line of inequality: that between the rural and urban population. This is very much the case in China. India also has a similar geographical and rural-urban divide. It is of course to be expected that the development process will be prone to polarization, and all four BRICs are going through this process. But how have their individual development policies sought to contain this polarization, and what success they have had in doing so?

China

China shares with Russia a history of communist pursuit of an egalitarian society. While this society may have been more an ideal than a reality, the nations also share the social disintegration that followed the collapse of the communist regimes and the introduction of capitalist reforms. It is not clear whether the specific experience of transition to a different economic system or the general experience of developing country reform has had the greatest repercussions on inequality. Does it make a difference to current patterns that China and Russia once had a degree of equality and lost it, while India and Brazil have always been unequal societies? Not necessarily. China and Russia set out on such an extreme reconstruction of their economic systems that it seemed to uproot any residue of previous egalitarian values, which were purposely discarded due to associations with failure. With the rejection of the communist economic system came a transition to a very particular kind of market economy, one that concentrated power at the level of production (resulting in quasi monopolies) and at the level of income, with obvious repercussions on efficiency and equality. With the switch to this type of market economy, China and Russia could soon have income inequality levels dangerously close to those achieved by Latin American countries with a history of inequality going back to colonial times.

In the last five years, Chinese GDP growth has averaged 10 per cent (it reached 10.3% in 2010), fuelling a decline in the poverty rate from 64 per cent at the beginning of reform to 10 per cent in 2004, according to David Dollar.[58] The extent of the reduction in absolute poverty is impressive: between 1978 and 2007 the annual real income per capita of rural residents increased from 133.6 (US$19.60) to 4140.6 renminbi (US$606.20), and for urban residents it went from 133.6 (US$50.30) to 13,785.8 renminbi (US$2018.40).[59]

Still, one in ten Chinese live on the equivalent of US$1.50 a day or less. What is more, growth has not helped to suppress inequality; quite the contrary. As Niall Ferguson notes, 'an estimated 0.4 per cent of Chinese households currently own around 70 per cent of the country's wealth'.[60] In that context, one has to ask whether it is a coincidence that Prime Minister Wen Jiabao lowered the Chinese growth target to 7 per cent from 7.5 per cent in February 2011.[61] This decision amounts to a partial acknowledgement that overambitious growth targets and little attention to the most vulnerable may have resulted in increased inequality. At the time it seemed that the prime minister was vindicating the thesis that China needs to address inequality and lack of innovation, as he mentioned specifically the priorities of fighting income inequality and corruption and fostering 'creative spirit and independent thinking' instead of building the nth skyscraper. Wen Jiabao's rhetoric raises doubts as to Ferguson's comment that 'the capitalist-communist regime currently enjoys uniquely high levels of legitimacy in the eyes of its own people';[62] if it did, the Chinese leaders would not be making such comments. No doubt the regime enjoys legitimacy in the eyes of the minority 0.4 per cent of the population who benefit from it, but when it comes to the poor, legitimacy is less than clear.

As was noted above, high levels of inequality have ironically become one of the central economic problems of a country where communist leaders had once striven for an egalitarian society. In 1978 the Gini indices of urban and rural areas were, respectively, 16 and 21.[63] China's overall Gini index of inequality, 31.7, made it one of the world's most equal countries. This was especially remarkable considering its size and the fact that it was a low-income economy. Beyond the income dimension, it was a country whose development strategy was focused on fulfilling the 'basic needs' of health and education of the population. Huang notes that 'in 1976, under Mao, China had more doctors, nurses, and hospital beds than virtually any other country at its level of development'.[64] To a large extent, though recent progress has been less than impressive, China is still living off these basic-need achievements. For instance, progress in raising literacy rates came early, and the 91 per cent literacy rate registered in 2003 has more to do with this *acquis* (i.e., historical legacy) than with recent improvements.

Similarly, life expectancy at birth was already a remarkable 67.8 years in 1980 – quite an achievement for a low-income country.[65] It had risen to 73.5 years in 2010, but the improvement in life expectancy was much slower than the improvement in income growth over these years. Life expectancy only rose by five years between 1981 and 2009. In countries that had similar life expectancy levels in 1981 but slower economic growth thereafter – Colombia, Malaysia, Mexico and South Korea, for example – by 2009 life expectancy had grown by 7 to 14 years.[66] In China, HIV/AIDS, tuberculosis, viral hepatitis, rabies and other viral and microbial diseases are a serious concern. More than 130 million people are infected with hepatitis B; that amounts to about one-third of all carriers in the world. Also, incommunicable diseases which are common causes of death in developed countries – cardiovascular disease, chronic respiratory diseases, cancer and the like – account for 85 per cent of deaths in China, a figure much higher than the worldwide average of 60 per cent. A major national survey conducted between 2001 and 2005 found that 17.5 per cent of the population, one of the highest rates in the world, suffered from some form of mental problem (e.g., mood and anxiety disorders). Last but not least, the Chinese suicide rate is 23 per 100,000 population, twice that of the United States. Yet government spending on health fell from 1.1 per cent of GDP in 1980 to about 0.8 per cent in 2002. Instead, the government prioritized economic growth.

A basic contradiction is at work here. The case for improving health care can be based precisely on the negative economic impact of a dysfunctional health care sector. According to Huang, the economic cost of disease in China in 2005 was about 13 per cent of GDP. As he notes, poor health suppresses domestic demand, especially in the absence of a social safety net. Between the mid-1990s and 2006, more than 50 per cent of total health care spending was in the form of patient out-of-pocket payments, which is money not spent on other goods. More directly, the burden of infectious diseases also threatens China's economic development. Eberstadt developed a model suggesting that even a mild HIV/AIDS epidemic, with a peak HIV prevalence rate of 1.5 per cent, would shave more than 0.5 per cent a year off China's growth rate over the following 25 years.[67] All these health indicators suggest that behind the apparently satisfactory life expectancy of 73.5 years, there are many reasons to be concerned about China's health achievements, especially when it comes to the poorest.

While the communist *acquis* at least provided the Chinese with a foundation in health and education that could not collapse instantly, there was no historical buffer to moderate the shock of transition when it came to income inequality. From 31.7 in 1978, the Gini index had risen to 40 by 2001 and 41.5 by 2007. According to Naughton, 'there may be no other case where a society's income distribution has deteriorated so much, so fast'.[68] Especially from 1990 to 2000, a development process driven by an export-oriented strategy exacerbated interregional inequalities, with foreign trade and investment liberalization heading exclusively to particular coastal areas which benefited from public infrastructure growth and export promotion incentives. The result has been a dense concentration of high incomes in Guangdong Province, Shanghai and Beijing.

Beyond the obvious geographical divide, a growing urban-rural gap lies at the heart of inequality in China.[69] To a large extent, this growing gap can be attributed to market reform, as it resulted in greater urbanization. While in 1990 three out of four Chinese lived in the countryside, 45 per cent of people now live in the cities.[70] At the same time, inequality within the urban sector has increased as well, and a growing disparity has arisen between highly educated urban professionals and the urban working class. A prime contributor to urban inequality is wage and employment inequality. Galbraith, Krytynskaia and Wang,[71] who investigated these inequalities across 14 economic sectors, found that the greatest losers from economic transition have been construction, manufacturing, mining and farming; the banking sector is the major winner. Interestingly, those employed in health and education are not among the main income losers. This is no accident: these sectors have been propped up by the Chinese government, which has sought to stimulate domestic consumption by raising average wage levels in these particular state-owned industries. In fact, Galbraith et al. found that the education sectors in Shanghai and Beijing are among the most rapid gainers of income in all of China during the late 1990s.

While the government managed the effects of transition on the wages of social service workers, on the demand side it failed to maintain the access of the poor, especially the rural poor, to these basic services in part because China's decentralized fiscal system relies on local government to fund health and education. Since poor villages cannot afford to provide good services and poor households cannot afford the high costs of basic public services, private health care and education have increasingly replaced government provision of such services. Here, too, the rural sector has been particularly hard hit: rural-urban health disparities worsened as of 1985, and in 2002 under-five mortality was 15 per 1000 in urban areas but 40 per 1000 in rural ones.[72] The maternal mortality rate in rural China was nearly double the urban rate. Education displays the same rural-urban disparity. At the regional level, the poorer regions have fared worse in terms of higher education; they also suffer from outward migration the most.

Still, inequality is higher in the United States, with a Gini index of 45, than in China. As noted above, the United States is among the most

unequal developed countries; its Gini coefficient has displayed an uninterrupted upward trend in the last 40 years in what could be interpreted
as a precursor of the its current economic decline. Yet it is important to
note that the United States has been a relatively unequal country since
1770. A Gini above 30 did not prevent its economic development. In that
sense one might ask why China's inequality could be more damaging
to development than US inequality was. At a basic level, China and the
USA may share high levels of inequality as measured by the Gini index,
but China's high Gini is more of a concern because of its lower GDP per
capita. At equal Gini index levels, income inequality in a poorer society,
measured grossly by GDP per capita, is likely to have more serious consequences (see Figure 4.1).

Furthermore, the distinction between 'constructive' inequality and
'destructive' inequality can be helpful in a USA-China comparison. As
noted by Nancy Birdsall, 'some inequality represents the healthy outcome of differences across individuals in ambition, motivation and
willingness to work. This constructive inequality provides incentives
for mobility and rewards high productivity. Increases in this constructive inequality may simply reflect faster growth in income for the rich
than the poor – but with all sharing in some growth. But inequality
can also be destructive, when for example it reflects deep and persist-
ent differences across individuals and groups in access to the assets that

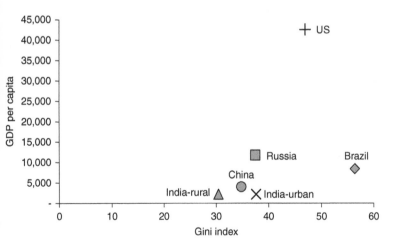

Figure 4.1   GDP per capita versus Gini index: US and BRICs compared
Source: World Bank, PovCalNet and US Census.

generate income – including not only land but also education'.[73] It has been suggested that constructive inequality is synonymous with the US's equal opportunity society, while destructive inequality has prevailed in China, where access to the assets which enable income generation has been unequal. While it is hard to describe the United States as the poster child of constructive inequality these days,[74] the hypothesis that China is characterized by destructive inequality is in line with a primary focus on inequality of opportunity and assets. The research of Yingziang Zang and Tor Eriksson suggests that 63 per cent of Chinese inequality in outcomes is due to inequality of opportunity.[75] They look at the income, education and employer of a person's parents and the person's place of birth and gender as elements beyond individual control. They find that a 10 per cent increase in parental income is associated with a 4.5 per cent income boost for the offspring. Furthermore, they find that having parents employed by the state improves a person's prospects dramatically – something which is examined in more depth below as a BRIC characteristic.

So what, if anything, is the Chinese government doing about inequality? The OECD[76] notes that it has recently increased welfare spending in rural areas. For instance, the 2007 budget nearly doubled funding for a programme of rural medical insurance and scrapped tuition fees for rural students. Similarly, the 2011 budget involves a 14 per cent increase in expenditures on education, social security and employment and a 35 per cent increase in expenditures on low-income housing.

Yet while China is very good at throwing money at problems, this may not solve them (see Chapter 5 on the subject of innovation). After all, the ratio of average urban incomes to average rural incomes is still two to one, according to the OECD itself. In order to further reduce this ratio, the OECD highlights the need for improvements in rural education and the abolition of the household registration system, or hukou. As it happens, the government has already identified rural education as a key priority, as suggested by the abolition of rural tuition fees. But since local governments in rich areas will continue to spend much more on education, educational quality will continue to be unequal despite being free. To deal with this problem, Dollar suggests the setup of equalizing transfers among locations.[77] Similarly, minimum support payments for social protection have been put in place; ironically, because they are funded by local government, wealthy Beijing benefits from high support payments, while rural area payments pale in comparison.

As for the hukou, in the days of central planning, it tied individuals to their birthplace and gave them a household-based residence status at birth. Only urban hukou holders were entitled to receive the social service benefits in the urban areas, thereby preventing rural migrants from settling in the cities permanently. Originally, the system was set up to ensure adequate labour supply in the rural areas and thus guarantee the supply of food. In the 1980s the hukou system was relaxed somewhat so as to allow some rural migrants access to temporary residence permits and some social services. Yet (1) migrants have to pay excessively high fees compared with urban residents; and (2) a majority of migrants do not even qualify for the temporary residence permits and are confined to working in the informal sector. Worse, they are charged 'administration fees' which accentuate inequality. In reality, local governments have a vested interest in maintaining the hukou because the last thing they want is a mass of rural migrants taking jobs from local urban workers and exacerbating local unemployment problems. This is unfortunate, as migration could be one of the most potent means of rectifying inequality,[78] and it would seem to be the most natural antidote to polarization.

Another problem to be tackled by the Chinese authorities is the inexistence of a proper rural land market, one that would allow peasants to sell or mortgage their land use rights. Being able to do so would allow them to finance rural investments or training, which would position them for an improvement in their standard of living. The main problem now is that when land is taken out of agriculture for urban use, peasants get relatively little compensation. As noted below, this is fuelling significant discontent among owners of rural land who are being expropriated. Here again, the government is coming up with a quantitative response to the problem. It comes in the form of the 2011 budget, which organizes the construction of 36 million units of social housing, with low-income housing expenditure up 35 per cent, at 103 billion renminbi. This is no substitute, however, for a market for rural land; that is what really needs to be created.

Finally, apart from these specific changes in micropolicy, a change in macroeconomic policy would also reduce inequality. While export-based growth increased interregional inequality in China, it also aggravated inequality at an aggregate level. Slow as the process may be (the Chinese trade surplus was still an astounding US$170 billion in 2010), the government's recent attempts to rebalance growth towards consumption could help reduce inequality. David Dollar explains why:

an artificially competitive exchange rate stimulates the growth of an export sector that is no longer an important source of job creation (it is too capital-intensive and too high-productivity) and is driving up the incomes only of urban residents who are already wealthy. In that sense, while it may not be an inequality-specific policy, perhaps the most pro-equality policy of all could fall within macroeconomic policy at large – to let the renminbi appreciate further and cool the export sector. This action would also have the benefit of addressing the inflation problem and thereby kill two birds with one stone on the inequality front. At the same time, a higher exchange rate would rebalance the economy towards consumption and shift the economy from manufacturing to services, consumption being primarily services-based. Because services are more labour-intensive than industry, they would contribute to the reduction of inequality, all other things being equal. As Dollar concludes, 'rebalancing toward the domestic market would make China produce more for its own people's needs'. Specifically, it would involve the poorest people in employment by encouraging greater labour intensity.

Yet that is at best a distant prospect, one requiring significant amounts of optimism. The dismantling of structural inequalities will be a long-term operation; while steps are being taken in this direction, dissatisfaction with inequality is likely to grow in the short-term. Reprogramming the Chinese economy towards consumption-based growth will take years, as will allowing the exchange rate to appreciate significantly. In fact, instead of exchange-rate adjustment, Chinese leadership is more likely to tolerate a rise in wages to achieve the same results. It has already announced that it expects China's average minimum wage to grow at least 13 per cent between 2012 and 2017. Similarly, in a country where many cities have separate substandard schools for migrant children, it will take a long time to get rid of the stigma associated with migration.

While rising food prices are disproportionately affecting the poor Chinese and exacerbating inequality, they have not created enough momentum for significant political unrest yet. Rising housing prices have been more of a catalyst for the latter. No doubt the poor are becoming mobilized around this issue; it seems that the threat of immediate homelessness is proving more tangible than a long-term structural rise in food prices. Also, the social asymmetries created by the housing boom are more acute, as the relative nature of housing deprivation in the middle of a housing boom is much more flagrant than that created by high food prices, which, on the face of it, seem to affect everyone. What better encapsulates the 'unfairness' of inequality than property speculation, which fuels the anger and bitterness that is conducive to political unrest? According to a Chinese state think tank, 'grey income' amounting to US$1420 billion is not declared to the tax authorities. Much of it is channelled into property speculation.[79]

In the context of rising house prices, land is being repossessed on a massive scale in order to build high-rise housing developments and sell them to the urban middle class. This process is facilitated by the lack of a proper market for rural land described above. Repossessions are occurring even inland, as urbanization is now spreading away from the coast with the help of the stimulus programme set up by the Chinese government to deal with the 2008 financial crisis. The result: poor farmers kicked off their land are engaging in violent protests against forced demolitions organized by local governments. According to the Chinese Academy of Social Sciences, 65 per cent of large protests in rural areas are related to such demolitions. They are a flagrant sign that the poor have the will and ability to stand up against growing social polarization, as long as it is a manifestation of polarization to which they are sensitive. If there are no attempts to slow this polarization, significant political instability could ensue and put the growth miracle at risk.

Russia

It is striking that while Russian GDP at PPP is on a par with that of France (around US$2.1 trillion), poverty levels in Russia are remarkably high.[80] As Joseph Stiglitz noted, 'in 1989, only 2 percent of those living in Russia were in poverty. By late 1998, that number had soared to 23.8 percent, using the $2 a day standard. More than 40 percent of the country had less than $4 a day, according to a survey conducted by the World Bank. The statistics for children revealed an even deeper problem, with more than 50 percent living in families in poverty'.[81] On the other hand, between 2000 and 2010 the number of people worth over US$10 million in Russia grew by a factor of 21, from 1000 to 21,000.[82] As of 2008, the ratio of the income of the population's top 10 per cent to that of its bottom 10 per cent was 16.9. The richest 5 per cent received about 47.9 per cent of total income.[83] Russia's Gini index increased from 25.9 in the period 1987–90 to 43 in the 1990s. In 2009 it was at 42.2.

It is not only inequality in incomes per se which is shocking; it is especially inequality in access to health care services, once considered virtually a human right in communist Russia. Even for the rich, how tempting would it be to live in a country where life expectancy is 66.6 years, 10 years less than the EU level and well below communist-era levels?[84] Eberstadt noted that 'by various measures, Russia's demographic indicators resemble those in many of the world's poorest and least developed societies'.[85] Male life expectancy is particularly low, due to a high mortality rate among working-age males from preventable causes (alcohol poisoning, smoking, violent crimes, etc.). Mortality rates among Russian men are four to five times higher than in Europe. At the same time, 'social diseases' are spreading fast: since 1992 the annual increment in the number of people suffering from tuberculosis has been 10 to 15 per cent.[86] All of these troubling statistics are related to the fact that since the fall of communism, free health care has been very restricted and poor in quality. A mandatory health insurance emerged from the public health system, offering limited coverage and requiring complementation by private insurance, which only a very few can afford. The result is greatly diminished access to health services for the poor.

Is transition entirely to blame for the worsening of Russian inequality? Even before the transition, the social system of Russia was meritocratic, not egalitarian per se. The nomenklatura controlled the allocation and distribution of resources, professionals were privileged, blue-collar workers had job security and more privileges than the peasantry. With the transition, the winners of the process became the young, the well educated, the well connected and the entrepreneurial. The losers were the old, pensioners, the less educated, women, those with little or no skills and rural people. All wage earners were affected by inflation and unemployment in the early years of transition. Yet the process of privatization in particular shaped the nature of post-transition inequality: the most important source of inequalities was the transfer of wealth from state ownership to domestic or foreign individuals. One of the consequences of restitution, voucher privatization, public auctions or direct sales of state assets was the increasing importance among income sources of capital income directly related to ownership; the same thing occurred in China. Only a small minority of the population received this type of income.

Delving further into the various aspects of post-transition inequality, Galbraith, Krytynskaia and Wang[87] use the Theil measure of inequality as an alternative to the Gini index. Because it is additive across subgroups or regions in the country, it allows them to reveal regional and sectoral patterns of inequality. Their analysis leaves no room for doubt: over the 1990–2000 decade Russian inequality increased significantly. They find that after the industrial collapse and hyperinflation of 1991 and the financial collapse of 1998, inequality rose considerably: it doubled from 1991 to 1992 and rose 39 per cent from 1998 to 1999. In particular, they find that inequality increased across both regional and sectoral dimensions, especially during the critical transition crisis of 1991–2. However, inequality increased much more across regions than sectors. As noted by Galbraith et al., 'choice of place mattered more than choice of occupation or industry'.[88] They found that as the 1990s wore on, there was a pattern of very rapidly rising relative incomes in just three places: Moscow, Khanty-Mansy and Tiumen. The latter two are lightly populated West Siberian oil and gas regions; hence, the concentration of income in these areas is a good summary of post-transition income distribution in Russia! The main sectors of the Russian economy – energy production and transportation – account for a rising share of incomes; there is also a notable increase in the share of the financial sector, which was insignificant in Soviet times. The major losers are agriculture, science, culture and the arts, education, health and sports; all were strong sectors in Soviet times. This performance contrasts with that of Chinese incomes in the science, education and health sectors, which remained strong in China after transition.

Is it at all surprising that the transition was associated with greater inequality? That is entirely dependent on the transition's goal and on how much the outcome deviated from it 'Transition to what?' is the question one needs to ask. In Russia the transition, instead of leading to the goal of a market economy built on competition, has led to monopoly capitalism at its worst. Monopoly capitalism refers to a concentration of power in terms of who controls supply, the result being the concentration of production. Transition concentrated market power in the hands of big players controlled by the state in the transportation, energy and financial sectors, instead of resulting in the competitive economic fabric of many firms, which is often associated with the ideal of the perfectly competitive market economy. This monopoly structure under state control can be described as a form of 'supply-side inequality'. There are no signs of this inequality lessening, judging from recent developments: 20 years after the first economic reforms were attempted in Russia, state-owned gas producer Gazprom agreed in 2011 to merge significant power assets with those of Russian tycoon Viktor Vekselberg.[89] In April 2012, Gazprom and Vekselberg failed to agree on price and abandoned their plans, which would have given the state control over 70 per cent of power generation. Still state-controlled monopoly capitalism is becoming ever more entrenched. To be fair, President Medvedev has called for the state to sell off controlling stakes in its national champions, resulting in the dismissal of

Igor Sechin, the deputy prime minister, from his position as chair of state oil firm Rosneft. But even here, Sechin's replacement recently described the privatization of Rosneft as a 'very exotic' proposition. Clearly the dismantling of a state-controlled monopoly structure will not happen overnight.

At the same time, transition resulted in the geographical concentration of income, in that it benefited mainly the regions involved in hard currency export earnings, such as the oil-producing regions, just as in China it benefited the coastal export-oriented regions. Transition has resulted in Russia and China producing goods that cater to the needs of other countries instead of fulfilling the needs of their own people. In summary, one of the main features of the imbalanced economic system that resulted from transition was inequality, whether one looks at it in terms of access to supply or to demand.

Who was left behind by the transition, and what policy changes are in order? The main victim was the agricultural sector, and strong agricultural support programmes and security systems are particularly relevant here. At a more general level, the losses of the education, health care and science sectors are problematic. Indeed, the Russian state is doing away with the science, health and education sectors, which were at the core of communist values. The shortcomings of the current health sector have already been noted, and those of the science sector were commented upon in Chapter 1. As for the education sector, after the fall of communism the quality of state-financed education deteriorated quickly. A large number of research institutes ceased to exist, as tens of thousands of scientists, researchers and engineers emigrated.[90] Yet the state does not seem concerned; the share of public education expenditure averaged around 5 per cent of GDP in the early 1990s, but it had fallen to 4 per cent of GDP by the end of the decade.[91]

Should not health, education and science be a central focus in the context of the current global capitalist race, just as they were at the time of the Cold War? Surely they have to be at the core of any development project, especially one based on innovation. Scientific excellence and human capital are the future of all BRIC economies; science and human capital are direct inputs into innovation, while health is a necessary condition of human capital development. Russia's weakness in these sectors is a major shortcoming which it needs to overcome if it wants to remain a key player in the global political economy.

Better still, by supporting the health and education sectors in particular, Russia will sustain its economic growth – hence its power in the global political economy – and reduce domestic inequality. Conversely, a couple of statistics make it plain that if Russia does not address its deficit in these areas, given its impact on the labour force, Russia's share of total global output will only shrink: between 2005 and 2025, according to the US Census Bureau, Russia's share of the global working-age population is projected to drop from 2.4 to 1.6 per cent.[92] Thus, if Russia is to maintain its share of global output, its long-term improvements in labour productivity must average 2 per cent more per year than the rest of the world's. As Eberstadt noted, 'such prospective accomplishments can hardly be taken for granted given Russia's health and educational problems'.[93]

India

In comparative perspective, India displays better performance than the other BRICs in terms of inequality, as measured by the Gini index. Its reading was 36.8 in 2004, while the other three BRICs are in the 40s and 50s.[94] Unlike other countries, which measure the Gini in terms of the distribution of income, the standard way of measuring it in India is in terms of the distribution of consumption expenditure. Because the rich save more than the poor, their consumption tends to be less than their income; hence, the distribution of consumption expenditure tends to be less skewed towards the rich than the distribution of income. Based on the income distribution data from a 2004–5 household survey, Bardhan derives a Gini coefficient of income (not consumption) inequality of 53.5, which is on a par with Brazil's and much higher than China's.[95]

In looking at data on inequality other than the summary measure provided by the Gini index, Bardhan's assessment of India's inequality record becomes all the more valid. More than 250 million people live below the poverty line, and the richest 20 per cent hold close to 50 per cent of household income.[96] According to Forbes, in a country of 1.2 billion inhabitants, India has 69 billionaires controlling more than 30 per cent of annual gross domestic product.[97] At a lower cut-off point, the growth in the number of people worth over US$5 million is striking. Kotak Mahindra Bank and Crisil forecast that households with a net worth of more than US$5.6 million will triple within five years, to 219,000.[98] The growth of the number of very rich individuals is directly reflected in the rise in the sales of luxury cars; the numbers rose to 15,702 cars in 2010 (still well below China's 727,227), according to IHS Global Insight.[99] This phenomenon is not new to the noughties, given that through the 1990s the real incomes of the top 1 per cent of earners in India already increased by about 50 per cent, according to Banerjee and Piketty.[100] In fact, they found that the degree of wage inequality widened significantly between 1983 and 2005. Between 1983 and 1993 the range of wage rates was reduced, but in 1993 it started widening; by 2004 it had returned to 1983 levels. The rise in wage rates during the 1993–2005 period was much higher among the high-wage-earning groups than the low-wage groups, which implies the perpetuation of inequality. During the period 1999–2004 wage inequality even widened in absolute terms, with low-wage earners earning less in 2004 than in 1999, while high-wage earners earned more than in 1999.

Inequality in India is structured along a number of fault lines: rural/ urban, rich/poor regions, and lower/upper castes. The rural sector contributed 45 per cent of national income in the period 2000–8, down from 58 per cent in the 1980s. Together with this decline in the contribution of the rural sector, the rural-urban income differential worsened. In the early 1980s per capita income in urban areas was around 220 per cent of the per capita rural income; in 2005–6 it was 300 per cent.[101] Ravi blames relatively low agricultural growth and the shrinking rural share in income from services, which is the fastest-growing sector in GDP.

Similarly, the sharp increase in regional inequality during the 1990s had not improved by the early noughties.[102] In 1983 Bihar, Madhya Pradesh, Orissa and Uttar Pradesh accounted for nearly half of the Indian poor in rural areas. By 2004–5 their share had grown to 61 per cent. In 2002–3 the per capita net state domestic product of Punjab, the richest state, was 4.7 times that of Bihar, the poorest, up from 4.2 times in 1993–4.

How does one explain India's unequal income distribution? An important question to address is the role of economic reform in aggravating inequality. This issue remains hotly debated, but most accounts of Indian inequality suggest that rural inequality went up between 1993–4 and 1999–2000, which were key periods of reform. For instance, Pal and Ghosh[103] note that consumption disparities between the rich and the poor and between rural and urban India increased during the 1990s. In general, one can relate the rise in inequality levels to economic reform through a logic which is well summarized by Ravi: 'with a spurt in the demand for skilled labour, especially in the information technology and communication sectors, inequalities in wages may have increased. The most intensively used factors of production in the newly emerging sectors that are strongly linked to the world market do not come from poor households'.[104] As was noted above, the same applies to China.

It seems that reform aggravated inequality through its impact on employment growth. During the 1990s, as employment growth plummeted, it affected the rural sector disproportionately, thereby aggravating rural-urban inequality. This was a serious issue given that 60 per cent of India's working population was employed in agriculture.[105] The annual growth of rural employment fell to 0.67 per cent between 1993–4 and 1999–2000. At the same time, the fact that real agricultural wages grew only 2.5 per cent in the 1990s partly explains the rise in rural-urban inequality. In particular, agriculture's employment of 75 per cent of the total female workforce led to the feminization of poverty. The 1990s also coincided with a casualization of the rural labour force, a situation that still prevails. Only about 7 per cent of rural workers now find regular employment; interestingly, it is mainly among men that the share of casual workers has steadily increased.

What of Ravi's 'newly emerging sectors that are strongly linked to the world market', which benefited from economic reform?[106] Could their expansion not compensate for such effects? What of the services sector, which is often publicized as the success story of India? It is true that in all of the services subsectors employment grew at a much faster rate in the 1990s than in the rest of the economy, especially in information technology, communications and entertainment, but the total number of those employed in the services sector remains very small relative to the size of the labour force. As a result, services sector employment growth could not compensate for poor performance in agriculture and some industrial sectors. Consequently, the overall rate of employment generation slowed significantly: its growth rate from 1993–4 to 1999–2000 was 1.07 per cent, well below the 2.67 per cent rate registered between 1983 and 1993–4.[107]

The combination of the above factors is most likely to blame for the increase in income inequality. Yet inequality of opportunity is also pervasive in India and precedes income inequality. Unequal access to assets is one of its manifestations. In the 1990s the small peasantry lost many assets which were, a crucial claim to income. Many small and marginal peasants who lost their land were forced to search for work as landless labourers. One determinant of inequality of opportunity is the caste system. Dalits, who are outside the caste hierarchy, are the victims of the worst forms of discrimination, yet they represent 19.7 per cent of the population. The Adivasis, which are native tribal communities, are also affected by extreme discrimination; they account for

8.5 per cent of the population. Together these groups represent nearly a third of the population, yet 62 per cent of them have no land or assets! High levels of poverty, illiteracy and malnutrition inevitably result. The share of the poor among the Dalits (44% in 2004–5) and Adivasis (32%) is much higher than their share in the general population (25%). The most serious impact of the caste system is that it prevents intergenerational mobility and thereby perpetuates inequality. It has often been suggested that social mobility is greater in China than India due to the absence of a Chinese caste system (although measures of mobility are hard to come by). Caste has a significant bearing on inequality of opportunity through its impact on unequal land distribution, unequal access to health and unequal education.

Yet inequality of opportunity can be independent of caste. Irrespective of caste, according to Bardhan, the Gini index of inequality of land distribution in rural India was 62 in 2002, compared with 49 in China.[108] If land quality is taken into account, the Gini index of distribution of asset ownership was 63 in 2002 in rural India versus 39 in China.

On access to health care, India's record is equally poor. This is no doubt partially due to the level of public health expenditure, which, at 5.1 per cent of GDP, is among the lowest in the world, although not as low as Russia's 4 per cent.[109] Given that less than 14 per cent of the population is supported by health insurance, treatment is only available to the rich.[110] The country's richest 7 per cent account for 30 per cent of spending in private health care and over 40 per cent of inpatient spending, reflecting the skewed access to private health care. Hence, it is no surprise that while there have been improvements in life expectancy – from around 40 years at the time of independence in 1947 to 64 years in 2003 – general indicators of health and nutrition remain poor. In some respects India fares worse than Sub-Saharan Africa: 53 per cent of children are undernourished, and the proportion of females to males is worse than in Sub-Saharan Africa.[111] The actual number of physicians per 1000 population is only 0.5 (compared with 2.7 in the USA), and since approximately 70 per cent of doctors are located in urban areas while the same proportion of the population lives in the rural areas, expensive travel limits actual access to health care. Furthermore, there are considerable interstate variations in health care quality. From 1993 to 1997, life expectancy at birth was 55 in Madhya Pradesh and more than 73 in Kerala. While Kerala's health indicators are comparable to those of high-income countries, those of Uttar Pradesh and Bihar have been worse than Sub-Saharan Africa's.

Educational inequality is also acute. According to Bardhan, the Gini coefficient of the distribution of adult schooling years in the population was 56 in the period 1998–2000, versus 37 in China and 39 in Brazil.[112] Literacy also displays interstate variations. At 65 per cent in 2001, the overall literacy rate was up from 52 per cent in 1991.[113] But even in 2001 Bihar, the state with the lowest rate, was about 18 percentage points below the national average. In contrast, Kerala had an average literacy rate of 90.9 per cent. There are also large disparities between the rural and urban sectors, and the literacy rate is still very low among rural women in particular. Ultimately, these disparities reflect changes in the form of teaching, with the rapid growth of private schools over the 1990s. Mostly located in urban areas, they cater to the richer sections of the population, thereby aggravating educational inequality.

Finally, gender discrimination has long been a significant factor in inequality of opportunity in India. What is striking and surprising is that it is most pronounced in Punjab and Haryana, which are two of the most prosperous states in India. Indeed, in the 1990s, there was a decline in the female-male ratio in these states. The female-male ratio among children declined from 945 girls per 1000 boys in 1991 to 927 girls per 1000 boys in 2001[114] – this statistic has given rise to the expression 'India's missing women' (China displays similar, if less pronounced, characteristics; see Table 4.2). One interpretation of the cause of the missing women is that income growth in these states may have facilitated the spread of sex-selective abortion by making sex-determination technology more affordable. If that is the case, then economic growth can be associated with (1) increased inequality in income but also with (2) increased inequality in non-income dimensions.

Brazil

Despite recent improvements, income inequality is a serious concern in Brazil, with a Gini index of 53.9 in 2009. The poorest 20 per cent of

Table 4.2   Males per 100 females in the marriage-age population

Country	India	China	Vietnam	World
Males per 100 females in marriage-age population, 2011 (15–24 years)	111.5	110.2	106.7	105.6

Source: US Census Bureau.

Table 4.3 Evolution of income inequality in Brazil, measured by the Gini coefficient, 1977–2007

	1977	'78	'79	'81	'82	'83	'84	'85	'86	'87	'88	'89	'90	'92
Gini	62.3	60.4	59.3	58.2	58.9	59.4	58.8	59.6	58.7	59.9	61.5	63.4	61.2	58

	'93	'95	'96	'97	'98	'99	2001	'02	'03	'04	'05	'06	'07
Gini	60.2	59.9	60	60	59.8	59.2	59.3	58.7	58.1	56.9	56.6	55.9	55.2

Source: Pesquisa Nacional por Amostra de Domicilios, 1977–2007.

the population command only 2.8 per cent of national income, whereas the richest 20 per cent command 61.1 per cent of it. While the worst period of inequality in Brazil was the 1980s – hyperinflation exacerbated income concentration, resulting in a Gini index of 63.4 in 1989 – the current situation is also characterized by negative influences on the distribution of income. In particular, as is the case in Russia and China, returns on property have become an important component of national income through the expansion of the property-owning middle classes, whose growth has aggravated inequality – so much so that between 1980 and 2005, the participation of labour income in national income fell from 50 to 39 per cent.[115]

Geography-based inequality prevails; the northern and north-eastern regions of the country display much lower incomes than the southern and south-eastern regions. Just like India's caste-based inequality, Brazil's ethnicity-based inequality is a major problem: in 2006, among working people over 10, the poorest 10 per cent included 26.1 per cent of whites and 73.2 per cent of non-whites.[116] Among the richest 10 per cent, only 12.4 per cent were non-whites and 85.7 per cent whites. The average monthly income of white people was nearly twice the average income of non-whites. In sum, inequality in incomes is often just the outcome of inequality of opportunities: the assetless, non-white populations of the northern regions have consistently lower incomes and also have less access to schooling and infrastructure services.

However, Brazil has made giant strides in reducing inequality. As suggested by Table 4.3, the Gini index went from 59.3 in 2001 to 55.2 in 2007, an average decline of 1.2 per cent per year. For the period 2001–7 the bottom six deciles of the population, which account for only 18 per cent of income, accounted for 40 per cent of total income growth.[117] From 2001 to 2007, the per capita income of the poorest 10 per cent grew 7 per cent a year, nearly three times the national average of 2.5 per cent. Better still, while Brazil managed to more than halve the proportion of the population living in extreme poverty between 2000 and 2007, more than 60 per cent of this reduction was achieved through the reduction of inequality. Indeed, Barros, de Carvalho, Franco and Mendonca[118] find that if inequality had not changed between 2001 and 2007, the income of the rich and that of the poor would have grown at the national rate of 2.6 per cent a year. They find that since the income of the poorest 10 per cent actually grew 7 per cent a year – that is, 4.4 percentage points above the overall average – almost two-thirds of the income growth of this group came from declines in inequality. For the poorest 20 per cent, 60 per cent of the growth in income also originated from declines in inequality. This is no small feat, and it highlights that over this period Brazil managed to reduce poverty by tackling inequality, in contrast with China's reduction of poverty, which was largely growth-driven. This is also different from previous Brazilian history, where episodes of poverty reduction were driven by economic growth and not lowered inequality. Brazil shows that inequality reduction can be an efficient means of poverty reduction. Barros et al. calculate that to achieve the same reduction in extreme poverty without the decline in inequality, Brazil's overall per capita income would have had to have grown an extra 4 percentage points a year. Indeed, they find that from the point of view of the extremely poor, a 1 percentage point reduction in the Gini coefficient requires 4.2 percentage points higher growth in per capita income.

How did Brazil succeed in reducing inequality? In general, a supportive background has been provided by the resumption of economic growth in the context of the commodities boom, a gradual increase in the minimum wage, the growth of formal employment in the lower class groups and a decrease in the rural-urban wage disparity. More specifically, improvements in education and income transfer programmes have been at the core of the reduction in inequality. The workforce gained more equal access to education in the early and mid-1990s, thanks to universal admission to primary schooling and lower repetition rates, which ultimately contributed to lower wage inequality. At the same time Bolsa Familia and other income transfer programmes, which target exclusively the poorest of the poor, were introduced. They have helped reduce extreme poverty, and they are being copied all over the world, including New York City.

The now famous Bolsa Familia is a non-contributory cash transfer, which delivers a small grant directly to the poorest families, but it is conditional on them sending their children to school and meeting basic health care requirements, such as having children under the age of 6 years vaccinated and sending pregnant women to pre- and postnatal care sessions. The programme aims to reduce short-term poverty by direct cash transfer and fight long-term poverty by investing in the human capital of the poor. It is this dual system of income transfer combined with an incentive towards the acquisition of human capital that sets the programme apart. The benefits paid range from 20 to 182 reais, depending on monthly income per person in the family and the number of children and adolescents up to 17 years.[119] It reaches more than 46 million people, a large proportion of the country's low-income population. The programme has critics (the *Economist* has an excellent summary of its flaws; http://www.economist.com/node/16690887), but it has indisputably been a strong contributor to the reduction of the inequality of the noughties. It has also been cost-effective for the government, at only 1.5 per cent of GDP.

However, data from the period 2006–7 do not augur well. The average income of the bottom 5 per cent declined by 14 per cent, as a reminder that improvements in income distribution are reversible. One particular problem which has emerged is that the above policies have disproportionately benefited the rural sector, thereby bringing down its poverty, but new manifestations of poverty are emerging in the cities. Another issue to be highlighted is that in a country where 76 million people are poor, one cannot make a serious dent in the problem of poverty by focusing exclusively on the poorest of the poor. The sustainability of the reduction of inequality means that after tackling the emergency faced by the poorest of the poor, new means have to be employed to tackle the poverty of the rest. Yet dealing with those who are not in a state of emergency but can benefit from long-term, structural changes in society could be much more challenging.

Introducing these long-term changes could amount to tackling the root cause of inequality in Brazil. Brazilian inequality is deeply rooted in the structural mechanisms that perpetuate it, the most entrenched of which are the coalitions between social classes, particularly landowners and business, which oppose urban wage workers and the rural masses. Since colonization, these coalitions have prevailed in the concentration of land and political power. They have blocked attempts to change the distribution of income or provide social services for the poor. Hence the persistence of inequality, regardless of changing political regimes and development strategies. In this context Brazilian industrialization took place at the agricultural sector's expense instead of helping trigger the modernization of agriculture in line with that of industry. The result has been an ever greater disparity between productivity levels in agriculture and industry since the 1960s.

Reducing this disparity requires dismantling or at least countering the coalitions of landowners and business, whose concentrated power has blocked attempts to change the distribution of income. A challenging task likes ahead. Brazil has made significant improvements in reducing inequality, but a Gini index of 53.9 is still high, even by BRIC standards. A lot of work still needs to be done.

Conclusion: dismantling the political economy of inequality

Poverty reduction can be achieved either by absolute increases in economic growth or by a reduction of inequality. Judging from the above survey, Brazil stands out as the only BRIC where poverty has recently been reduced through significant inequality reduction, and China exemplifies the case of poverty reduction through growth. Two questions arise from this BRIC evidence. First, can a growth-focused strategy of economic development be equality friendly? In that sense, could Russia, India and China (RICs) have done it better? Second, if inequality reduction is taken as the main focus, what can the RICs learn from Brazil, and what aspects of inequality does Brazil itself still need to address?

To answer the first question, even a growth-focused strategy of economic development can be equality friendly. Two characteristics of such a growth strategy stand out. First, the case of China shows that all other things being equal, privileging an export-oriented strategy amounts to disregarding the needs of the people. Conversely, a growth strategy more driven by domestic consumption is likely to be more equality friendly. Second, whether one looks at Russia or India, it is clear that economic growth based on the capacity of a few oligarchs to accumulate wealth is by definition *not* equality friendly. Nor is this type of growth efficiency friendly in the long-term; the ensuing monopoly power can be as detrimental to the market's functioning as the resulting inequality is to social stability. Put otherwise, the biases of the economic reforms undertaken by the BRICs towards external demand and towards elite-driven capital accumulation seem to have created the 'wrong' kind of market economy, one that achieved skyrocketing rates of growth by ignoring domestic demand at large and by exacerbating inequalities.

It is too late to worry about how to create an equality-friendly growth process: the BRICs have already achieved impressive rates of growth. Yet they are left with unsustainable and flagrant inequalities, whose reduction must become a prime objective of economic policy. If inequality is the main concern, what can the RICs infer from the special case of

Brazil? The Brazilian reduction of inequality is largely the result of government transfers of the Bolsa Familia type. Barros et al., comparing the factors influencing the level of inequality – demography, non-labour income, employment and productivity – find that non-labour income, mainly transfers, has contributed the most to the recent inequality reduction. In other words, the government has directly attempted to change income patterns to reduce inequality and has succeeded. While it has been very effective, the government's direct transfer approach could have easily perpetuated the notion that the poor are victims, with little power to help themselves. Yet in the case of Bolsa Familia, the government transfer is strongly tied to the acquisition of human capital by the poor, which seems the most sustainable exit strategy from poverty. The genius behind Bolsa Familia is that it is a government transfer which gives the poor enough of a financial boost to let them take advantage of opportunities and achieve better outcomes. Not only does it rectify income inequality through the transfer, it also rectifies inequality of opportunity through an incentive towards human capital acquisition. This is exactly in line with this book's view that the only way to address inequality as a long-term consideration is to give the poor the ability to help themselves.[120]

On the other hand, even in Brazil, it can be argued that the changes in the pattern of inequality are still cosmetic. They have not overturned the structural foundations of inequality: coalitions of landowners and business have largely succeeded in maintaining concentrations of power. This particular configuration of social forces, or 'political economy', perpetuates inequality. The key to sustainable reduction of inequality lies in destroying such constellations of social forces – across all the BRICs.

As was mentioned above, Russia and India display a similarly vicious political economy of inequality. In these countries, the most salient social alliance is that between business and the political class. In India and Russia, coalitions perpetuate inequality by ensuring that the rich keep getting richer. India's corporate landscape is dominated by a handful of family-led companies: the Tatas, the Ambanis, the Birlas, the Godrejs, the Bajajs, the Mahindras. The *Financial Times* calls them 'the Bollygarchs'. This is a characteristic of emerging market business in general, but in India and Russia the unhealthy alliance between influential family businesses and politicians has assumed dramatic proportions. Scandals in India, especially in the telecoms sector but extending to property and construction, have exposed the corruption of powerful entrepreneurs who manipulated bureaucrats and regulators for decades. An official audit claimed that the national exchequer lost as much as US$39 billion in potential revenues from irregularities in the awarding of mobile phone licenses in 2008.[121] This scale of corruption can be seen as an extreme version of unbridled capitalism gone wrong, where monopolistic power rules both political and economic life. India could not be further away from Adam Smith's vision of a market economy characterized by atomistic competition. As Brahma Chellaney, professor of strategic studies at Delhi's Centre for Policy Research, notes, 'the capability of big business to influence policy now is much greater than it was prior to 1991'.[122]

Similarly, Russia has been synonymous with the crony capitalism of the oligarchs for years. While the government has decided to remove ministers from boards of state companies and has engaged in a US$30 billion privatization drive in order to offload state stakes in big corporations, it is impossible to sever corporate from political power overnight and that is clearly visible in the mixed messages which newly elected President Putin has been sending on privatisation since March 2012. Back-door arrangements are likely to prevail for a long time.

Currently, the process of wealth creation in Russia occurs in tandem with a lack of social mobility: the only realistic path to success is to be the son or daughter of a top provincial official. Hence, Russia finds itself with a generation of students whose sole aspiration is to become a bureaucrat. After the end of communism in 1991, economic liberalization allowed Russians to climb the social ladder through business. In the noughties President Putin achieved two separate results. On the one hand, a doubling of real incomes between 2000 and 2008 lifted the living standard of all the masses. On the other hand, it became harder to join the elite, as the state reclaimed its stranglehold on business. The state generated an elite that now controls both government and business, and the private sector is no longer available as a route to social advancement. According to Rosstat, between 1999 and 2009 the number of Russian federal employees increased by 634,000 to reach 1.5million.[123] Arguably, there is an economic reason for the growth of the public sector: given that oil and gas, the main sources of employment in Russia, do not require large amounts of highly qualified labour (jobs for highly qualified labour account for only 15 per cent of GDP), there are only two paths available to the highly skilled: they can emigrate or go into the public sector. Until structural economic reforms create private sector jobs for the highly skilled – the government's current project is to create a Russian Silicon Valley in Skolkovo to shift the highly skilled into technology services (see Chapter 5, on innovation) – the onus is on the increasingly saturated public sector. Hence, new college graduates find it harder than ever to get a job, while at least half of those who do use family connections. It is rather ironic that Russia has returned to the system which prevailed under socialism: the state controls the channels of social mobility.

Similarly, in China almost 90 per cent of the country's top leaders in sectors encompassing finance, foreign trade, property development, construction and stock trading were 'princelings', or offspring of Communist Party leaders, and about 90 per cent of China's billionaires are the children of high-ranking officials.[124] These princelings seem to shy away from the limelight of politics in favour of the corporate sector. The family of former Premier Li Peng, for example, controls the country's energy sector.[125] His daughter Li Xiaolin is chairman of China Power International Development, an electricity monopoly. His son Li Xiaopeng used to head Huaneng Power, another energy heavyweight. Former President Jiang Zemin's family moved into telecommunications, and the offspring of former Premier Zhu Rongji are strong figures in banking. His son Levin Zhu is the chief executive of China International Capital Corporation. Even outside the princelings' cocoon, the blending of political and business powers is evident, and its most natural locus is the state-owned enterprises: Guo Shuqing, the chairman of state-owned China Construction Bank, used to be deputy governor of Guizhou province, and the chairman of Sinopec has just become governor of Fujian province.[126]

Beyond the BRICs, the United States confirms the central role of crony capitalism in increasing inequality. George Packer discounts other explanations quite effectively when he notes that global competition, cheap goods made in China or technological changes could not have been decisive in increasing inequality in the United States, given that they also occurred in Europe. But inequality remained much lower there than in the USA. Packer seems right in saying that 'the decisive factor has been politics and public policy: tax rates, spending choices, labour laws, regulations, campaign finance rules', in that 'the government has consistently favoured the rich'.[127] At the bottom of rising inequality, both in the BRICs and in the United States, there is an alignment of political and social forces.

In the case of the United States, Packer also notes that political changes were aided by deeper changes in norms of responsibility and self-restraint. 'In 1978, it might have been economically feasible and perfectly legal for an executive to award himself a multimillion-dollar bonus while shedding 40 per cent of his work force. But no executive would have wanted the shame and outrage that would have followed. These days, it is hard to open a newspaper without reading stories about grotesque overcompensation at the top and widespread hardship below'.[128] In contrast, such stories have defined the BRICs for decades. If the reduction of inequality in the BRICs requires a positive change towards responsibility and self-restraint, it will be a very long-term process. But it is definitely one worth undertaking, as the social and economic costs of a continued rise in inequality are too high for the BRICs to ignore.

This chapter has shown that across the BRICs, the fight against inequality, far from being over, is an ongoing process. It is a necessary process, and not just from a moral perspective (in any case the boundaries between moral and efficiency motives have become blurred since the 2008 financial crisis); it is also necessary from a pure efficiency perspective. Indeed, if the BRICs manage to create less unequal societies, they will reap multiple benefits, which will ensure the sustainability of their economic miracles. (1) They will avoid the political instability that could put their growth miracles in jeopardy, especially in the context of inflation. (2) They will also increase the range of national resources they can draw on to fully realize their economic potential. Just as innovation constitutes an engine of sustainable growth – as Chapter 5 will explain – the reduction of inequality has a similar effect. It releases dormant economic resources by creating new, diversified sources of demand. It rebalances the economy, away from a focus on elites' demands and towards a more diversified demand profile catering to all social groups. In other words, reducing inequality amounts to (1) ensuring that there is a buy-in for sustainable economic growth on the part of the masses, not least to prevent them taking to the streets; and (2) unlocking demand and hence economic growth potential. Conversely, the sustainability of the BRICs' growth miracle will be in question if they fail to address their inequality problem. The next chapter will examine the second biggest threat to this sustainability: the BRICs' inability to produce breakthrough innovations.

5
Limit No. 2: BRICs and the Silent Power of Ideas

> Many of us are old enough to remember America's ignominious scramble out of Saigon in 1975 and the way Japanese factories drove Western rivals out of business in the 1980s. Even more of us now have the sense that everything we buy is made in China. Yet it is also obvious that in the last hundred years or so Westerners have shipped armies to Asia, not the other way around. East Asian governments have struggled with Western capitalist and Communist theories, but no Western governments have tried to rule on Confucian or Daoist lines. Easterners often communicate across linguistic barriers in English; Europeans rarely do so in Mandarin or Japanese (p. 11 of the Ian Morris theories, *Why the West Rules for Now*, London, Prfile Books, 2010).

This is an excerpt from Ian Morris's 'Why the West Rules – for Now',[1] which captures the spirit of the times: westerners are in awe of the potential for Asian domination, but at the same time, the transition to an Asian domination regime has not been completed. Similarly, while the media love a story of BRIC ascendancy and Western demise, the jury is still out on whether this will be the BRIC century. There is good reason to think that the BRICs are not taking over the world and Western influence is set to remain in place, at least for the medium term. Amongst the few books on the subject which share this conviction, most take the stance that this is so because the West continues to command the key resources for domination. Parent and MacDonald, for example, find that using the benchmarks of military capability and economic strength relative to rivals, 'there is a strong case to be made that although US decline is real, its rate is modest'.[2] In contrast, it seems more likely that (1) it is less the superiority of Western resources that explains continued Western domination than the inability of the BRICs to take the position of leading power; and 2) taking over the world requires dominating the domain of ideas, a space from which the BRICs are largely absent.

To begin with, there is something disturbing about the fact that the BRICs did not even come up with the BRIC concept themselves. The acronym BRIC, which is meant to celebrate the coming of age of emerging markets, was in fact a Western coinage: it was the brilliant creation of a Western investment bank, and it caught on around the world. Everyone refers to the BRICs nowadays and wants to have financial exposure to them. It was not merely by virtue of high economic growth rates that emerging markets arrived on the world's ideational map; rather, it was because Goldman Sachs made them stand out by repackaging them under a catchy acronym. And when it came to discriminating among emerging markets, Goldman Sachs had the power to declare who was trendy – that is, the BRICs – and who was not; namely, the rest of the emerging world (at least before the trendy shortlist was expanded and renamed the N11). This phenomenon exemplifies nothing so much as the continued superiority of the West in spinning out concepts that reverberate across the world. It is the best piece of evidence of the West's continued domination of ideas.

This chapter begins by first zooming into the relationship between power and ideas, which was touched upon in Chapter 3 in the summary of the main international relations theories on power. While finance gives a country the capacity to buy ideas, a country's ability to create and spread them is a major determinant of its power. The chapter continues by demonstrating that the era of gunpowder, the printing press and other pioneering Chinese inventions is far behind and that the BRICs currently lack the capacity to generate ideas or innovations. What of the much-celebrated Chinese supercomputer Tianhe-1? Has it not been ranked the fastest in the world by the Top 500 survey of supercomputers? The reality is that the bulk of its hardware is still designed by Intel and Invidia in California. Similarly, China's recent rail catastrophe is a symbol of two Chinese weaknesses: (1) lack of innovation and (2) the contradictions inherent in innovation by authoritarian government. Indeed, the high-speed train built by China's CSR Corporation, which seemed a technological feat before it was involved in a crash leaving 39 people dead and more than 200 injured in July 2011, is in fact a poor quality copy of the technology used by Canada's Bombardier and CSR's former partner Kawasaki Heavy Industries, which manufactures Japan's bullet train. Even a former senior railway ministry official said in June 2011 that the core technology was still foreign, although it underwent a process of 'technology importation, digestive absorption, independent reinnovation and localization'. When China bought the foreign technology, the contracts specified that the trains should not run faster than 300 km/h. These instructions were not followed, as suggested by the rail catastrophe.[3] Chinese train manufacturers are likely to pay a heavy price for this deviation: their first overseas sale of 28 high-speed trains, which was destined for Malaysia and had gone through just before the catastrophe,[4] is unlikely to materialize. Weeks before, the foreign competitors Alstom (France) and Kawasaki Heavy Industries (Japan) seemed outdone by Chinese manufacturers, which seemed to have mastered their technology while selling cheaper trains. Beyond these commercial repercussions, the crash has deep political implications: the knee-jerk reaction of the official propaganda bureau was to immediately bury the remaining evidence of the crash, as the high-speed technology was a pillar of legitimacy for China's authoritarian government. Any trace of failure had to be removed, especially as it might have revealed the role of corrupt officials in maintaining a dysfunctional railway system. Instead of being showcases of modernity, Chinese high-speed trains now merely stand for the unhealthy conflict between innovation and authoritarian government.

This chapter explains that for China and Russia, the capacity to generate ideas is blocked by these contradictions between creativity and authoritarian rule. In Brazil and India, on the other hand, the scaling up of innovations is flawed, as there is no attempt to link the innovations of national champions with the rest of the economy.

Why ideas matter: a key input into power

Power may be defined as the ability of a state to get what it wants, whether through coercion or goodwill. Direct inputs into power are economic, military, cultural and scientific dominance. Dominant states tend to combine many such inputs, but as Halper notes, 'the waning value of raw military power has coincided with the development of international economic power. [...] [W]ar has receded as the principal vehicle for the accumulation and safeguard of power'.[5] In that respect it may be a sign of the US' waning power that it spent more than US$2000 billion in wars in Afghanistan and Iraq (according to US TV networks) that culminated in the capture of Osama Bin Laden. This US military focus seems a classic case of what Paul Kennedy calls 'military overstretch', which often produces a civilization's decline. Such was the fate of the Habsburgs, as he notes: 'they steadily over-extended themselves in the course of repeated conflicts and became militarily top-heavy for their weakening economic base'.[6] While the United States chased Bin Laden, China accumulated economic might at US expense.[7]

To rectify this imbalance, Parent and MacDonald suggest that the United States should seek savings amounting to a minimum of US$90 billion annually from changes in procurement, a slightly swifter draw-down in Afghanistan and Iraq and a somewhat smaller army and marine corps. Given that 'the United States is already past the point of diminishing returns when it comes to defense spending',[8] they suggest spending what is saved on directly stimulating the US economy and making it more competitive.

Yet even if the United States were to recover some of its economic might through the recycling of a 'military dividend', one has to ask whether it would suffice to restore US supremacy. What about the role of ideas in maintaining power? Ideas are central to the exercise of power as inputs into (1) economic dominance, which is powered by innovation; (2) cultural and scientific dominance; and (3) military dominance. Ideas tend to stand out relative to the more standard determinants of power: population, education and economic resources. Goldman Sachs singled out the BRICs as a rising economic power largely on the basis of the growth prospects implied by their massive populations. Forecasts of a 'BRIC century' are largely the result of a gross forecast of growth potential based on a quantitative concept of economic power. In his projections on BRIC economic growth, Goldman Sachs's Jim O'Neill does include productivity, which can be seen as a proxy for ideas and innovation. Yet the power implications of the quality of the BRICs' ideas is seldom discussed, despite the fact that ideas confer greater stability than other determinants of power, as their ability to become embedded in the cultural values of non-dominant states exercises long-term influence on the latter. For example, Western dominance of the global political economy has been associated with rationality, democracy, tolerance, free markets, the technological revolution and other dominant ideas that have been global values for centuries. The populations of non-Western states have come to identify with many of these ideas, the most obvious one being the consumer society concept built into the free market idea. It follows that national identity is partially shaped by a Western cultural orientation. Because people generally resist cultural change and Western ideas are embedded in the social fabric of non-Western states, the West's power to shape the rest of the world through ideas is largely self-sustaining. Seen thus, the Western dominance of ideas could well outlive the West's material domination.

Not so, says Ian Morris, whose theory offers an interesting counter-point to the preceding one. The West's domination is about to end, and its rule until now has had nothing to do with ideas. It is instead the material forces of geography which have created the West's dominance, according to Morris. Ironically, he is a historian who believes that 'latitudes, not attitudes' ultimately explain why the West and not another power has come to rule the world. His argument goes as follows. At the end of the Ice Age, global warming marked the emergence of a band of 'Lucky Latitudes' (20 to 35 degrees north in the Old World and 15 degrees south to 20 degrees north in the New). In this band, warm weather combined with a local geography favouring the evolution of plants and animals that humans could domesticate. This environment resulted in more food, people and innovation. The so-called Hilly Flanks of Southwest Asia (now Iran, Iraq, south-eastern Turkey, Jordan, Israel) were especially blessed, as their latitudes were particularly conducive to farming. Western societies are descendants of these farmers. About two thousand years later, farming took off in China, where latitudes were also favourable, if less so than in the Hilly Flanks. Eastern societies descend from these farmers. From then on, the West's lead grew at some times and shrank at others. Around 550, the Western lead disappeared altogether, and for the next 1200 years the East led the world. Then phases of Western and Eastern domination alternated, until the current phase of Western domination, which, for Morris, started with the industrial revolution. It occurred in Britain and not elsewhere because of its proximity to the New World. The fact that Britain was only 3000 miles from it while East Asia was 6000 miles away started to matter in 1600 with the invention of ocean-going ships and in the perspective of the colonization of America. As Britain created a new market economy around the Atlantic Ocean, there was what Morris calls a 'shrinkage of the Atlantic'. With new resources available to Britain through colonization, its sharpest minds started to think about ways to dominate nature – hence, the development of science. Finally, as increasing wages in Britain were pricing British goods out of the European continent, the British decided to channel their new scientific talents into substituting technology for human labour. Enter the coal and steam technology that powered the industrial revolution. The result: in 1600, per capita GDP in Britain was 60 per cent higher than in China. By 1820 even in the United States per capita GDP was twice that in China and by 1913 nearly ten times.[9]

To be fair, Morris does emphasize that geography has not locked in Western rule. His theory seeks to explain the dynamics of shifts between global power centres: as great empires develop, with the help of geographical advantage, social change causes these very empires to fall apart and others to emerge with new geographical advantages. Morris's theory is therefore a theory of change. A case in point is the US replacement of Britain as a superpower as Britain gradually lost its competitive edge in industrialization. Morris – who believes that a similar fate is now befalling the United States as the 'shrinkage of the Pacific ocean' turns Asia into a global power – concludes that a power shift from West to East in the twenty-first century is inevitable. While there might be a shift in wealth, the only certainty is that the ascent and descent of civilizations is unpredictable, as the example of the Roman Empire's collapse testifies. Perhaps the strongest evidence that the eastern shift of power is not going to happen any time soon is that everyone expects it.

While Morris's interpretation is fascinating, especially for the wealth of its historical analysis, his geographical interpretation is devoid of a crucial aspect of power, that which gives it longevity. Even though his interpretation benefits from the objective detachment afforded by a perspective focused on geography, in glossing over the role of ideas as a means of maintaining power, his conception of power is too passive. Put otherwise, Morris seems so biased towards providing a theory that can explain changes in global power that he ignores what makes power sustainable: ideas. For even if we accept the logic that a power dominates because of geographical factors, is it not the case that the sustainability of its domination will depend on the ideas it circulates? Morris's theory better explains the emergence of new powers than their continued domination. Even if a power has emerged as the result of an advantageous geographical endowment, it will stand the test of time only if it is legitimized by a set of ideas that ground its supremacy. As was explained above, a power grounded in ideas is likely to last longer: as its impact on global culture becomes deeply ingrained, it becomes increasingly difficult to displace it from the centre of global culture. That is why this book grounds its analysis in an idea-driven theory of global political economy, and this analysis thus leads to a conclusion on the future of Western power which differs vastly from Morris'.

The current battle for ideational supremacy

Hang on a minute. Is it not precisely in the realm of ideas that the West currently faces a crisis of confidence – thereby, opening a vacuum which could be filled by the BRICs? Western economic free market models, especially those of unbridled financial and trade globalization, are being questioned, as was suggested in Chapter 3. So is another favourite building block of Western economics: regional monetary union. The threat to the Eurozone presented by Portugal, Ireland, Italy, Greece and Spain has ironically produced an exodus of capital flows to safer emerging markets. Worse, it has eroded the credibility of a regional mode of economic organization without a political backbone (a shortcoming the BRICs might want to bear in mind). With globalization and regionalism in question and the West drifting into ideational crisis, does a clean slate of ideas open up for the BRICs? Not really. The fact that there is a crisis of ideas is normal from an evolutionary perspective; 'creative destruction' is an engine of human thought, just as it is an engine of economic growth. That some Western ideas die is inevitable. What matters in terms of future dominance of the global political economy is that the new ideas that emerge will still come disproportionately from the West.

Arguably, the greatest economic idea emanating from the West – some call it the worst – is capitalism. From the perspective of ideational evolution, its fate is crucial to the West's future as a case study in the evolution of a Western idea. Anatole Kaletsky argues that the crisis in capitalism, which the current questioning of its key concepts implies, is only a means for this economic system to emerge stronger than ever in a new form.[10] Through ideological flexibility, Kaletsky continues, capitalism can prevail. Flexibility, he believes, is what will allow the West to demonstrate that its capitalism is more adaptive and durable than Chinese capitalism.[11] He acknowledges that in its next era capitalism's most distinctive feature will be a recognition that governments and markets can both be wrong and that sometimes their errors can be near fatal.[12]

Regardless of the West's talent for creative destruction in ideas, the most important part of the question may be whether the BRICs are themselves capable of making ideational contributions. This goal will be harder to achieve than financial domination, whose challenges the BRICs have overcome with a great deal of success (see Chapter 2). A perfect illustration of this challenge is the debate surrounding the Harvard portfolio investment model, a highly diversified model of portfolio management, including investment in private equity and real estate. The model was invented by the Harvard University endowment fund, a paragon of Western ideational superiority, long before the financial crisis. Since then, it has been under heavy criticism, as private equity and real estate were ravaged by the crisis, thereby exposing investors adopting the Harvard model to significant losses. Sure enough, Singapore's illustrious sovereign wealth fund, the Government Investment Corporation (GIC), has been questioning its validity.[13] The problem is that the GIC, has not presented a strong alternative approach, and stands as a perfect symbol of the challenge which the BRICs, just like Singapore (the BRIC equivalent of the eighties), face. The West may be in an 'insecure' phase of ideational development which the BRICs can take advantage of, but how *constructive* can they be? The answer depends on their creative ability, on whether they can come up with ideas. In particular, China, by being the best at intellectual piracy, has made its reputation as the copycat of the world. Can it upgrade to being the world's brain?

Some, like Patrick Smith, believe that the new century will see Asia become the home of the world's ideas. Smith provides a fine, profoundly intellectual discussion of what it is to be Asian and how the Asian approach can rule the world. His argument is the following. In the nineteenth century, under Western influence, Asia turned its back on its own values and embraced the West's assertive notions of time, the self and nature: 'past and present were to be reconceived as discontinuous, the one inaccessible to the other. The self was to be the ego-centred self, not the embedded self, the self within a larger community of one kind or another [as it is in Asian culture]. Humanity was distinct from nature and acted upon it; it was not simply a constituent in the physical world [as it is in Asian culture]. The West brought segmentation, not continuity or conceptions of the whole. And this was taken to be what it meant to be modern'.[14] Fortunately, Smith argues, Asia has entered a process of 'revaluation', whereby it has reconnected with its history and can combine it with the new. Smith collects anecdotal evidence of this revaluation through his reportage-style conversations with Asian friends; one has to take his word for the fact that this revaluation is the new Asian 'spirit of the times'.

One emerges from reading Smith with the conviction that being Asian means being satisfied with contemplative 'being'. This seems to be a bit of a caricature. In particular, while Smith does not fail to report Asia's desire to engage in the material world, most notably through its consumer urges, he does not acknowledge that a mimetism of the West is another Asian aspiration. At least partly, Asia 'sources' modernity from the West through this mimetism, and the enthusiasm with which Asia has embraced aspects of Western modernity has ensured that they have become entrenched in Asian identity. Also at least partly, Asia sources history from the West; there is no getting around the fact that some of Asia's cultural aspirations are achieved vicariously through Western associations. According to the president of Christie's Asia, auction houses there achieved total sales of US$3.8 billion in 2010,[15], with Chinese mainland buyers contributing a large part of the amount. Surely this fact speaks for itself. With large amounts of Chinese cash chasing fine art, antique jewellery and wines around the world, the Chinese appetite for all things Western, far from being on the wane, is on the rise. This behaviour is a long way off from just 'being'; China embraces Western culture actively: it buys it. Ironically, this also signifies that the West's 'declining' culture and ideas are flourishing in the very countries which are supposed to be eradicating Western civilization.

Furthermore, Smith's suggestion that 'power without purpose' is the intrinsic philosophy of Asian leadership cannot possibly be applied to Chinese rule. One look at the recent build-up of the Chinese navy[16] (see Chapter 3) highlights that there is a lot of purpose to Chinese rule, and the leadership is unlikely to be happy asserting itself through 'the active practice of inaction'. The 'soft power' which Smith celebrates is not what an observer of contemporary China picks up on.

Smith then describes a 'post-Western' world whose beginnings he traces to the fall of the Berlin wall, when 'the line between East and West started to become erased'. In this world he advocates 'conversations', as opposed to power relations, between East and West, and he calls for the West to re-examine its values through the eyes of a foreign, Eastern culture. His is a beautiful analysis of the philosophical underpinnings of what the East-West relationship should be. But even if one accepts his premise, the world is unlikely to conform to these principles, valuable as they may be. While Smith is right to point out that the association of the state with the exercise of power and purpose has wrought much destruction in history, it remains the main foundation of interstate relations. One may strive towards a horizon of Asian-inspired 'power without purpose', but the reality-based principle of 'power with a purpose' rules for now. Importantly, as argued below, even ideas that might seem to belong in the Asian concept of being are in fact key inputs into the power machine.

Smith operates mainly at the level of culture and values. While culture, values and science are 'pure' ideas, innovation – the form ideas take when applied to the economy – provides a useful measure of applied ideational power. Innovation is this chapter's focus. It represents both ideational power and the primary source of economic growth, hence its impact on power is doubled.[17] First, the relationship of innovation and growth is documented. Then the BRICs' innovation profiles are examined. If the BRICs are able to innovate, they will already have a very strong claim on global power.

Main economic approaches to innovation

What are the basic debates around innovation and growth from an economic perspective? Innovation can be defined as the process by which firms master and implement the design and production of goods and services that are new to them. Given the theories of economic development laid out in Chapter 1, no one will be surprised that the hands-off neoliberal approach to economic development is echoed in the neoliberals' call for complete laissez-faire in the sphere of innovation. In a nutshell, their view is 'let private businesses be, and they will come up with the best outcome possible in the area of innovation'. For neoliberals innovation increases productivity, which in turn increases economic growth. While the productivity of the three inputs into production – land, labour and capital – used to be thought of as the engine of economic growth, neoliberal economists showed that up to 60 per cent of growth is caused by a factor other than inputs called total factor productivity (TFP). TFP describes the key growth factors over which a country has limited direct and immediate control, including geographical factors, the rule of law, property rights, human rights, freedom of expression and, above all, technological change and innovation. Ultimately, neoliberals treat innovation as a black box, in that for them innovation is merely that part of economic growth not accounted for by labour and capital growth. This approach is well illustrated by the macroeconomic models of 'new growth theory' found in the work of Paul Romer,[18] for instance. Goldman Sachs's forecast of BRIC economic growth rates is predicated on one such model.

In contrast, Joseph Schumpeter began to look at innovation at the micro level of the firm in the 1930s.[19] Schumpeter defines 'innovation' as the emergence of new combinations of materials and forces. An important concept contained within innovation is the implicit existence of a 'combinator' or 'entrepreneur', who produces the new combination through his individual creativity. Because Schumpeter's theory of innovation is based on his definition of the entrepreneur, innovation is not merely technological but always by definition organizational, as it is impossible without the entrepreneur combining firm resources, including technology, in a novel way.

The key to Schumpeter's understanding of innovation is the idea of creative destruction, which we already pointed out as the survival condition of out capitalism as an idea. 'Creative destruction' implies that economic growth is a disruptive process. Desai illustrates this in the case of the industrial revolution:[20] 'steam-powered cotton-spinning made cottage spinning redundant; the same applied to weaving. Prices of products and services fell precipitously, output expanded, but many older businesses were ruined'. Creative destruction through innovation ensures a regular self-cleansing of the capitalist system rather than the type of once-in-a-century apocalypse some feared when the 2008 financial crisis broke out. Innovation strengthens the evolutionary tendencies of the capitalist economy. Because it is the mechanism propelling the economy forward while destroying its inefficient segments, it is the underlying foundation of long-term growth.

The main contribution of Schumpeter seems to be his belief that the creative act of innovation has to be brought back to the firm and the entrepreneur. This contrasts with the thinking of neoliberal economists, who try to link technology and growth through macroeconomic models that fail to examine either the industry level or the micro level of the firm in the creation of innovation. Inspired by Schumpeter, contributors to the field of industrial organization, including Kenneth Arrow[21] and later Richard Nelson,[22] looked at innovation as a firm-specific and, in particular, organization-specific process. They pointed out that innovation could be organizational; that is, it could consist in a specific way of combining the firm's resources as opposed to being purely technological. In the nineties an important issue addressed by industrial organization has been the role of networks inside and outside the firm in the creation of innovation.[23]

While the industrial organization approach has helped refocus analysis on a firm's internal organization and on the interaction between the firm and its related industry, it lacks a historical awareness and a sensitivity to local context. The most insightful contemporary alternative to the neoliberal approach to innovation is that presented by Freeman's[24] national system of innovation (NSI) approach; it is the one emphasized in this book. To Freeman, the system of innovation is a 'system of different institutions that contribute to the development of the innovation and learning capacity of a country, region, economic sector or locality'.[25] In the NSI approach, innovation is a localized, context-specific and socially determined process. From this perspective, the firm is only one innovator among many, which implies that leaving innovation to a firm's private decision is inadequate, while the role of policy in shaping innovation patterns becomes paramount. In part, this role is made essential by the fact that mere exposure of the NSI to international trade does not in and of itself produce innovation or economic development. Policy initiatives are required to assist the acquisition, use and internalization of foreign innovation, as well as the independent creation of national innovation.

One key implication of the NSI approach is that the acquisition of technology abroad does not substitute for local efforts. On the contrary, a lot of knowledge is needed to interpret information and select, buy, transform and internalize technology. Another important implication of this approach is that innovation in small and medium-sized enterprises and in traditional industries is at least as important as large-scale innovation projects. Finally, innovation capacity results from a combination of specific social, political, institutional and cultural factors and from the environment in which economic agents operate. In other words, firms are not isolated agents producing innovation; they interact with others in a system. Crucially, they are also set within a historical process of development and its specific social, political, institutional and cultural characteristics. To sum up, the NSI approach puts innovation in perspective.

Given the interdisciplinary outlook of this book, this approach to innovation is a natural choice, the one that best suits the book's analysis, as it captures the specific challenge of innovation in a developing-country context better than any other framework. To understand this specific challenge, one needs a perspective that is sensitive to (1) the contextual and historical specificity of innovation and hence development and (2) the implications of innovation for inequality. The NSI approach[26] fulfils both requirements.

One of the defining characteristics of the approach is that it starts from the highly specific socio-economic and political building blocks of a nation's system of innovation. Not only are these building blocks different across developed countries themselves; they differ even more between developed and developing countries. The NSI approach examines these differences and, in essence, emphasizes innovation as a social process and as the outcome of the particular historical accumulation of technology emerging from particular institutions.

At the same time, the NSI approach stresses that the accumulation of knowledge and innovation is heavily localized. Innovation breeds innovation; it creates a dynamic pole that contrasts with the 'innovation laggards' in other regions or sectors. The immediate implication is that innovation may bring polarization and inequality between regions or sectors if there are no policies to prevent polarization and to ensure that the innovation laggards are not left behind. In that sense the NSI approach brings out the fact that the relationship between innovation and economic development is not as virtuous as one might expect. Innovation is not a neutral input into economic growth, it can alter the distribution of growth in a way that worsens the prospects of certain productive sectors or regions while it improves those of others. Innovation might generate economic growth through the accumulation of knowledge; yet it also has a 'shadow effect' which leaves a systemic and historical trail by dividing an economy into innovation 'haves' and 'have-nots'. The beauty of the NSI approach is that it captures this shadow effect.

Beyond theoretical approaches and in the face of evidence on the role of innovation in economic growth, it is now widely accepted that innovation has a significant effect on productivity and growth at the levels of the firm, industry and country, whether measured by R&D spending (see the definition in Chapter 1), patenting or innovation counts.[27] As Cameron has noted,[28] many researchers have examined the output elasticity of R&D – that is, the additional percentage by which output increases for a given additional percentage increase in R&D: among others Griliches,[29] Nadiri and Bitros,[30] Nadiri,[31] Patel and Soete,[32] Nadiri and Prucha,[33] Verspagen,[34] Srinivasan,[35] Mansfield,[36] Sassenou,[37] Cuneo and Mairesse,[38] Mairesse and Cuneo,[39] Bartelsman et al.[40] and Englander and Mittelstädt,[41] as well as Coe and Helpman.[42] The majority of these studies found a strong, enduring link between R&D capital and output (typically a 1% increase in the R&D capital stock leads to an output rise of between 0.05% and 0.1%).

If one decomposes R&D into public and private components, there is more evidence of its effectiveness in the private than the public sector. Still, Jaffe[43] and Acs, Audretsch and Feldman[44] find that university R&D can have significant spillovers, with an elasticity of corporate patents with respect to university R&D of around 10 per cent. Nadiri and Mamuneas[45] find that government-financed R&D can also have an impact on the productivity of the manufacturing industry. As for the impact of patenting on output, Geroski,[46] who examined the effect of firm entry and innovation on TFP growth using a sample of 79 UK firms from 1976 to 1979, argued that innovation (measured by the Science and Technology Policy Research Unit Significant Innovations Database) accounted for 50 per cent of TFP growth and entry for 30 per cent.

Finally, Budd and Hobbis[47] estimated a model of UK manufacturing productivity between the first quarter of 1968 and the fourth quarter of 1985. They found that patenting by UK firms in the USA and imports of machinery from abroad have a significant and positive effect on productivity. Notwithstanding the role of foreign sources of technology, the present study agrees with Budd and Hobbis, as does the NSI approach, that international technological spillovers cannot account for most growth in a mature economy. This conclusion can be extended to developing countries. Even if economic development is understood as the overall result of the introduction and diffusion of new technologies, the innovative efforts of domestic firms are most important since a substantial domestic research effort is necessary to exploit the results of foreign research and since domestic research plays an important role in human capital formation. Hence, countries cannot source much innovative capability from abroad; ultimately it must become home-grown. By extension, this also confirms that there is no innovation, as opposed to the adaptation of foreign technology, without genuine creativity. Both these conclusions will be key in the context of the BRICs, as will be seen below.

The BRICs' innovation record

For each BRIC, the record of innovation at the country, corporate and sectoral levels is examined below.

Country level

At the country level, a useful piece of anecdotal evidence is the following: out of the 50 top inventions of 2010 ranked by *Time* on 22 November 2010,[48] only five were from emerging markets (South Korea, Israel, Hungary, China), including just one from China, which invented the 'straddling bus', a partly solar-powered bus which will span two lanes and carry up to 1200 people in a carriage raised two metres above the roadway; by allowing cars to pass underneath, it responds to the traffic jam problem in Chinese cities.

Going beyond the anecdotal level and looking at BRIC productivity in general, the weight of history suggests that the United States is still far ahead of the BRICs in labour productivity (see Figure 5.1). In the BRICs, capital productivity growth has been constrained by excess labour, as businesses have relied on low wages for competitiveness and have therefore been able to put off capital investment. However, as factories and call centres have come to replace subsistence farming, land productivity has increased, while labour productivity has also increased with industrialization and commodity resource exploitation. Overall, TFP growth improved from 1995 until 2007 in China, Russia and India (2007 Chinese productivity growth was close to 6%, Russian growth was above 4% and Indian growth above 2%, whereas Brazilian

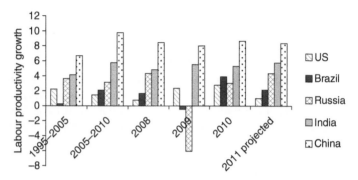

Figure 5.1 US versus BRIC labour productivity growth, 1995–2011 (%)

Source: Conference Board Total Economy Database, January 2011.

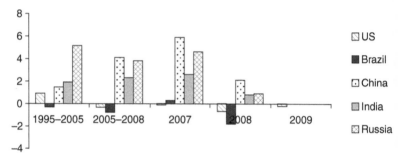

Figure 5.2 US versus BRIC total factor productivity growth, 1995–2009 (%)

Source: Conference Board Total Economy Database, January 2011.

performance was consistently poor), while US TFP growth became negative in 2000 and has been ever since (see Figure 5.2).

Still, it is doubtful whether high TFP growth rates in the BRICs are sustainable, especially in China. According to the Asian Development Bank, most of the efficiency gains which have resulted in China's skyrocketing GDP and TFP growth rates can be attributed to the catch-up effect, whereby personal income rises towards global averages because China is starting from a low base.[49] Back in the 1970–80 decade, the contribution of the catch-up effect to TFP growth was estimated at 2.47 per cent; by the period 2000–7 it had fallen to 0.54 per cent. Needless to say, as a country proceeds along its growth trajectory, diminishing returns to growth from the catching-up process set in. The bank suggests that in the next 20 years Chinese TFP growth will fall from an average of 7.4 to 1.6 per cent – below that of South Korea (2.5%), Malaysia (1.9%), the Philippines (2.6%) and even Pakistan (1.8%). Consequently, Chinese GDP growth is expected to slow to 5.5 per cent on average for the 20 years ending in 2030, compared with 9.4 per cent between 1981 and 2007 and 10.3 per cent in 2010.[50]

In terms of innovation per se, a systematic measure of national innovation is contained within the World Economic Forum's Global Competitiveness Index rankings. The ranking is based on 12 competitiveness factors, including innovation. The score on the innovation subcomponent is heavily biased towards so-called innovation inputs, as it combines capacity for innovation, quality of scientific research institutions, company spending on R&D, university-industry collaboration in R&D, government procurement of advanced technological products, availability of scientists and engineers, and only one innovation output – utility patents per million population. As is clear from Table 5.1, BRIC overall innovation scores are strong: out of 139, China comes 26th, India 39th, Brazil 42nd, and Russia 57th.[52] Still, even China pales in comparison with the US's number 1 ranking. More interesting is the breakdown of individual components, where countries score on a scale from 1 to 7, with 7 the top score; note that triadic patents are the only component which is not measured by such a score.[53]

Table 5.1 World Economic Forum innovation rankings/scores/data, 2010–11

	Brazil	Russia	India	China	USA	Mean score
Innovation ranking out of 139	42	57	39	26	1	
Capacity for innovation score[51]	3.8	3.5	3.6	4.2	5.3	3.2
Company spending on R&D score	3.8	3.2	3.6	4.1	5.4	3.2
University/industry collaboration in R&D score	4.3	3.7	3.7	4.6	5.8	3.7
Government procurement of high-tech goods score	3.9	3.5	3.5	4.5	4.7	3.7
Quality of research institutions score	4.2	3.9	4.7	4.3	6	3.8
Availability of s cientists score	4	4.3	5.2	4.6	5.7	4.1
Triadic patents per million population	0.36	0.45	0.14	0.39	OECD average: 44	

Source: World Economic Forum Global Competitiveness Report 2010–11.

Overall, these results are in line with expectations that BRICs would score at the top of the developing-country group but still well off US scores. Note, however, that in a cost-cutting rationale the financial crisis has reduced the scope for US corporate innovation and public spending on science, technology and universities. This fact might help the BRICs close in on the United States in the near term, but US historical advantages in innovation are unlikely to vanish, temporary financial effects notwithstanding. President Obama's reference to the US' 'Sputnik moment' in his January 2011 State of the Union address presented innovation as a panacea, in the context of a country plagued by subdued demand and needing dynamic companies to create highly paid jobs.[54] Whether Obama will increase R&D from 2.65 to 3 per cent of GDP in the middle of a fiscal crisis remains to be seen, but he is no doubt aware that innovation is central to the leadership struggle between the United States and China.

The traditional measures of innovation are patents (output) and public and private R&D investments (input). By the standard of triadic patents per million population, the 'inferiority' of the BRICs in the area of ideas is evident. Triadic patents are a set of patents on the same invention taken at the European Patent Office, the Japan Patent Office and the US Patent and Trademark Office. They are adjusted for economic size and therefore allow for cross-country comparisons. US inventors account for a 32 per cent share of the triadic patent total, and BRIC ones for a 0.2 per cent share.[55]

Yet beyond cross-country comparisons at a point in time, which can only reflect the large-scale of catching-up required of the BRICs, the evolution of BRIC patents over time is equally important; here the picture is much different, as Table 5.2 suggests. China has made a huge effort to boost its global patent applications since the year 2006, according to the World Intellectual Property Organization.[56] Already in 2007 China had overtaken Germany in terms of the number of new patent applications. In terms of patents granted, China had already overtaken

Table 5.2   Change in global patent applications, 2006–9, USA versus China

Global patent applications	USA	China
2006	420,000	210,000
2009	450,000	337,215

Source: World Intellectual Property Organization.

Table 5.3 Government versus business R&D expenditures as percentage of GDP, 2008

	Brazil	Russia	India	China	OECD average	USA
Government R&D expenditure, % of GDP	1.09	1.03	0.71	1.54	2.5	2.62
Business R&D expenditure, % GDP	0.49	0.72	0.14	1.02	1.17	1.84

Source: OECD.

Britain in 2004, Russia in 2005 and France in 2006. There has also been an average annual 20 per cent growth rate in patent applications in India since 2000.[57] Still, cross-country comparisons allow one to see that China's and India's acceleration in patent applications mainly reflects the low base from which these countries began catching-up with the developed world.

China has already registered significant R&D improvements; ranked seventh in the world overall, it is the most R&D-intensive of the BRICs in terms of government-financed R&D (see Table 5.3). Once again, these achievements are the result of recent efforts. Since 2006 China's annual government R&D investment as a percentage of GDP rose 279 per cent, reaching 1.6 per cent of GDP in 2011.[58] The government is following a 15-year plan to increase expenditures on R&D to the average level of developed countries; that is, 2.5 per cent by 2020 (see below). The other BRICs are still a long way from the average of OECD countries. As for business expenditure on R&D, the same conclusion holds.

Characteristics of BRIC NSIs

Beyond these macroeconomic measurements of innovation, each one of the BRICs' national systems of innovation displays specific features.

Russia

Russia's strength is its higher education. In 2006 more than 72 per cent of the school-age population was enrolled in higher education, which was especially strong in mathematics and physics. The good performance at this level follows through into working life: in its share of researchers in the population, Russia is on a par with South Korea. Russia is not, however, on a par with South Korea in government expenditure on R&D

as a percentage of GDP; it is the second worst performance among the BRICs in this respect at 1.03 per cent. Still, Russia is not a bad performer when it comes to innovation inputs taken as a whole.

This decent level of inputs does not translate into a decent level of outputs. Here Russia lags behind the OECD countries, although it does well relative to the other BRICs as it has a relatively low number of tri-adic patents and scientific publications per capita. Ultimately, the country's policymakers have failed to convert the major asset of scientific knowledge into commercial innovation.

At this juncture there are two main weaknesses of the Russian NSI. (1) Government research institutes, many of which were transformed into joint-stock companies in the 1990s but remained government owned, have no links with the private sector or the international scientific community. They are currently at the centre of the NSI, as they produce much of Russia's innovation, while firms have yet to take a central role in the system. (2) At the firm level there is less utilization of advanced technologies than in Indian or Chinese firms. One reason for that is that there is a negative correlation between the adoption of technology and political and macroeconomic uncertainty. Why would a firm's managers make a long-term investment in sophisticated technology when they do not know whether unforeseen regulations will put them into bankruptcy in a year's time? Small and medium-sized enterprises are particularly affected by this logic. Since 2000 the Russian Ministry of Economic Development has enacted a series of administrative reforms that have reduced red tape and barriers to business start-ups, but these enterprises particularly vulnerable remain to rent extraction by government bureaucrats.

As a response to these weaknesses, President Putin chose precisely to increase state control over the NSI. The current policy agenda emphasizes public procurement for advanced technologies, support for the production of technology-intensive goods through government-owned venture capital funds and government-owned development banking. Also, the Russian Corporation for Nanotechnology, a state corporation, was set up in 2007. It has co-invested in companies with knowledge in memory communications, plastic electronics and photovoltics. Finally, in a country where the oil and gas sector has created US$1 trillion in revenues since Putin became president, the current policy agenda does not neglect the goose that laid the golden eggs even as it encourages diversification away from it. Indeed, it promotes innovation in the energy, oil and gas industries themselves.

These measures may not be an adequate response to the bottlenecks in Russia's NSI. Russian policy needs to refocus its priorities. Specifically, it needs to (1) improve the national R&D institutes and encourage their links with both private sector and international research, and (2) provide firm-level incentives to absorb advanced global technologies, adapt production processes and engage in commercial R&D. Yet as mentioned above, specific innovation policies are probably less important than a change in the greater policy environment: ultimately, the prime requirement of innovation in Russia is a general effort towards greater certainty and stability in policy and less bureaucratic rent extraction. State involvement in the NSI is not a problem per se; quite the contrary. But in Russia it comes with a political economy of rent-seeking by officials, which, far from facilitating innovation, hinders it. Hence, solving the innovation problem in Russia means dismantling this perverse political economy. Also, as was noted in the previous chapter, solving the inequality problem requires the same process. Needless to say, rectifying the political economy is a mammoth task; hence, the main obstacle to Russian innovation and social improvement is not about to be removed.

India

India is a country of contradictions. It has become a world-class innovator in biotechnology pharmaceuticals, automotive parts and assembly, information technology, software and IT-enabled services, partly due to the fact that the stock of its scientists and engineers engaged in R&D is among the world's largest. The latter characteristic also explains why India has a strong record in the production of internationally refereed scientific and technical publications. Yet unequal access to higher education is a major weakness in India, with only 11.85 per cent of the school-age population enrolled in higher education in 2006 – the lowest percentage among the BRICs (Russia is at 68%, South Korea is at 90%). This asymmetry in higher education finds its way into the innovation potential of various productive activities. There is a significant gap between the productivity of formal enterprises in manufacturing sectors and that of the informal sector. In fact, this spread is greater in India than in the three other BRICs. Furthermore, the productivity spread within sectors is even wider. In this respect, improving India's innovative capability does not involve merely an effort to assimilate foreign technologies; first and foremost, it involves spreading innovation across the domestic economy. In that sense, the reduction of inequality in access to innovation becomes paramount.

India also stands out for its high share of government R&D in total R&D, at 75 per cent of the total in 2004. This is noteworthy in that in the other BRICs, the ratio is between 21 and 26 per cent. Yet although government is the highest contributor to total R&D, its expenditure as a percentage of GDP is actually the lowest among the BRICs, at 0.71 per cent of GDP. The public sector's dominant presence in R&D has had strongly negative repercussions from a national welfare perspective. R&D is very much strategically oriented towards defence, space and energy and is applied a lot less to agriculture, industry and health. This emphasis explains why India is much better at producing basic knowledge than commercializing innovation. India needs to strengthen incentives to commercialize public R&D, especially as it does not have a law prohibiting patenting development or commercialization derived from public research funds.

Furthermore, commercialization prospects would improve if linkages between the public and private R&D sectors, still very weak, were promoted. The symbol of Indian innovation that is Bangalore is no exception: here are several hundred information businesses set in the middle of numerous science colleges and high-end public sector research institutes, yet even here, the cross-fertilization of new ideas between these actors is limited.[59] According to D'Costa, the information technology industry's export-oriented model, whereby software services are developed offshore and targeted mainly to the United States, is to blame. While D'Costa offers a plausible sector-specific explanation for the NSI components' lack of integration, this feature applies across India's productive sectors, implying that it is a fundamental weakness in the NSI. To promote integration, government could encourage mobility of personnel among public R&D labs, universities and industry through competitive awards or by promoting spin-offs from universities and public research labs to create new companies. Also, government should build on the success of SPREAD; as its first programme to encourage collaboration between Indian technology institutes and firms, it provides matching grants and requires collaborative commercialization. For instance, it could focus on small and medium-sized enterprises.

Beyond the lack of integration between NSI components, there is a similar lack of integration between the NSI and foreign sources of innovation. India has had a history of highly reluctant and selective trade and investment liberalization (see Chapter 1), and even though by now most sectors, other than telecoms and energy, have been liberalized, the process has not been channelled into domestic innovation. While more than 300 multinational corporations have set up R&D centres in India, there has been little effort to tap into the technological spillovers offered by these centres. At the same time, it can be argued that the history of selective trade and investment liberalization has allowed large domestic entrepreneurial groups to catch up with Western innovations.

Some of these large groups became world-class multinational players: the Tata Group; Cipla, Ranbaxy, Dr Reddys and several other pharmaceutical firms; and Mittal and other steel groups. Now that these groups have achieved critical mass and innovative capability, there is little reason not to encourage technological spillovers from multinational R&D centres into the NSI. Integration between the NSI and foreign sources of innovation should no longer be perceived with scepticism by Indian policymakers.

Brazil

In Brazil the government carries out and finances about 60 per cent of R&D activity, but two-thirds of government spending on R&D is directed to higher education institutions, which places them at the heart of the Brazilian NSI.[60] With patenting activity also dominated by the government, it is consequently one of the greatest challenges for Brazilian innovation policy to encourage the development of firm R&D. This situation is very symptomatic of the Brazilian innovation system's historical features, which are characterized by dynamic poles of innovation that were originally powered in the 1960s by mostly public innovation institutes in combination with firms, many of which were state-owned. Many of these firms went on to create their own R&D labs. Brazil's poles of innovation exist in petroleum and gas, aeronautics, biofuels, agro-industry, minerals and paper and cellulose, and they are very much the product of a state-driven innovation effort, at least to begin with. Some of the firms that became involved in these poles are now Brazil's top innovators, and some of them are still at least partly state-owned, such as Embraer and Petrobras, which happens to be Brazil's most important holder of triadic patents. They are now viewed as Brazil's leaders in corporate innovation (see the corporate innovation section, below), but it is crucial to understand that they never would have had sufficient innovation capability without the support of state innovation policy. This kind of collaboration between public- and private sector institutions needs to be increased in the future, as it is localized only within a few poles of innovation. Still-nascent efforts are being made to encourage collaboration between universities and firms. For instance, in 2002 the University of Campinas set up an agency for innovation, called Inova, to foster cooperative ventures in R&D, consulting and intellectual property licensing. By 2006 it had already filed 40 patents and three non-proprietary technologies in 21 contracts.[61] Before Inova, the university itself held only 8 filed patents.

The other major weakness of the Brazilian NSI is the shortage of skills. The challenge here is to expand the supply of higher education while reducing the gap in the quality of education between private and public universities. The number of private universities more than doubled between 1997 and 2003. During the same period the public universities, which are free of charge, experienced an increase in enrolment: the ratio of applicants to accepted students rose from 6.6 to 8.4, while it fell from 2.4 to 1.5 in private institutions.[62] Drop-out rates in public universities remain high because the academic performance of students issuing from private high schools is higher than that of those from public high schools. This fact defeats the whole purpose of public universities being free: with so many free places being taken by students who attended a private high school, the few students from disadvantaged backgrounds who make it into a public university often cannot follow and drop-out. Most of these students are left with no choice but to pay for a private university they can barely afford. It is hardly surprising, then, that students from federal public universities score higher than those from private universities, both in general knowledge and career-specific tests.

Thus, the increase in private universities, which are mostly focused on low-cost programmes in management and social sciences, does little either to address the quality gap between public and private universities or to increase the innovation potential of universities through the production of engineering graduates. The stock of engineers graduated per thousand population is only 0.08 in Brazil, compared with 0.22 in the United States and 0.8 in South Korea.[63] From this perspective, it is crucial for Brazilian innovation policy to adjust educational output to market demands.

China

The contrast between India and China could not be sharper, given that 68 per cent of total R&D expenditure in China is generated by firms. That being said, one has to bear in mind that with the state having prioritized the capital and technology-intensive high-tech sector, hence it comes as no suprise that the 'pillar industries', which are the innovative core of Chinese firms, are state-owned.

However, state control has not been a recipe for success. While China ranks second in the world after the USA in number of researchers and publication of scientific papers,[64] the main weakness of its NSI is the imbalance in its R&D mix: Chinese firms do much more development (that is, applied innovation) than fundamental research – the opposite of the situation prevailing in India.[65] As with firm R&D, so too with government research: only a quarter of government R&D expenditure is devoted to applied research, and only 6 per cent to basic research.[66] The other 70 per cent of government expenditure is devoted to experimental development. The main problem with this focus is that barely any research gets patented. While innovation should not be strictly equated with patents, patents remain the only hard measure of innovation. It is not for nothing that patents are protected by intellectual property rights, while development is not.

In the 2011–15 five-year plan the government launched an effort to boost China's innovation and research capability. In its wake the ratio of R&D to imports of technology increased considerably. Furthermore, a growing number of Chinese multinationals have become involved in mergers and acquisitions to acquire knowledge and innovation capability.

High-tech zones have been promoted and linked to universities, which were allowed to set up and control firms in the zones. (The golden example of these firms is Lenovo, examined below.) One important consequence of these high-tech zones has been the boom in the value-added share of high-tech goods in GDP, from 2.12 (1998) to 4.44 per cent (2004)). That being said, much of this high-tech boom is more closely associated with the exports of multinational corporations located in these zones than with high-tech products made by Chinese firms (cf. Chapter 1). There has been little attempt to link innovation producers beyond the confines of R&D parks and incubators and even less to bridge innovation producers in innovative regions with potential consumers in low-innovation regions. The OECD's remark that China presents 'a large number of "innovative islands" with limited synergies or spillovers' is hard to dispute.[67]

Interestingly, this description of the Chinese NSI is very similar to the one made earlier about the NSIs of Brazil, India and Russia; it suggests that the immature and barely integrated NSIs of the BRICs have some commonalities. Whether in China, India, Brazil or Russia, there is a clear need for linkages between NSI actors. These linkages could be achieved through internal networks involving national firms, public research institutes and government, but linkages between the NSI and foreign innovation sources should also be encouraged through external networks.

Another conclusion valid across the BRICs is that integration between producers of innovation and between producers of innovation in innovative regions and potential users in low-innovation regions are both lacking. This weakness is particularly relevant to the present analysis in that it implies the scope for increased inequality from innovation systems which aggravate underdevelopment in regions which do not produce innovation, as the aforementioned uninformed potential users are unable to take advantage of innovation. This relationship between innovation and inequality – a crucial issue not only in the context of China, where it is particularly obvious, but also in that of the BRICs as a whole – is examined in more depth in Chapter 6.

Sectoral level

From the above data on BRIC innovation and the description of BRIC NSIs, it is hard to maintain that the BRICs have joined the playground of innovators. What do the sectoral data suggest? An examination of OECD patent data leaves no doubt as to the still marginal contribution of BRICs to world patents, regardless of the sector. More important, they are extremely telling as to the sectoral concentration of BRIC innovation, which is focused on information and communication technologies (ICT) and renewable energy. A look at the picture of the relative country share in total ICT patents (2005) shows that the USA still leads at 35 per cent (see Table 5.4).[68] A better indication of a sector's concentration is its share in a country's patents relative to its share in total patents – its 'revealed technological advantage'. By this standard, the BRICs' ICT sector has the greatest technological advantage: ICT patents amounted to 36 per cent of total patents in the 2003–5 period (exactly equalling the US share and above an average share of 35 per cent), and twice the 1995–7 levels. In China in particular, more than 50 per cent of patents were in ICT, compared with an average of 35 per cent of total patents. China is the most-ICT intensive BRIC, followed by Russia, India and Brazil.[69]

Similarly, the picture of the relative country share in total renewables patents shows the BRICs at 6.5 per cent, their highest global weight across sectors (see Table 5.4). In terms of national sectoral concentration,

Table 5.4 Shares of various countries in total patents in ICT, renewables, nanotechnology and biotech, 2005 (%)

	USA	Brazil	Russia	India	China
Share in total ICT patents	35	0.1	0.4	0.4	4.2
Share in total renewables patents	20.2	1	1.6	1	2.9
Share in total nanotechnology patents	41.8	0.3	0.5	0.4	1.4
Share in total biotech patents	40.6	0.3	0.4	0.7	1.3

Source: OECD.

renewable energy patents were another BRIC focus, at least in comparison with other countries; in the period 2003–5 they amounted to 0.7 per cent of total BRIC patents, versus only 0.25 per cent of total US patents and only 0.45 per cent of the total world patents. The BRICs have bet on outpacing the rest of the world in this new technology; as it is new for all countries, the BRICs have less of a technological deficit to make up for. In other words, they are specializing in a sector where there is more scope for technological leapfrogging.

Yet in patents in cutting-edge innovation sectors, the BRIC contribution amount to very little. Nanotechnology – which covers equipment and methods for controlled analysis, manipulation, processing, fabrication or measurement with a precision below 100 nanometres – is a case in point. The European Union, Japan and the USA have filed 84 per cent of all nanotechnology patents; the BRICs only 2.6 per cent (see Table 5.4). In terms of revealed technological advantage, 0.6 per cent of BRIC patents are in nanotechnology, compared with 1.3 per cent of US and 1.1 per cent of world patents. Like renewables patents, nanotechnology patents do not constitute a large share of most countries' total, but while nanotechnology and renewables patents constitute a similar share of BRICs' patents, their nanotechnology share is lower than other countries'. The opposite occurred with renewables; in other words, renewables is a niche for BRICs, but nanotechnology is not. This is also clear from the fact that the nanotechnology share of BRIC patents fell to 0.6 per cent in the period 2003–5 from 0.8 per cent in the period 1995–7. Of the BRICs, India is the most nanotechnology-intensive, and China the least.

Biotechnology is not a BRIC niche either. In 2005 the BRICs filed 2.7 per cent of all biotechnology patents (see Table 5.4). In terms of national sectoral concentration, the BRICs' 4 per cent share of biotech to total patents falls below the 5.8 per cent average. They are also below the US share of 7 per cent.

In sum, innovation is very sector-specific in the BRICs, with ICT and renewables emerging as clear foci. Some explanations for this selectivity are offered in Chapter 6.

Corporate level

At the individual corporation level, Antoine van Agtmael celebrates 'a new breed of world-class companies [that] is overtaking the world';[70] they are the pillars of an 'emerging market century'. Similarly, the Boston Consulting Group's list of '100 new corporate challengers' features 72 BRIC firms, highlighting 13 companies from Brazil, 6 from

Russia, 20 from India and 33 from China.[71] Van Agtmael believes that the rise of emerging market corporate champions is occurring through innovation, but his case studies raise major concerns. First, his show-cases of innovation are all Taiwanese firms, not BRIC ones. Crucially, one of his Taiwanese star cases, Taiwan Semiconductor Manufacturing Company (TSMC) – 'TSMC was the first company to spot the innova-tive opportunity of being a dedicated integrated circuit foundry while leaving the designing and branding of chips to others' – stole its genius idea from the United States. Van Agtmael has to admit that 'the idea for an independent foundry had originated with an American professor at Caltech. The revolution in the semiconductor industry that TSMC envisioned was already occurring in a small way, yet it was limping along in low gear until [TSMC] came along to jump-start it backed by the clout and resources of the Taiwanese government'. Point made. Van Agtmael's second showcase of Taiwanese 'innovation' is High Tech Computer Corporation, an original design manufacturer (ODM) of wireless devices, which it supplies to Windows Mobile equipment vendors. What van Agtmael does not say is that because ODM firms are under tighter and tighter deadlines to supply their vendors, they do not get a chance to develop new products. In fact, the relationship between an ODM and its client encourages the ODM not to question existing product architecture and to become locked into incremental, marginal innovation within this architecture. It is unlikely to come up with breakthrough innovation.

Three conclusions are in order here.

(1) What is labelled corporate 'innovation' needs to be examined closely. In general, all cases of emerging market corporate innovation fall into the category of commercial innovation, leading to better products, services and processes. That is not to say that it is useless innovation; it is usually a very clever commercial adaptation of a developed country technology to emerging market conditions.[72] An excellent example is the development of low-cost electronic chips by Taiwan's Media Tek as inputs for Chinese electronics manufacturers, especially Chinese mobile phone manufacturers seeking to use cheaper prices to compete with developed country leaders.[73] The beauty of Media Tek's business idea was that instead of just selling the chip, they provided Chinese manufacturers with reference designs and a suite of 'turnkey software solutions' to enable small, newly founded Chinese electronics manufac-turers to compete. As one would expect, the manufacturers themselves were not innovative; they came to be known as the manufacturers of 'bandit phones': their products, which were copies of branded models,

became an instant hit in emerging markets. The innovation came from Media Tek, a managerial innovation responding to emerging market conditions: Media Tek sold a product – the chip – but it also sold designs that would allow companies often lacking any experience to enter the mobile phone manufacturing industry. In a sense, Media Tek, by selling knowledge where it was scarce (i.e., in a developing country), created a virtuous circle of knowledge and entrepreneurship.

Sometimes emerging market innovations are re-utilized in developed country contexts. In Bangalore, India, Doctor David Shetty devised mass heart surgery at his 1000-bed Narayana Hospital. 'Narayana's 42 surgeons performed 6,000 heart operations in 2009 including 3,000 on children. This makes the Bangalore hospital the busiest facility of its type in the world. By contrast Great Ormond Street, Britain's largest centre for paediatric heart surgery, did 568 ear operations on children. The sheer volume enables profits to be earned despite many patients being poor'.[74] As the adaptation of a Western technique of mass production, Fordism, to health care, Shetty's innovation is a secondary commercial innovation deriving from an original Western innovation. Still, it is no surprise that some Western governments, including the UK's, are considering replicating Shetty's innovation in their countries.

Similarly, Kenya's Safaricom, by refining the mechanism of mobile phone banking, came to cover 23 per cent of the Kenyan population, something unheard of in the European countries, such as Norway, which invented Wireless Application Protocol (WAP)-based mobile banking in 1999. Above all, these innovations are lucrative; hence, the short-term economic payoffs seen in emerging economies, including the BRICs'. However, they do not constitute an Internet-type transformative innovation, one that spurs a technological revolution giving its country of origin an ability to rule the world.

(2) Van Agtmael forgets to mention that for every successful commercial innovation by an emerging market corporation, there is a disaster. China's high-speed rail catastrophe immediately springs to mind. In India, in 2007 it looked as if Tata had achieved a commercial coup in inventing the cheapest car in the world, the Nano. By the autumn of 2010, however, sales were at an all-time low, as security issues and pricing that was still above its target customer's reach turned out to be fundamental concerns.

(3) Just as the BRICs have niche sectors of innovation, such as ICT and renewables, so too are there cases of outstanding BRIC commercial innovators not mentioned by van Agtmael (a shortlist might include Embraer, Natura and Petrobras in Brazil; Kaspersky Laboratories in

Russia; Bharti Airtel, Ranbaxy, Reliance and Tata Motors in India; Huawei, Mindray and Haier in China). Yet the individual BRICs lack a critical mass of innovation, be it at the sector or corporate level, to power innovation-based domestic growth.

This critical mass is what BRICs are desperate to build, as they are well aware that therein lies the key to sustainable growth. In theory, one means of building a critical level of corporate innovation could be for BRIC companies to acquire developed country corporations with a strong innovation record. This is what India's Tata consortium did when it acquired the UK's Corus, Jaguar Land Rover and Tetley. Tata was looking to use Land Rover's off-road technology for its truck and car business in India, but the acquisition of know-how was also behind the purchases of the other two firms. Yet as the *Economist* noted, 'any fears that Tata would strip out technology and ship it home have proved baseless. British staff say Tata was a preferred bidder for their firms because it could be relied upon to support research and product development'.[75] Arguably, Tata's strategy can be put down to the fact that the United Kingdom has both the skills to fulfil these tasks and the legal, accountancy and branding expertise which may be lacking in India. The key point remains that Tata, like most BRIC multinationals, did not repatriate UK-based innovations to India. Consequently, this example indicates that one cannot count on the channel of corporate innovation acquisition to spill over into improved national innovation capability for an emerging country. Any benefits are likely to be confined to the emerging market corporation.

As BRIC governments have become aware of the shortcomings of this kind of reliance on individual corporations' acquisitions of innovation, they have refocused their efforts on the promotion of domestic innovation. Barry Naughton has suggested that the promotion of national high-technology industry at home has arguably become 'the central economic development policy of the Chinese government today'.[76] One reason for that was presented in the conclusion of Chapter 1: China's original economic development model, one based on low-cost labour, is faced with a serious challenge in the form of its ageing population. As the working-age population becomes smaller and smaller, low-cost labour is ever less an option. What then? Innovation has become the new credo.

Hence, the Chinese government is heavy-handedly directing a national innovation effort through its National Programme 2006–2020 for the Development of Science and Technology. This programme, set on boosting indigenous innovation, is a follow-up on earlier reforms focused on sourcing global knowledge (see Chapter 1). It is meant to end China's dependence on foreign technology and FDI via three means. (1) By increasing R&D expenditure to 2.5 per cent of GDP by 2020. (2) By enacting a new tax policy to stimulate R&D at the corporate level. In making company R&D expenditure 150 per cent tax deductible, a net subsidy will result. The policy also allows accelerated depreciation for R&D equipment worth up to 300,000 renminbi. (3) By public procurement of technology. This policy instrument is no doubt the most potent; it is also the one that causes the most concern in the Western world, as suggested by the protests raised by US corporations upon Hu Jintao's visit to President Obama in January 2011. After all, in a country where government accounts for one-third of GDP, government procurement is big business. Indeed, this may be China's literal 'Buy China' answer to Obama's 'Buy American' act. Except where goods or services cannot be provided by a Chinese company, the new policy requires government agencies to prioritize innovative Chinese companies by procuring their goods or services, even if these are not as good or as cheap as those of foreign companies. Within the list of those foreign companies wishing to sell to the government, those willing to transfer technology to local companies and let them assimilate it will be given priority over other candidates. Indigenous companies are also given priority in pricing: if indigenous products are not priced higher than others, they will be selected. This is nothing if not a plain application of innovation protectionism. While President Jintao, bowing to US pressure during his January 2011 visit, did promise to dissociate promotion of Chinese indigenous innovation from government procurement, the Chinese government is known for making a concession on one measure and replacing it with an equally strong alternative. It is unlikely to act any differently in this instance.

Still, for all its impressively improved indicators, China's National Programme 2006–2020 seems bound to fail. Scale is not a challenge for an authoritarian communist regime capable of channelling national resources into the production of a yearly growth rate of 8 per cent in a bad year. But this quantitative miracle has been achieved through an efficiency-based growth strategy relying on cheap labour. As China seeks innovation-based growth, it seems to be taking an identical quantitative approach to the problem, one embodied in the goal of R&D expenditure at 2.5 per cent of GDP. Though there is no denying China's improving statistics on patent applications, R&D expenditure and even scientific paper publications,[77] the same drive and incentives that allowed China to succeed in its efficiency-based growth strategy can produce these outputs. The problem is that innovation-based growth does not work like efficiency-based growth. A national innovation strategy based on quantity, one where the government merely throws resources at 'forced innovators' via carrots or sticks, is unlikely to succeed in the long run. According to Liu and Liu, 'scientists cannot do work that takes them more than five years to accomplish. Science is increasingly subordinate to the political and economic agenda'.[78] Worse, improving indicators of patents and R&D spending will merely mask the increasing weakness of Schumpeterian innovation at the micro level. For instance, the government spends huge amounts of money on developing digital machine tools, but few related commercial products are put on the markets.[79] Entrepreneurs must find the space to express their creativity – this is the prime condition of sustainable innovation. Its absence is the Achilles' heel of China.

The most successful cases of Chinese corporate innovation resulted from 'freeing' innovative corporations from the hold of the state to let them become partly independent spin-offs. During the 1980s institutes and universities were allowed to contract with enterprises to establish their own commercial subsidiaries. 'This led to the creation of a number of new enterprises that became important in the development of China's high-technology industry. They were "owned" by the state entity that spun them off, but they were considered "civilian" in the sense that they had no direct bureaucratic supervisor'.[80] Among them, Lenovo, a spin-off from the Institute for Computer Technology of the Chinese Academy of Sciences, stands out. Lenovo started out as a distributor of foreign desktop computers and concentrated on labour-intensive production of motherboards and video cards; it later became a major assembler of personal computers for the Chinese market. Finally, its takeover of IBM's personal computer business in 2004 turned it into a household name. Spin-offs like Lenovo are arguably the best product of Chinese technology policy to date. What has happened since then? The fact that until 1999, only large state-owned enterprises entering high-technology sectors were supported by the government says it all. Though high-tech private firms are now also entitled to tax breaks, access to low-interest credit lines and preference in procurement, to some extent things are even worse for them, as the government uses its provision of financing and contracts as another formal means to shape the direction of innovation projects.

The Chinese government is so keen to parade the innovator label that it names as innovation the technologies it imports from abroad and adapts marginally. How does China get away with that? Once again, it is a case of tit for tat: China gives Western innovators its highly sought-after market, subject to their pouring out the details of their technology (witness Westinghouse Electric's recent transfer of nuclear technology).[81] Once the transfer has taken place, the Western innovator finds itself with a new competitor, in the form of a Chinese state-owned enterprise selling a slightly amended version of its products. That the Chinese government feels compelled to orchestrate what could be called adapted theft of foreign technologies by state-owned enterprises only confirms its desperation to catch up. This desperation is even more visible in the outright theft of intellectual property through industrial espionage. Renault's electric vehicle programme comes to mind,[82] [83] as does Motorola's US$600 million claim of R&D costs for data allegedly stolen by a Chinese employee, Jin Hanjuan. In turn, such desperation is yet more evidence that innovation capability is absent from Chinese private companies.

Overall, whether innovation at the national, sectoral or corporate level is the subject, the BRICs cannot be described as strong innovators. The next chapter examines the reasons behind the lack of innovation capability across the BRICs.

6
Conclusion: The Innovation–Equality–Development Triangle

This chapter investigates the causes of the BRICs' innovation deficit. The investigation focuses first on the cases of China and Russia, where authoritarianism has a negative impact on innovation, and, second, on Brazil and India, where despite authoritarianism's absence, inequality keeps innovation from achieving its full potential. Then the focus shifts to what is missing from the BRICs: a relationship linking innovation, equality and development – the so-called innovation-equality-development triangle.

As was noted in the Introduction, because China is the only BRIC to have increased its weight significantly in the world economy since 2000, some explanation for the bottleneck in Chinese innovation would be helpful before the other BRICs are examined. China raises the question of whether a country's innovative capability is related to its political regime (see also Chapter 1). It seems likely that there is such a relationship and that it plays itself out in two stages, based on two successive types of growth: investment-based and innovation-based. Investment-based growth, consisting in capital accumulation, catch-up and imitation, tends to be based on the assimilation of foreign technology through learning-by-doing. It is achieved by relying on existing firms and managers to maximize investment. In contrast, innovation-based growth is based on the indigenous creativity of highly skilled managers and firms.

Corresponding to these two types of growth are the two stages in the relationship between politics and innovation. In the first stage authoritarian rule is good for investment-based growth: it sets the infrastructural foundations of innovation by providing development incentives, efficiency and order. Hence, investment-based growth is compatible with the notion of the 'developmental state';[1] that is, one where a state bureaucracy guides the economy, sets social goals, creates national champions and directs resources to favoured industries. An authoritarian government's ability to channel subsidies and resources to existing firms can be seen as an advantage for investment-based growth.

The Chinese economy embodies investment-based growth: from 2000 to 2010, growth of gross fixed investment averaged 13.3 per cent, while growth of private consumption averaged 7.8 per cent.[2] Over the same period the share of fixed investment in GDP rose from 34 to 46 per cent, while the private consumption share collapsed from 46 to 34 per cent. The role of the Chinese state in creating this investment-led growth was clear: it engineered suppression of wages, huge expansions of cheap credit and exchange-rate repression, which together ensured an income transfer from households to business and a change from consumption to investment. According to Michael Pettis from Peking University, 'the Chinese development model is mostly a souped-up version of the Asian development model. The Asian model channels wealth away from the household sector and uses it to subsidize growth by restraining wages, undervaluing the currency, and keeping the cost of capital extremely low'.[3]

The Chinese government is well aware of the need to phase out the investment-based model, but in the course of transition out of this model, there is scope for major damage to the Chinese economy. Japan offers ample evidence of the sort of damage to be expected, as it had to undergo a similar transition in the 1990s, its 'lost decade'. In Japan's recent economic history provides a measure of the significant risks threatening the Chinese economy. Just like China is today, until 1990 Japan was seen as a major threat to Western economic dominance. Its gross domestic product per head at PPP grew from a fifth of US levels in 1950 to 90 per cent in 1990, while China's grew from 3 per cent in 1978 to a fifth of 2012 US levels.[4] Yet Japan's GDP per head corrected from 90 per cent of US levels in 1990 down to 76 per cent by 2010. Similarly, Michael Pettis notes that Japan had grown from 7 per cent of global GDP in 1970 to nearly 18 per cent in the early 1990s, only to decline to 8 per cent of global GDP today.[5] Will China follow in its footsteps?

According to Michael Pettis, Japan kept boosting investment to generate high growth well into the early 1990s. But less than twenty years later, 'after a terribly long struggle to adjust to high debt levels and massive overinvestment, Japan has given back almost all the entire GDP share it had taken in the two decades that preceded'.[6]

In planning their nation's transition from investment-based growth, Chinese leaders would be wise to contemplate the example of Japan, where transition led to a sudden standstill in the expansion of capacity, as it was no longer artificially propped up by subsidization and financial repression, and then a collapse in output and investment. Relative to Japan, the most worrying factor for China is that, according to Pettis, investment is now much higher in China than it was in Japan before the crash. Hence, the output and investment collapse is likely to occur earlier in the growth process than it did in Japan. A comment by Martin Wolf well summarizes the challenge facing Chinese leaders: 'it is hard for a country investing half of GDP to decelerate smoothly'.[7] While Pettis and Wolf could be exaggerating the scope of the output collapse resulting from corrected investment levels, the argument remains a very solid one and is undoubtedly a concern for Chinese growth prospects.

The perverse political economy of innovation under authoritarian rule

Transition away from investment-based growth is not solely a transition towards consumption-based growth. At least as important is the transition to innovation-based growth. A society that fails to move to innovation-based growth or to make advances in frontier technologies will exhaust its economic potential. The BRICs may well be overtaken by countries lower on the development ladder if they do not effect such a transition.[8] A major concern with investment-based growth is non-sustainability. It seems inevitable that the learning-by-doing approach that underpins the investment-based paradigm will yield decreasing returns. This situation becomes all the more likely the closer the catching-up economy comes to the technology frontier, as other economies will become increasingly territorial over their own innovations. Thus, innovation has to become home-grown.

China is likely to come up against yet another set of challenges in its transition to innovation-based growth, since such growth requires ever more creativity as the catching-up process comes to an end and as individual freedom in the creation of ideas becomes more of a key ingredient. Meanwhile, as Schumpeter's microeconomic concept of the entrepreneur as the trigger of productive revolutions suggests, the notions of entrepreneurial spirit and creative destruction are completely at odds with political repression, because creative destruction threatens the stability of the political system. Acemoglu and Robinson identify a 'political replacement effect': although elites would benefit from innovation, all other things being equal, the fact that change may erode their political advantages relative to other groups leads them to block it.[9] They add that this explains the different paths of industrialization across Europe. While Britain and the United States adopted new technologies and industrialized rapidly, Russia lagged. In Britain and the USA, the elites were sufficiently entrenched not to feel quite so threatened, while in Russia, out of fear that industrialisation would bring political change, they blocked it. Morris makes a similar argument in noting that China's admiral Zheng He (1371–1435), who made seven oceanic voyages between 1405 and 1433 with 300 vessels, was prevented from continuing his voyages in the latter 1430s. Chinese emperors worried more about how trade might enrich merchants and other undesirable groups than they did about getting more riches for themselves. There were no incentives to exploit Zheng's voyages, which were tantamount to innovation in those days, because centralized government opposed them.

One point worth noting is that the damage of authoritarian rule to the creativity required to innovate is not uniform across sectors; because the institutional preconditions for innovation are not the same across sectors. According to George Magnus, 'in some of the most sophisticated and complex technologies, such as tissue engineering, genetics and genomics, and those incorporating the fusion of information, bio- and nanotechnologies, the Chinese are not expected to overcome barriers to the most sophisticated forms of innovation in the next 10–20 years'.[10] These technologies do not require the same institutional foundations as the production of information technology goods and green energy products, which the Chinese are penetrating successfully through massive government spending.[11] In screen-based goods and green energy, government spending is a sufficient substitute for innovation-friendly institutions. But there are only so many products that can be created without the rule of law or political freedom. Imagine innovating in sensitive areas like genomics or genetics without them.

Finally, universities in authoritarian developmental states do not lend themselves to innovation even though they are essential to it. If there is one place where innovative ideas need to be found, it is in vibrant university centres and their networks with industry. It is hard to argue that the quality of Chinese universities approaches the supremacy of those in the USA, where there are high levels of academic freedom, free enquiry and meritocratic organizational structures. A statistic mentioned by Magnus puts the matter in a nutshell: China has 13 universities of the world's top 600, whereas the United States has 13 of the world's top 20.[12]

Forty per cent of total world spending on scientific R&D takes place in the USA,[13] which also employs 70 per cent of the world's Nobel Prize winners. Ironically, when the 2010 Nobel Peace Prize was awarded to a jailed Chinese democracy activist, Liu Xiaobo, China put pressure on other countries to boycott the ceremony. This is a powerful symbol of Chinese contradictions.

China's education system is also riddled with contradictions. China displays a quantitative 'output' approach to the educational sector: it has more than doubled the number of its higher education institutions since the year 2000, from 1022 to 2263, with more than 5 million Chinese students enrolled in degree courses, compared with 1 million in 1997.[14] With the Chinese government spending at least 1.5 per cent of GDP on higher education, Richard Levin, the president of Yale University, stated that Chinese universities could rank in the top 10 in 25 years' time.[15] But here again, throwing resources at the higher education sector does not guarantee success. Yes, China enrols 15 per cent of the world's university students and 40 per cent of new degrees are in science and engineering, compared with 15 per cent in the United States,[16] but the quality of Chinese higher education's output is nothing like its quantity. Levin is the first to admit that Chinese universities lack focus on critical thinking, and a high incidence of plagiarism characterizes China's whole education system.[17]

What is at work here? Does a cultural attachment to the notion of community clash with individual creativity and competition? Levin explains that in China, all parts of the community can be used by its members. This philosophy is in direct contradiction with the notion of intellectual property rights, which constitute the main incentive for innovation in the West. But apart from the Western reference point, innovation based on cooperation rather than competitive individualism does not necessarily sound like such a bad thing. Of course, the individual capitalist's reward of intellectual property rights is not the only possible incentive for innovation. That being said, however, the problem remains that in the area of innovation, China has not come up with anything resembling a constructive alternative through community-based creativity. Plagiarism is the antithesis of creativity, not an alternative to it.

The greatest contribution of the above analyses of innovation and political freedom may lie in the fact that they draw attention to the political economy of innovation. Innovation and ideas do not exist in a void; they are affected by political processes, and their impact is directly dependent on the nature of their politicization. The economics of innovation is always overridden by the political power defining its constraints. In particular, because innovation is the main engine of sustainable growth, political repression is indirectly threatening growth – which is the BRICs' main contribution to the world.

Without excessively dwelling overly on the prospects for China's democratization, a few words on the subject are in order. Some argue that democratization will result from the tension between rising levels of wealth and the intolerance of political dissent. Perhaps. Alternatively, as Chapter 4 suggests, pressure for democratization could come from the falling wealth of those at the bottom as inflation increases. Note that consumer prices remain stubbornly above the official 4 per cent inflation target. Another factor that could fuel popular discontent is rural house repossessions, as was also shown in Chapter 4.

But neither factor in itself need spark democratization; it might merely create political instability. Instead, for the unease of political instability to generate full-blown democratization, the middle class, discovering that it has similar aspirations, would probably have to join the lower class in pushing for democratization. It would be difficult for the Chinese government to stand in the way of such a critical mass of pressures. So far, the rising middle class has shown no aspiration towards a new Tiananmen Square revolt. After all, the current middle-class generation benefits from the opportunities to travel, learn and make money that Chinese-style capitalism has offered them. The first signs of middle-class aspiration to democracy are only now appearing, specifically in relation to home ownership and in the form of a spread of homeowners' committees in the new middle-class urban compounds for private owners, which are managed on the basis of democratic principles and display significant homeowner activism. These owners are, for the first time, exercising their rights, as they no longer have to deal with the controls involved in state-owned flats. For instance, in Shanghai people living in a suburb next to the planned extension of the high-speed rail line organized protests and got the project cancelled.[18] While it is a big step from the democracy of a homeowner committee to the democracy of a political system, the crucial point is that the middle class is affirming its political identity and rights, albeit in the microcosm of housing. While the poor may organize for less inequality and the middle class for other interests, the fact that there are stirrings of a growing cross-class political identity in China constitutes a threat to Chinese authoritarianism. Maybe the long-expected process whereby economic forces bring about political change will unfold. Nor would this be China's first democratic revolution. In 1911 Sun Yat-Sen, leading the Chinese to topple the imperial Qing dynasty in the Xinhai democratic revolution, created the Republic of China. Apart from the carving up of China by foreign powers, the main motives behind the Xinhai revolution have been described as political inertia, economic inequality and corruption, all of which are again in abundant supply. But while the Xinhai revolution ended two millennia of imperial rule, communist rule has existed only since 1949.

The perverse political economy of innovation in cases of economic inequality

While China provides evidence for the idea that innovation requires political freedom, the argument is incomplete without a discussion of the other BRICs. Russia can be categorized as another innovation failure in the context of authoritarianism, although its greatest weakness is probably the fact that its commodity-driven economy tends towards boom and bust cycles, which are not consistent with a sustainable innovation effort. But what about India and Brazil? They have political freedom, but their innovation record is even poorer than China's. Only 3.6 per cent of Brazilian firms introduced new-to-market product innovations in the period 2003–5, and a below-average 36 per cent of firms undertook non-technological innovation.[19] Science and engineering degrees increased to a still negligible 11 per cent of new degrees in 2007, around half the OECD average. As for India, both its government and business R&D expenditures are the lowest of the BRICs.

That political freedom is a necessary but not sufficient condition for innovation can be seen in the democratic contexts of India and Brazil, where socio-economic weaknesses hold up innovation capability. To be sure, in China the creative act is doomed before it begins; innovation is strangled by political repression. Yet in India and Brazil, where the creative act is at least possible, inequality prevents, innovation from reaching full potential. Thus, even if China, which is both undemocratic and unequal, becomes democratic, innovation will remain weak unless China resolves its inequality problem. Innovation requires reduced inequality to create the long-term conditions to overcome underdevelopment. In that sense, resolving the structural problem of social inequality may be more important than acquiring innovative capability. If inequality imbalances the structure of the economy, the engine of growth that is innovation cannot function effectively.

To understand why, consider the demand-side perspective on innovation developed by Foellmi, Wuergler and Zweimuller.[20] They differentiate between two types of innovations: (1) product innovations, those that open up completely new product lines and cater to the advanced wants of the rich; and (2) subsequent process innovations, those that transform the luxurious products of the rich into products for the poor by finding ways of decreasing costs per unit of quality. This implies that there is a product cycle, whereby a product changes as it addresses the needs of different classes. That was the fate of the automobile which was originally a luxury and eventually became more widely accessible thanks to the process innovation of Fordism. From this perspective, Foellmi et al. demonstrate that 'an egalitarian society creates strong incentives for process innovations (such as the Model T) whereas an unequal society creates strong incentives for product innovations (new luxuries). Inequality determines the direction of technical change.'[21] By way of illustration, they note that the fall in US income inequality between the Great Depression and World War II was associated with a boom in consumer durables. A related implication is that through the process of development, inequality's impact on innovation and growth can be divided into two phases: in the early stages of development, before mass production technologies are introduced, inequality is good for growth because innovation is mainly driven by the introduction of new products for the rich. After mass production technologies are introduced, process innovations become the important drivers; hence, inequality becomes harmful. With the BRICs having just reached the stage of development where innovation is driven by mass production technologies through the advent of the middle class, inequality would be bad for innovation, if one believes Foellmi et al.

So much for the theory; what about the practice? On the demand side of innovation, a significant share of the Brazilian and Indian corporate sectors ignores demands for innovation from the large lower-class market and focuses instead on those from the middle and upper classes. In Brazil and India innovation consists in product innovation, which is unsurprising given the extent of inequality and its relationship with the type of innovation, as described by Foellmi et al. Innovation, biased towards the middle and upper class, creates an imbalanced internal system of consumption, which is a significant threat to the sustainability of growth. Presenting to the world a facade of showcase innovations catering to the elites can only mask social polarization for so long. Worse, the elites' tastes often mimic those in developed countries;[22] the domestic productive system thus must constantly adapt to an imported pattern of demand that is artificial, not being based on existing domestic technological capability, and detrimental to the development of endogenous innovation. Furthermore, since this type of production requires imports of technology and capital-intensive techniques with low potential for employment generation, it increases productivity while raising unemployment and thereby exacerbates inequality.

At the same time, in a few Brazilian corporations the same manufacturing unit may cater to both the rich and the poor segment, resulting in the coexistence of productive systems catering to different income markets within a single factory. One manufacturing unit may combine a technologically modern line of production that manufactures products aimed at higher income groups, along with a production line of low technological complexity responding to the demands of the low-income sector of the population. In this case the dual production structure ensures the survival of low-productivity activities based on low wages and other competitive advantages. Such a heterogeneous productive pattern helps only to perpetuate inequality, precisely because these dual productive patterns serve the 'market for inequality'.

On the supply side, most innovation produced in these countries exists in a world of top national champions, a world separate from the rest of society. Why so? In India and Brazil high inequality restricts the development of broad-based human capital and education, especially given credit constraints; what results is a microcosm of elite students at top universities, who go straight to the top innovative corporations. Innovation occurs in contradiction with the rest of the economy, in the islands of economic efficiency that are the emerging market champions. At the corporate as well as the sector level, the same phenomenon can be observed: in the BRICs, especially Brazil and India, a few top innovative sectors are localized success stories, but they have not been sufficient to galvanize the development of innovative capability across the country. Islands of high performance, whether they be corporations or sectors, have not yet shown that they can provide sustainability to innovation and growth.

Therefore, whether one looks at demand- or supply-side perspectives on innovation, inequality prevents innovation from scaling up to its full potential; in this respect state intervention to reduce inequality is of the essence. Given that the elites' demand, typically aligned on foreign patterns of consumption, diverts industry away from the development of endogenous innovative capability, national innovation policy should be designed to focus on inequality reduction from the point of conception, not as an afterthought. A less unequal system of innova-

tion is likely to be less driven by foreign technology and more conducive to development of endogenous innovative capability.

Finally, having suggested that inequality can be bad for innovation,
one should also consider the reverse relationship: that innovation can
worsen inequality. Indeed, for obvious reasons a positive correlation is
often observed between advances in science, technology and innovation and the widening of socio-economic gaps. Innovation relies on
highly skilled labour, which is rarely extracted from the low-income
segments. Low-income usually goes with low skill; hence, a knowledge-
and innovation-based economy often leads to concentration of learning capabilities and, by extension, innovative capabilities and power.
The benefits of an innovation-based economy are typically not distrib-
uted equally.[23] Therefore, although innovation does not constitute the
main factor influencing inequality, innovation policy needs both to
take inequality into account and to attenuate the divide between the
'knows' and the 'know-nots'. How so? In general, through more equal
access to education, health, knowledge and financial and R&D infrastructure. More specific policy recommendations can be found India's
experience.

India is a country characterized by duality between innovation and
inequality. India is home to innovative multinationals and represents
the world's fastest-growing market for mobile phones, but it is also a
country where a quarter of the population lives below the poverty line.
The greatest weakness of the Indian NSI is that the poor remain on the
sidelines of modernity and innovation. The best way to capture the
poor's isolation is to note that less than 3 per cent of the workforce is in
the private sector, with 90 per cent in the informal sector. To lower this
divide, it is essential to create incentives for formal innovation by public
and private actors, and incentives aimed at the informal sector's needs.
Governments can increase preferential matching grants for projects
which finance pro-poor innovation through the collaboration between
public R&D entities, industry, universities, non-governmental organizations and global poverty alleviation networks; prizes and awards can
also act as incentives. In the Indian context, grants would fulfil two
goals: (1) by addressing the lack of integration between India's public
and private R&D, they would increase the NSI's innovation potential in
general, as was suggested in Chapter 5; (2) in addition, putting this integration in the service of pro-poor innovation would contribute to this
specific goal. Utz and Dahlman[24] suggest that the Indian government
could set up a pilot pro-poor innovation fund to support collaborative
ventures that disseminate innovations to the population living on less

than US$2 a day. According to Utz and Dahlman, if its projects proved successful, a small percentage of the federal public R&D budget could be allocated to permanently fund pro-poor innovation projects all the way from scaling up to marketing. Such a fund seems like a good idea, at least in principle.

Yet while collaboration between multiple entities seems an ideal vehicle for pro-poor innovation, in some cases it can be challenging and not always realistic as the approaches of different NSI entities can be too far apart for collaboration to be successful. When it does proves difficult, policy can fall back on strengthening individual institutions. First, it can strengthen public institutions, which in and of themselves have a role to play in making innovation pro-poor. In India a good illustration of the positive implications of this role is the public sector–driven agricultural R&D which occurred in the context of the green revolution and helped generate income and employment for the poor. This revolution included investments in technology – high-yielding seed varieties, chemical fertilizers, agricultural research and extension – through public investment in supportive infrastructure and price incentives. Utz and Dahlman[25] mention in particular the space technology and preventive medicine sectors, where public institutions have come in as brokers to facilitate the pro-poor impact of innovation. For example, Sujala, a watershed development project, relied on space technology through satellite remote sensing and information technology.

Another institution whose strengthening could contribute to pro-poor innovation is the university. University-led initiatives to make innovation pro-poor are a growing trend. Utz and Dahlman mention an Internet service for rural areas, called n-Logue, that was developed at Chennai's Institute of Technology; they also mention Baluchari Institute of Technology of Kharagpur, a computer-aided sari design programme spearheaded by that city's Institute of Technology, which has made this type of expensive sari accessible at low prices and expanded the size of the market while keeping the production process household-based.

Another institution with an important role in making innovation more pro-poor is the firm. Private sector research on its own has significant potential. As noted by Prahalad,[26] a large company can use its considerable technological, organizational, and marketing capabilities to create and deliver products and services for people at the bottom of the economic pyramid – and profit from it. For example, the Shell Foundation's programme of solar home systems helps the poor by making loans to rural households seeking to buy solar lighting. Reliance Industries, India's largest private sector company, gives poor farmers access to cold-storage supply chains through a retail network of 2000 supermarkets and 1000 larger hypermarkets. Reliance connects farmers to this network through a distribution system guided by the latest logistics technology, with a view to creating enough surplus to generate US$20 billion in annual agricultural exports.

Yet the most sustainable solutions to the innovation deficit of the poor seem most likely to come from the poor organizing themselves. Chapter 4 has already looked at the merits of Brazil's Bolsa Familia in reducing inequality by encouraging the poor to become educated and find their own means of emancipation. In a similar spirit, India has started to experiment with self-help groups that develop mutual insurance schemes, lending and savings operations and marketing strategies for new agricultural products. These experiments are at least a first step in making innovation accessible to the poor. India's Agriculture Technology Management Agencies do just that through their Strategic Research and Extension Plans,[27] which are defined by village groups on the basis of consultations with farmers. The agencies contract nongovernmental organizations to conduct extension responsibilities and form partnerships with input providers for farmer training. Training volunteer farmers in technology is crucial to the success of these plans. In diversifying production systems towards the cultivation of high-value crops, they have increased farmers' incomes and enabled better natural resource management, integrated pest management, organic farming, well recharging, resource conservation technologies and development of new enterprises (including cashew processing and bee-keeping). Another example of the poor helping themselves is the Prayog Pariwar movement, which organizes farmer meetings to provide them with information on scientific practices. In particular, it has carried out the Scientific Grape Revolution in Maharashtra state. Implementing this 'revolution' with Prayog Pariwar's help, farmers with little experience in scientific farming have become India's leading grape cultivators in the space of 20 years.[28]

One conclusion to be drawn from India's experience is that what one might call the ideal triangle of economic equality, innovation and development is not a natural construct. If it were, all the countries of the world would be like Finland. Still, it is at least partly within the scope of innovation policy to adjust an economy towards this triangle. A country like China has a lot on its plate. It must not only acquire genuine innovation capability; to spread the benefits of innovation as equally as possible, it has to ensure that acquiring this capability does not contribute to aggravating its other weakness, inequality.

Conclusion

It was noted above that in the BRICs governed by authoritarian states, the dismantling of authoritarianism is a necessary but not a sufficient condition for innovation to flourish. Rather, the common challenge faced by all BRICs is to align their economies' progression towards genuine innovation with the reduction of inequality.

That being said, the BRICs may well rule the world in the short term, even if they refuse to address any of these challenges. If the West's economy collapses altogether, it could ensure BRIC rule in and of itself. One thing is for sure: if that scenario does come to pass, it will be a dull rule resulting in a world devoid of originality. In that sense, hoping that the BRICs decide to take on the challenges of inequality and innovation is in their own long-term interest and the West's, too.

Finally, it has been emphasized that BRIC innovation must be the result of domestic creativity. BRIC ideas can put their stamp on the world only if they are BRIC originals. The BRICs can become a global force by affirming their difference in the way they exercise power, not by becoming a new West. One powerful means for the BRICs to affirm their power would be to promote the unique idea of development to the least developed countries. Of course, this idea assumes that they have addressed their shortcomings in terms of innovation and inequality; otherwise the world would become an experiment, in which a multiplicity of least developed countries tries to imitate the BRICs' unsustainable and imperfect model, resulting in multiple development failures. Hence, one should add that the existing Chinese model is not a valid candidate. Assuming the BRICs succeed in addressing the above concerns, they could provide an alternative development model to the Western one, which has been heavily criticized for being a post-colonial imposition on the least developed countries. Such an alternative model has the potential to be the greatest idea that the BRICs could contribute to the global political economy. Their unique experience could be their ultimate 'comparative advantage'.

But before they can qualify as a successful alternative development model, they must work towards implementing the innovation-equality-development triangle. If they were to do so, how impressed Ulysse Merou would be with the resulting Planet of the BRICs! In this brave new world, iPhones would offer networks connected to other planets.

Trains would run at the speed of light in a comfort and safety worthy of the Orient Express. Inhabitants would enjoy a decent average standard of living, and inequality of income, assets and opportunity would be low. Ulysse would return to a utopia, a million miles away from the Planet of the Apes.

Notes

Introduction

1. Also called renminbi.
2. See Beausang 2003.
3. Nothing captures the public's imagination like the fact that, according to Forbes in 2010, for the first time the number of billionaires in the BRICs (301) surpassed the number of those in Europe. This fact seems to substantiate the public's perception of a power shift from the Old to the New World.
4. Recently, the acronym 'BRICs' has sometimes been interpreted as 'BRICS', with South Africa being the S. However, economically South Africa is not really in the same economic or demographic league as the other countries and seems to be included primarily to give better geographic coverage (i.e., including Africa).
5. The BRIC acronym was introduced in O'Neill 2001.
6. See O'Neill 2011.
7. O'Neill mentions the following determinants of productivity growth: a stable macroeconomic background, supported by sound macroeconomic policies designed to keep inflation low and public finances in order; strong and stable political institutions; openness to trade and foreign investment; adaptation of modern technologies; and high levels of education (ibid., 34). In 2005, as a measure of these determinants in the BRICs, Goldman Sachs compiled 13 World Bank Development indicators (inflation, government deficit, investment spending, external debt, degree of openness, use of mobile telephones, use of the internet, use of computers, life expectancy, education, rule of law, corruption, stability of government) and combined them into a 'growth environment score'. This score became Goldman's main means of forecasting BRIC productivity. The higher the score, the higher the productivity.
8. See Wilson and Purushothaman 2003.
9. The G6 countries are the United States, Japan, Germany, France, the United Kingdom and Italy.
10. Note that there are several methods of calculating PPP estimates (e.g., the IMF and Maddison use different ones). Depending on which one is used, quantitatively different values GDP will be obtained. Hence, throughout the book, values for GDP differ depending on which data source was used. They have not been corrected for, because in general I am more interested in the qualitative trends than the exact quantitative result, which will always be an approximation anyway. See Maddison 2010.
11. See Magnus 2011.
12. Despite the objections of political commentators and academics, such as (Yang, 2011).
13. See http://www.ggdc.net/MADDISON/oriindex.htm, under statistics on world population, GDP and per capita GDP, AD 1–2008.

14. See Chapter 4 for a deeper analysis of Russia's demographic indicators.
15. See Eberstadt 2011, 105.
16. See Magnus 2011.
17. See Moyo 2011.
18. Fukuyama (2011) also argues in his conclusions that liberal democracies currently suffer from an inability to tackle difficult problems.
19. See Ferguson 2011.
20. Ibid., 325.
21. Rodrik (2011) comes to a similar conclusion while focusing on a different set of limitations, which are related to the limited space for policy intervention in the emerging markets.
22. This does, however, remain the subject of debate (see Wade vs Wolf in the *Financial Times*).
23. While O'Neill claims that he singled out the BRICs because he wanted investors to stop seeing them as emerging markets, I affirm the BRICs' emerging market identity. In my view, while their GDP performance will soon make them more closely resemble developed than emerging markets, when it comes to other characteristics (e.g., inequality and innovation), they remain far from having emerged; hence, they cannot be dissociated from the emerging markets.
24. See O'Neill 2011, 104.
25. Interestingly, Held, McGrew, Goldblatt and Perraton come up with a different set of four globalization dimensions, although this book does not draw from their perspective. These dimensions are the extensity of global networks, the intensity of global interconnectedness, the velocity of global flows and the impact propensity of global interconnectedness. The first three dimensions are self-explanatory. The last refers to the fact that the impact of distant events is magnified, so that the local and the global become more deeply intertwined (see the introduction to Held et al. 1999).

1 BRICs: Beyond Developing?

1. Beyond these two main approaches, there exists an intermediary model, which is that adopted by most of continental Europe. Here, the state provides for public goods – i.e., goods which benefit everyone but whose costs cannot be imputed to one person, such as a lighthouse – but private markets are given free reign. Higher income taxes are required to finance public goods. They are also used to reduce poverty. For example, according to the *Economist* (2011c), Sweden's tax benefit system cuts its poverty rate by 80 per cent. The intermediary model might be termed a 'lightly managed market'.
2. See Chang 2010.
3. See Halper 2010.
4. See Moyo 2011.
5. Back then, NICs were defined as countries whose economies had not yet reached developed country status but had, in a macroeconomic sense, outpaced their developing counterparts through high economic growth rates. In the seventies and eighties the first NICs were South Korea, Taiwan, Hong Kong and Singapore, which have long since graduated to developed country status. Current NICs include Turkey, South Africa, Mexico, Brazil, China,

India, the Philippines, Malaysia and Thailand, but somehow no one remembers that three out of four BRICs are also NICs. This is a measure of the trendiness of the BRIC concept. For the purpose of the present analysis, however, in the focus is on the first wave of NICs.

6. The exact year of this symbolic event is a contentious issue, as is explained in the Introduction.

7. Kenya and Zambia are excellent illustrations.

8. Note, however, that South Korea has become highly globalized, as illustrated by its trade-to-GDP ratio of 105.8 per cent in 2008–10.

9. South Korea is not ranked relative to the BRICs, as it is in a different category on every indicator.

10. See Chang 2008.

11. Ibid.

12. Ibid.

13. Most-favoured nation, or MFN, stipulates that based on multilateral trade liberalization, the lowest tariff deal which a country grants to its favourite partner has to be granted to everyone else.

14. Countries that join the WTO agree on bound tariff rates, which are the maximum tariff allowed by the WTO on a particular product. Members have the opportunity to increase or decrease their actually applied tariff rates as long as they don't raise them above the bound rate.

15. See Naughton 2007.

16. See Srinivasan 2007.

17. As in the case of trade, this has changed since then, with FDI inflows now accounting for 12.6 per cent of GDP.

18. Ibid.

19. See Yu 2007.

20. Yet that has not dissuaded the Chinese from resorting to informal channels as well: Motorola is now suing one of its Chinese employees for industrial espionage with a US$600 million claim.

21. Yet it is interesting that other FDI restrictions have since appeared, such as sectoral restrictions on energy and mining FDI, while FDI in high-tech, advanced materials and equipment manufacturing are encouraged.

22. See Liu, Xu and Liu (2002) for a review of the theoretical limitations.

23. See Zhao 2006.

24. Research and development (R&D) activities are often used as a synonym for innovation – wrongly so, given that they account only for formal innovation efforts, while there are also more informal forms of innovation, like reverse engineering or learning by doing, which are not accounted for by R&D. Still, R&D activities typically constitute a large percentage of innovation activities carried out by government and firms. Research is equivalent to scientific investigation, while development is experimental, applied research. R&D expenditures by government and by firms are therefore a good measure of the innovation inputs of an economy. Once R&D activities have been carried out, at the end of the process of innovation, there can be patents and other innovation outputs. However, few patents result from experimental development as opposed to research.

25. See Liu, Xu and Liu 2002.

26. See Naughton 2007.

27. See Aslund 2007.
28. See Vasiliev 1999.
29. See Stiglitz 2003.
30. Ibid.
31. See   http://business.timesonline.co.uk/tol/business/industry_sectors/natural_resources/article4124325.ece.
32. See Gokhberg et al. 2011.
33. Ibid.
34. Ibid.
35. See Cassiolato and Vitorino 2011.
36. See Furtado 1959.
37. While the thesis of deteriorating terms of trade has been contested, the argument that commodity exporters suffer from the volatility of the income generated by commodity exports remains valid nonetheless. See Harvey 2008.
38. See the *Financial Times*, 20 September 2011.
39. See Koeller and Cassiolato 2011.
40. Ibid.
41. See Saith 2008.
42. Dumping occurs when a company exports a product at a price lower than the price it normally charges in its home market. When a material injury is done to the competing domestic industry, the WTO agreement allows a government to act against dumping by charging an extra import duty on the particular product from the exporting country in order to bring its price closer to the 'normal' value and thus remove the injury to domestic industry in the importing country.
43. http://www.wto.org/english/tratop_e/adp_e/ad_init_rep_member_e.pdf.
44. http://www.unctad.org/en/docs/webdiaeia20111_en.pdf.
45. See Joseph and Abrol 2011.
46. See Naughton 2007.
47. See the *Financial Times*, 22 February 2011.
48. See Eichengreen, Park and Shin 2011.
49. See Saith 2008.

2 BRICs and Global Economic Power

1. Kose and Prasad (2010) include the following countries in their list of emerging markets: Argentina, Brazil, Chile, China, Colombia, Egypt, Hong Kong, India, Indonesia, Israel, Jordan, the Korean Republic, Malaysia, Mexico, Morocco, Pakistan, Peru, the Philippines, Singapore, South Africa, Thailand, Turkey, Venezuela.
2. Ibid.
3. Kose and Prasad (2010) include the following countries in their list of advanced countries: Australia, Austria, Belgium, Canada, Denmark, Finland, France, Germany, Greece, Iceland, Ireland, Italy, Japan, Luxembourg, the Netherlands, New Zealand, Norway, Portugal, Spain, Sweden, Switzerland, the UK, the USA.
4. Ibid.
5. See the *Financial Times*, 'War of the Worlds', 26 January 2011.

6. See the *Financial Times*, 'Talk of Currency Wars Fades As Emerging World Battles Inflation', 14 April 2011.
7. See Kose and Prasad 2010, 43.
8. See Halper 2010, 186.
9. See Kose and Prasad 2010, 46.
10. Ibid., 185.
11. See Bartlett 2009.
12. See the *Financial Times*, 'China Cements Role as Top of the BRICs', 14 April 2011.
13. See Kose and Prasad 2010, 54. In general, these authors' discussion of emerging markets' global financial integration and their data tables are both excellent.
14. See UN Conference on Trade and Development 2010.
15. The financial crisis has had a major role in heightening China's increasing weight in global outward FDI flows. Indeed, at the end of 2008, when global FDI flows dropped an estimated 20 per cent to 30 percent, China's outward FDI stock doubled to US$170 billion. However, once again, this increase has to be put in perspective: average Chinese FDI outflows still account for only 1 per cent of global flows annually. For all the talk of China buying up the world, there are US$5 of FDI assets under foreign ownership in China for every US$1 of Chinese direct investment assets abroad. In other words, China is still being bought up more than it is buying up the world, at least from an FDI perspective. Clearly, claims that China is overtaking the world through FDI are as much of an exaggeration as wider claims that China will soon rule the world. That being said, the acceleration in Chinese outward investment at the end of the noughties is still a remarkable phenomenon.
16. For a bird's-eye view of Chinese outward investment flows in terms of host countries and sectors, see Tables 2.3–2.5.
17. See www.unctad.org/wir for the list of 'megadeals'.
18. See Rosen and Hanemann 2011. This paper provides an excellent survey of Chinese outward FDI and its outlook.
19. See the *Economist* 2008.
20. See Bank for International Settlements 2008.
21. http://www.swfinstitute.org. Last accessed 1 June 2012.
22. See UN Conference on Trade and Development 2010, 14.

3   BRICs and Global Political Power

1. http://ase.tufts.edu/gdae/Pubs/wp/09–01IPinWTOJan09.pdf. Last accessed 1 June 2012.
2. Ibid. 5.
3. Ibid., 6.
4. See Keohane and Nye 1977.
5. See Nye 2011. Last accessed 1 June 2012.
6. http://ase.tufts.edu/gdae/Pubs/wp/09–01IPinWTOJan09.pdf.
7. See Haas 1980, 1990.
8. According to the World Bank, debt is the entire stock of direct government fixed-term contractual obligations to others outstanding on a particular date.

It includes domestic and foreign liabilities such as currency and money deposits, securities other than shares, and loans. It should not be confused with external debt, which reflects the foreign currency liabilities of both the private and public sector and must be financed out of foreign exchange earnings.

9. See Parent and MacDonald 2011, 36.
10. These data come from the World Bank's World Development Indicators, with the exception of the Chinese number, which comes from the Central Intelligence Agency, as the World Bank does not publish Chinese public debt data.
11. See Gruenwald and Hori 2008.
12. Also see Barcena 2010.
13. See Stephens 2012.
14. Lawrence Summers describes how 'even as market outcomes seem increasingly unsatisfactory, budget pressures have constrained the ability of the public sector to respond. The basic solvency of too many capitalist states seems in question' ('Current Woes Call for Smart Reinvention Not Destruction', *Financial Times*, 9 January 2012). Yet he believes that a solution can be found in 'reinventing health, education and social protection'. In contrast, John Plender finds 'a greater mistrust of big government than of business', and he concludes pessimistically that 'efforts to re-regulate the banking system have failed to convince many experts that an even larger financial crisis can be avoided' (John Plender, 'The Code That Forms a Bar to Harmony', *Financial Times*, 9 January 2012).
15. Ibid.
16. See Erixon and Sally 2010, 9.
17. See World Trade Organization, *Overview of Developments in the International Trading Environment*, op cit., A3–A46.
18. See Evenett 2009.
19. See World Trade Organization, *Overview of Developments in the International Trading Environment*, op cit., A3–A46.
20. See International Energy Agency 2010.
21. See the *Financial Times*, 'US Threatens to Retaliate at EU's Green Levy on Airlines', 20 December 2011.
22. See the *Financial Times*, 'China's Rare Earths', 7 July 2011.
23. See the *Financial Times*, 'Rifts Emerge in WTO over Push for Pacts', 19 December 2011.
24. http://www.telegraph.co.uk/finance/recession/china-economic-slow-down/5556913/Chinas-Buy-Chinese-decree-with-400bn-stimulus-package-risks-US-protectionism-row.html. Last accessed 1 June 2012.
25. http://online.wsj.com/article/SB10001424052748703407304576154121951088478.html.AQ: please provide last date of access>
26. See the *Financial Times*, 'Huawei Goes on Attack against US Restrictions', 17 October 2011.
27. See Stiglitz 2011.
28. http://www.bloomberg.com/news/2011–01–04/mantega-threatens-more-capital-controls-to-prevent-brazil-currency-gains.html. Last accessed 1 June 2012. Also, see Sebastian Edwards's classic paper on the general subject of capital controls in Latin America, http://www.nber.org/papers/w6800, (Last accessed 1 June 2012) for an academic perspective.

29. See the *Financial Times*, 'Outsourcing: Thick Skins Shrug Off Protectionist Rhetoric', 16 January 2011.
30. See the *Financial Times*, 'China Fund Shuns Guns and Gambling', 13 June 2008.
31. See the *Financial Times*, 'Reject Sovereign Wealth Funds at Your Peril', 20 June 2008.
32. See the *Financial Times*, 'Asia: Eastern Billions Can Still Join the World', 3 January 2011.
33. In April 2010 quotas were changed so that the share of low- and middle-income countries on the governing board would increase from 44% to 47%; these changes have not been ratified yet
34. See Chang 2008, chap. 1.
35. Ibid.
36. See Kwa 2003.
37. See Wade 2004.
38. Alternatively, see Teune 2002.
39. See Wade 2003.
40. See Limao 2005.
41. http://www.pisani-ferry.net/base/re02-gouvernance-contributions.pdf. Last accessed 1 June 2012.
42. See O'Neill 2011, 229.
43. See the *Financial Times*, 'Chinese Trades Suggest Shift from US Dollar towards Euro Market', 21 June 2011.
44. See Buira 2005.
45. Ibid.
46. See Fox 2010.
47. See the *Financial Times*, 'China Launch Set to Boost Space Station Plan', 21 September 2011.
48. India's rocket launches have the same effect.
49. http://www.asiaing.com/chinas-naval-2007.html. Last accessed 1 June 2012.
50. See the *Financial Times*, 'Beijing Builds to Hold US Power at Bay', 19 January 2011.
51. See Parello-Plesner and Khann 2011.
52. See Brautigam 2009.
53. See the *Financial Times*, 'China to Ease Path for Investors', 19 December 2011. Last accessed 3 January 2012.
54. More than anything else, one could argue that the second reform was introduced as a response to China's experiencing capital outflows in October 2011, for the first time since 2007. Most emerging markets, including China, are concerned with sudden increases in speculative capital inflows; instead, October 2011 saw a spike in Chinese capital outflows, as investors fled due to concerns that the property market might collapse.
55. http://www.research.hsbc.com/midas/Res/RDV?p=pdf&key=HarTkXFDc9&n=286641.PDF. Last accessed 1 June 2012.
56. Brazil has also proposed an 'exchange rate antidumping' measure at the WTO for countries which engage in competitive devaluations of their currencies. See the *Financial Times*, 'Brazil to Seek New Arms for Currency Battle', 20 September 2011.

57. http://www.telegraph.co.uk/property/expatproperty/7887469/Brazils-government-plans-to-restrict-foreign-land-ownership.html. Last accessed 1 June 2012.
58. http://www.reuters.com/article/2010/06/10/brazil-oil-idUSN1025754820100610.
59. http://www.bloomberg.com/news/2011–04–01/vale-s-main-shareholders-group-seeking-replacement-for-ceo-roger-agnelli.html.

4   Limit No. 1: BRICs and Inequality

1. See Ferguson 2011.
2. http://www.businessdayonline.com/NG/index.php/analysis/commentary/18016-the-inequality-wildcard. Last accessed 1 June 2012.
3. See Packer 2011.
4. See Ravallion 2004.
5. Ibid, 24.
6. A poverty line can be set as a national standard or an international benchmark for comparison. The focus is on the international poverty line in this book, but the definitions of national and international poverty lines are summarized in this endnote. According to the World Bank, a national poverty line is the income level below which people are defined as poor. This definition is based on the income level people require to buy life's basic necessities – food, clothing, housing – and that allows them to fulfil their most important socio-cultural needs. The poverty line changes over time and varies by region. Alternatively, there is also an international poverty line, which is an income level established by the World Bank to determine which people in the world are poor – set at US$1.5 a day per person in 2005 international purchasing power parity dollars. A person is considered poor if he or she lives in a household whose daily income or consumption is less than US$1.5 per person. Although this poverty line is set for international comparisons, it is impossible to create an indicator of poverty that is strictly comparable across countries. The level of US$1.5 a day per person is close to national poverty lines in low-income countries but considerably lower than those in high-income countries.
7. See Bourguignon 2004.
8. See Mirlees 1971.
9. See Moore and White 2003.
10. http://www.business-standard.com/india/news/pranab-bardhan-how-unequalcountry-is-india/369106/. Last accessed 3 January 2012.
11. See Alesina and Perotti 1996.
12. Based on the OECD's estimate.
13. See Li and Zou 2002.
14. See Forbes 2000.
15. See Barro 2000.
16. See Lopez 2004.
17. http://codfishwaters.files.wordpress.com/2008/05/alesina.pdf. Last accessed 1 June 2012.
18. See Perotti 1996.
19. http://kisi.deu.edu.tr/yesim.kustepeli/w4499.pdf. Last accessed 1 June 2012.

20. http://qed.econ.queensu.ca/pub/faculty/lloyd-ellis/econ835/readings/deininger.pdf. Last accessed 3 January 2012.
21. See Birdsall and Londoño 1997.
22. See King Whyte 2010.
23. Ibid., 182.
24. See Zhang and Eriksson 2009.
25. See King Whyte 2010, 199.
26. See Hirschman and Rothschild 1973.
27. See Ferguson 2011.
28. This is the average of the annual inflation from January to November.
29. This is the Selic target rate.
30. This is the central bank refinancing rate.
31. This is the central bank repo yield.
32. This is the 12-month lending rate.
33. This is the average of the annualized quarterly GDP change for the first three quarters of 2011.
34. The central bank deems an inflation outcome acceptable if it is within 1.5 per cent above or below the central inflation target of 4 per cent. The latest December 2011 outcome of 6.5 per cent was at the upper limit of what is acceptable and even the 6.5 per cent upper limit was breached in 8 out of 12 months of 2012.
35. See Helbling and Roache 2011.
36. Ibid.
37. http://www.nytimes.com/2011/08/27/business/global/india-adds-a-slowing-economy-to-its-corruption-woes.html?pagewanted=all. Last accessed 1 June 2012.
38. See the *Financial Times*, 'Food Subsidy Bill To Test India's Finances', 19 December 2011.
39. See the *Financial Times*, 'The Price of Tea in China', 15 June 2011.
40. See the *Financial Times*, 'Labour Unrest Sweeps China', 29 December 2011.
41. See the *Financial Times*, 'Beijing Frets As Local Injustices Swell the Tide of "Incidents"', 15 June 2011.
42. Ibid.
43. http://online.wsj.com/article/SB10001424052702303714704576384890805560986.html. Last accessed 1 June 2012.
44. Whether the renminbi is undervalued is a hotly debated topic, which cannot be elaborated upon here for reasons of space. However, most academics support the hypothesis of undervaluation, at least on the basis of purchasing power parity. See, for instance, Lipman 2011, which suggests that the renminbi is undervalued by 37.5 per cent on the basis of purchasing power parity.
45. See Morgan Stanley 2011.
46. http://www.mittalgroup.co.in/future-real-estate.aspx. Last accessed 3 January 2012.
47. http://www.ft.com/intl/cms/s/0/27dbe920-b10f-11e0-a43e-00144feab49a.html#axzz1UYiHcPMn. Last accessed 1 June 2012.
48. See the *Financial Times*, 'Chinese Cities to Pilot Property Tax', 27 January 2011.
49. For the full series since February 2008, see http://www.fipe.com.br/web/index.asp. Last accessed 1 June 2012.

50. http://www.telegraph.co.uk/sponsored/russianow/business/8864306/House-prices-Russia-rise.html. Last accessed 1 June 2012.
51. China may present the greatest risks in this respect.
52. http://elsa.berkeley.edu/~saez/TabFig2007.xls. Last accessed 3 January 2012.
53. http://elsa.berkeley.edu/~saez/TabFig2007.xls. Last accessed 3 January 2012.
54. See the *Financial Times*, 'Brazil May Be Heading for a Subprime Crisis', 21 February 2011 and the *Financial Times*, 'China's Credit Growth', 30 April 2009.
55. See the *Financial Times*, 'Brazil Credit Bubble Fear As Defaults Rise', 20 June 2011.
56. Ibid.
57. Based on https://www.cia.gov/library/publications/the-world-factbook/fields/2172.html#br. Last accessed 3 January 2012.
58. http://china.usc.edu/App_Images/Dollar.pdf. Last accessed 1 June 2012.
59. See Zhang and Eriksson 2009.
60. See Ferguson 2007.
61. http://www.businessweek.com/news/2011–02–27/china-lowers-growth-target-as-wen-calls-for-sustainability.html. Last accessed 1 June 2012.
62. See Ferguson 2007.
63. See Zhang and Eriksson 2009.
64. See Huang 2011, 122.
65. See Naughton 2007.
66. See Huang 2011, 119.
67. Ibid., 130.
68. See Naughton 2007.
69. See Sengupta and Ghosh 2007.
70. See Naughton 2007.
71. See Galbraith, Krytynskaia and Wang 2003.
72. http://www.wpro.who.int/NR/rdonlyres/0267DCE8–07AB-437A-8B01–03D474D922CD/0/hsa_en.pdf. Last accessed 3 January 2012.
73. http://www.econ.yale.edu/alumni/reunion99/birdsall.htm.
74. One has to ask how constructive inequality can be in the USA, where the poor cannot use democracy to further their interests effectively because 'poor people don't make campaign contributions', as noted by Bob Dole in 1982. George Packer offers an excellent analysis of this mechanism. He demonstrates how organized money and the conservative movement began a massive generation-long transfer of wealth to the richest Americans in 1978, whereby the rich bought themselves the votes which would allow them to become ever richer through their monopoly on policy (see Packer 2011, 29). As he shows, this transfer of wealth was never questioned again; even Democrat politicians would soon pander to Wall Street and corporate America, which amounts to disenfranchising the poor. And if the poor are disenfranchised, they are more likely to take to the streets.
75. See Zhang and Eriksson 2009.
76. See Organization for Economic Cooperation and Development 2011.
77. See Dollar 2007.
78. Ibid.
79. *Financial Times*, 'China: A Democracy Is Built', 7 March 2011.
80. If the focus is on poverty itself, according to the UNDP, about two-thirds of the population in Russia belong to the lower-income group, with most members of this group coming from the peasantry or the working poor.

About half of the poor live in households where the head of household is employed. The largest subgroup is composed of households with children. The younger and more numerous the children, the more likely the family is poor. Single-parent households are more likely to be poor, and 90 per cent of such households are headed by women, which indicates the feminization of poverty. This already pre-existing vulnerability of women to poverty is aggravated by an unequal distribution of income in terms of wages. Indeed, in 2001, gender-income differentials were pronounced, with women earning 63.8 per cent as much as men in terms of estimated earned income. Considering that average real wages (male and female) in 2001 were only 53 per cent of those in 1989, one can imagine how bad it was to be a Russian woman leading a single household in 2001.

81. See Stiglitz 2003.
82. http://www.ft.com/intl/cms/s/0/01862e52–3793–11e0-b91a-00144feabdc0. html#axzz1UYiHcPMn. Last accessed 1 June 2012.
83. See Remington 2011, 1.
84. http://data.wordbank.org/country/russian-federation. Last accessed 1 June 2012.
85. See Eberstadt 2011, 97.
86. http://www.undp.ru/nhdr2010/National_Human_Development_Report_ in_the_RF_2010_ENG.pdf.
87. See Galbraith, Krytynskaia and Wang 2003.
88. Ibid.
89. http://www.ft.com/intl/cms/s/0/92ef58fa-a8c2–11e0-b877–00144feabdc0. html#axzz1UYiHcPMn. Last accessed 1 June 2012.
90. For a thorough investigation of the effects of health and education privatization in transition economies, see Bayliss and Kessler 2006.
91. http://data.wordbank.org/country/russian-federation. Last accessed 1 June 2012.
92. See Eberstadt 2011, 105.
93. Ibid., 105.
94. http://data.worldbank.org/country/india. Last accessed 1 June 2012.
95. http://www.business-standard.com/india/news/pranab-bardhan-how-unequalcountry-is-india/369106/. Last accessed 3 January 2012.
96. http://www.narayanahospitals.com/images/Harvard%20Business%20 School.pdf. Last accessed 3 January 2012.
97. http://www.forbes.com/2010/09/28/india-richest-40-ambani-mittal-premji-india-rich-10-intro.html. Last accessed 1 June 2012.
98. http://blogs.ft.com/beyond-brics/2011/06/08/indias-ultra-rich-embrace-risk/#axzz1UkpLvrkl. Last accessed 1 June 2012.
99. http://www.ft.com/intl/cms/s/0/603099b4–6917–11e0–9040–00144feab49a.html#axzz1UYiHcPMn. Last accessed 1 June 2012.
100. See Banerjee and Piketty 2001.
101. http://www.adb.org/documents/events/2009/poverty-social-development/ globalization-impact-on-inequality-in-India-Ravi-paper.pdf. Last accessed 3 January 2012.
102. See Pal and Ghosh 2007.
103. Ibid.

104. http://www.adb.org/documents/events/2009/poverty-social-development/globalization-impact-on-inequality-in-India-Ravi-paper.pdf. Last accessed 3 January 2012.
105. See Pal and Ghosh 2007.
106. http://www.adb.org/documents/events/2009/poverty-social-development/globalization-impact-on-inequality-in-India-Ravi-paper.pdf. Last accessed 3 January 2012.
107. See Pal and Ghosh 2007.
108. http://www.business-standard.com/india/news/pranab-bardhan-how-unequalcountry-is-india/369106/. Last accessed 3 January 2012.
109. http://data.worldbank.org/country/india. Last accessed 1 June 2012.
110. http://www.narayanahospitals.com/images/Harvard%20Business%20School.pdf. Last accessed 3 January 2012.
111. See Pal and Ghosh 2007.
112. http://www.business-standard.com/india/news/pranab-bardhan-how-unequalcountry-is-india/369106/. Last accessed 3 January 2012.
113. See Pal and Ghosh 2007.
114. Ibid.
115. See Barros, de Carvalho, Franco and Mendonca 2009.
116. See http://brics.redesist.ie.ufrj.br/proj_idrc/cp_report/NIS%20Comparative%20Report.pdf, esp. section II, on the Brazilian innovation system. Last accessed 1 June 2012.
117. See Barros, de Carvalho, Franco and Mendonca 2009.
118. Ibid.
119. Ibid.
120. Brazil does not have a 'monopoly' on these types of projects. Chapter 6 looks at projects in India, which have also allowed the poor to help themselves.
121. http://viewswire.eiu.com/index.asp?layout=ib3Article&pubtypeid=1162462501&article_id=547914439&rf=0. Last accessed 1 June 2012.
122. *Financial Times*, 'Writing Is on the Wall', 22 March 2011.
123. *Financial Times*, 'Ascent and Dissent', 12 July 2011.
124. *Straits Times*, Singapore, 25 July 2009.
125. Ibid.
126. http://www.ftchinese.com/story/001038465/en. Last accessed 1 June 2012.
127. See Packer 2011, 30.
128. Ibid., 30.

5   Limit No. 2: BRICs and the Silent Power of Ideas

1. See Morris 2010.
2. See Parent and MacDonald 2011, 34.
3. http://www.washingtonpost.com/opinions/the-politics-of-chinas-high-speed-train-wreck/2011/07/27/gIQAGedXdI_story.html. Last accessed 1 June 2012.
4. See the *Financial Times*, 'Beijing Sacks Rail Officials As Crash Kills 35', 25 July 2011.
5. See Halper 2010.
6. See Kennedy 1989.

7. Still, even in terms of economic might, the USA is not exactly collapsing: as noted by Parent and MacDonald, 'the US still exports more goods and services than any other country and is close behind China as the world's largest manufacturer. In terms of market exchange rate, the US economy is still more than double the size of the Chinese economy' (see Parent and MacDonald 2011, 36).

8. See Parent and MacDonald 2011, 46.

9. http://nationalsecurityforum.net/china/niall-ferguson-on-the-rise-of-china-and-the-decline-of-the-west/. Last accessed 1 June 2012.

10. See Kaletsky 2010.

11. Similarly, Morris notes that a geographical advantage at one stage of social development may be irrelevant at another, implying that the most important resource for world domination is adaptability.

12. That being said, one could argue that the greatest lesson of the collapse of the latest extreme 'version' of capitalism is the fact that 'markets do not create, regulate, stabilize, or sustain themselves', as noted by Rodrik (2011). Sadly, this is an old lesson that merely needs to be relearnt and possibly revisited in new, creative ways.

13. http://www.ft.com/intl/cms/s/0/edccd72a-432e-11df-9046–00144feab49a.html#axzz1V6SYhmON. Last accessed 1 June 2012.

14. See Smith 2010.

15. http://www.ft.com/intl/cms/s/0/42d64dce-fe3b-11df-abac-00144feab49a.html#axzz1V6SYhmON. Last accessed 1 June 2012.

16. See Wu and Zou 2009.

17. At the national level, having an entrepreneur base with a strong capacity for innovation can turn a country into a global power, in both the economic and ideational dimensions. Witness Britain's ascent with the Industrial Revolution and its steam-powered cotton-spinning wheel and railroads. This ascent was partly an economic phenomenon founded on the high rates of growth afforded by innovation. But it was also an ideational one, as the age of innovation and scientific progress gave Britain a leading position in producing the knowledge of the world, which added legitimacy and sustainability to its central economic position in the global economy.

18. See Romer 1989.

19. See Schumpeter 1934.

20. See Desai 2002.

21. See Arrow 1962.

22. See Nelson and Winter 1982.

23. For an investigation of how this debate applies to developing country firms, see Beausang 2003.

24. See Freeman 1987.

25. See Cassiolato and Vitorino 2011, 3.

26. See Freeman 1987.

27. See Cameron 1998.

28. Ibid.

29. See Griliches 1980.

30. See Nadiri and Bitros 1980.

31. See Nadiri 1980.

32. See Patel and Soete 1988.

33. See Nadiri and Prucha 1990.
34. See Verspagen 1995.
35. See Srinivasan 1996.
36. See Mansfield 1988.
37. See Sassenou 1988.
38. See Cuneo and Mairesse 1984.
39. See Mairesse and Cuneo 1985.
40. See Bartelsman, van Leeuwen, Nieuwenhuijsen and Zeelenburg 1996.
41. See Englander and Mittelstädt 1988.
42. See Coe and Helpman 1995.
43. See Jaffe 1989.
44. See Acs, Audretsch, and Feldman (1992) and Acs, Audretsch and Feldman (1994).
45. See Nadiri and Mamuneas 1991.
46. See Geroski 1989.
47. See Budd and Hobbis 1989.
48. http://www.time.com/time/specials/packages/completelist/0,29569,2029497,00.html. Last accessed 1 June 2012.
49. http://www.adb.org/documents/working-papers/2010/Economics-WP227.pdf. Last accessed 1 June 2012.
50. The flip side of China's deteriorating TFP is the limitations of its investment-based model; it is looked at in more depth in the conclusion. Here, note the similarities between contemporary China and Japan since the 1990s, as both economies faced the need to unwind an investment-based growth into a consumption-based growth. As is explained, there exists a significant risk that China will undergo difficulties similar to Japan's, which went through its 'lost decade' while meeting the challenges of this transition.
51. Scores are out of 7.
52. See World Economic Forum 2010.
53. For details of calculations and component definitions, see http://www3.weforum.org/docs/WEF_GlobalCompetitivenessReport_2010–11.pdf. Last accessed 1 June 2012.
54. http://www.whitehouse.gov/state-of-the-union-2011. Last accessed 1 June 2012.
55. See Organisation for Economic Cooperation and Development 2008a.
56. http://www.wipo.int/freepublications/en/intproperty/941/wipo_pub_941_2010.pdf. Last accessed 1 June 2012.
57. Ibid.
58. See Organisation for Economic Cooperation and Development 2008b.
59. See D'Costa 2006.
60. See Organisation for Economic Cooperation and Development 2006, 92.
61. See Organisation for Economic Cooperation and Development 2006.
62. Ibid., 110.
63. Ibid., 111.
64. China became the second-most prolific publisher of scientific papers after the USA in 2010; although the USA still leads the world, its share of global authorship fell from 26% (1993–2003) to 21% (2004–8), while China went from sixth to second place, with its share rising from 4.4% to 10.2%, according to the Royal Society (2011).

65. Usually a developing country first acquires development capability, as China has. Ideally, the closer an economy is to developed country status, the more it should become capable of basic research, so that the research-to-development mix should gradually become heavier on the research side. There are problems with both research-heavy and development-heavy models. Clearly, an economy with solid fundamental research and no product applications lacks commercialization prospects. Conversely, an economy with only marginal, applied innovations will never produce a breakthrough innovation, such as the Internet, with the capacity to change the global economy. In that sense, a degree of balance between research and development, which neither China nor India displays, has to be achieved.
66. See Organisation for Economic Cooperation and Development 2007.
67. Ibid.
68. See Organisation for Economic Cooperation and Development 2008a.
69. Ibid.
70. See Van Agtmael 2007.
71. See Boston Consulting Group 2009 or the *Economist* 2011a.
72. See Beausang 2003.
73. http://www.techworld.com.au/article/376938/taiwan_strategy_seen_making_low-end_phones_even_cheaper/#closeme. Last accessed 3 January 2012.
74. See the *Times* 2010.
75. See the *Economist* 2011b.
76. See Naughton 2007.
77. See Royal Society 2011.
78. See Liu and Liu 2011.
79. Ibid.
80. See Naughton 2007.
81. http://economyincrisis.org/content/westinghouse-electric-nuclear-secrets-given-china. Last accessed 3 January 2012.
82. http://abclocal.go.com/wls/story?section=news/local&id=6228552. Last accessed 3 January 2012.
83. http://www.bbc.co.uk/news/world-europe-12137714. Last accessed 3 January 2012.

6 Conclusion: The Innovation–Equality–Development Triangle

1. See Johnson 1982.
2. See the *Financial Times*, 'How China Could Yet Fail like Japan', 15 June 2011.
3. http://mpettis.com/2010/08/chinese-consumption-and-the-japanese-"sorpasso". Last accessed 1 June 2012.
4. See the *Financial Times*, 'How China Could Yet Fail like Japan', 14 June 2011.
5. http://mpettis.com/2010/08/chinese-consumption-and-the-japanese-"sorpasso". Last accessed 1 June 2012.
6. Ibid.
7. See the *Financial Times*, 'How China Could Yet Fail like Japan', 14 June 2011.

8. See Acemoglu, Aghion and Zilibotti 2006.
9. See Acemoglu and Robinson 2006.
10. See Magnus 2010.
11. In the second quarter of 2010, China spent US$10 billion on wind energy alone, twice the amount spent by the rest of the world. See http://www.ft.com/intl/cms/s/0/56c0f8e6-fbea-11df-b7e9-00144feab49a.html#axzz1VO9XoE4G. Last accessed 1 June 2012.
12. Ibid.
13. Insead Global Innovation Index.
14. CIA Factbook 2011.
15. See the *Guardian*, 'China's Top Universities Will Rival Oxbridge', 2 February 2010.
16. http://www.ft.com/intl/cms/s/0/1ebccad2-2f08-11e0-88ec-00144feabdc0.html#axzz1VO9XoE4G. Last accessed 1 June 2012.
17. See Chang 2001.
18. http://www.ft.com/intl/cms/s/0/07434446-48f6-11e0-af8c-00144feab49a.html#axzz1VO9XoE4G. Last accessed 1 June 2012.
19. See OECD 2008a. Note that the OECD includes Indonesia in its definition of BRICs. Unfortunately, the latest OECD data are for 2003–5.
20. See Foellmi, Wuergler, and Zweimuller 2009. The supply-side argument is less convincing (see Galor and Zeira 1993).
21. See Foellmi, Wuergler and Zweimuller 2009.
22. While this is an old idea developed by the dependency school, it appears now to be more applicable than ever.
23. See Saint-Paul 2008.
24. See Dutz and Dahlman 2007.
25. Ibid.
26. See Prahalad 2004.
27. See Dutz and Dahlman 2007.
28. Ibid.

Bibliography

Acemoglu, D., P. Aghion and F. Zilibotti, 'Distance to Frontier and Growth', *Journal of the European Economic Association* 4, no. 1 (March 2006): 37–74.

Acemoglu, D. and J. Robinson, 'Economic Backwardness in Political Perspective', *American Political Science Review* 100, no. 1 (February 2006).

Acs, Z., D. Audretsch and M. Feldman, 'Real Effects of Academic Research: Comment', *American Economic Review* 81 (1991): 363–7.

Acs, Z., D. Audretsch & M. Feldman, 'R&D Spillovers and Recipient Firm Size', *Review of Economics and Statistics* 76, no. 2 (1994): 336–40.

Alesina, A., and R. Perotti, 'Income Distribution, Political Instability, and Investment', *European Economic Review* 40 (1996): 1203–28.

Arrow, K. J., 'The Economic Implications of Learning by Doing', *Journal of Business* 35 (July 1962): 235–55.

Aslund, A., *Russia's Capitalist Revolution: Why Market Reform Succeeded and Democracy Failed*, Washington, DC: Peterson Institute, 2007.

Bank for International Settlements, 'Financial Globalisation and Emerging Market Capital Flows', BIS Paper no. 44, BIS, Basel, December 2008.

Banerjee, A., and T. Piketty, 'Are the Rich Growing Richer: Evidence from Indian Tax Data', in A. Deaton and V. Kozel (eds), *The Great Indian Poverty Debate*. Delhi: Macmillan India, 2006.

Barcena, A., 'Challenges and Opportunities for a State Role in the Post-Crisis', *Pensamiento Iberoamericano* (Santiago de Chile: UN Economic Commission for Latin America) no. 6 (June 2010).

Barro, R. 'Inequality and Growth in a Panel of Countries', *Journal of Economic Growth*, no. 5, 2000, 5–32.

Barros, R., M. de Carvalho, S. Franco and R. Mendonca, *Markets, the State and the Dynamics of Inequality in Brazil*, New York: UNDP Research for Public Policy, Inclusive Development ID-14–2009, 2009.

Bartelsman, E., G. van Leeuwen, H. Nieuwenhuijsen and K. Zeelenburg, 'R&D and Productivity Growth: Evidence from Firm-Level Data in the Netherlands', paper presented at the 1996 Conference of the European Economic Association, Istanbul, 1996.

Bartlett, D., 'African Investments by the BRIC Countries', Symposium on Foreign Investment in Africa, Bartlett Ellis LLC, http://www.sabusinesscouncil.org/wp-content/uploads/2009/04/african-investments-by-bric-countries.pdf, April 1 2009.

Bayliss, K., and T. Kessler, 'Can Privatisation and Commercialisation of Public Services Help Achieve the MDGs?', UNDP International Poverty Centre Working Paper no. 22, UNDP, New York, July 2006.

Beausang, F., *Third World Multinationals: Engine of Development or New Form of Dependency?*, London: Palgrave Macmillan, 2003.

Birdsall, N., and J. L. Londono, 'Asset Inequality Matters: An Assessment of the World Bank's Approach to Poverty Reduction', *American Economic Review* 87 (1997): 32–7.

Boston Consulting Group, *The 2009 BCG 100 New Global Challengers*, New York: BCG, January 2009.

Boulle, P., *Planet of the Apes*, London: Vintage Press, 1963.

Bourguigon, F., 'The Poverty-Growth-Inequality Triangle', mimeo, World Bank, Washington, DC, 2004.

Brautigam, D., *The Dragon's Gift*, Oxford: Oxford University Press, 2009.

Budd, A., and S. Hobbis, 'Cointegration, Technology and the Long-Run Production Function', Centre for Economic Forecasting Discussion Paper no. 10–89, 1989.

Buira, A., *Reforming the Governance of the IMF and the World Bank*, London: Anthem Press, 2005.

Cameron, G., 'Innovation and Growth: A Survey of the Empirical Evidence', http://hicks.nuff.ox.ac.uk/users/cameron/papers/empiric.pdf, July 1998.

Cassiolato, J. E., and V. Vitorino, *BRICs and Development Alternatives*, London: Anthem Press, 2011.

Central Intelligence Agency, *CIA World Factbook 2011*, Washington, DC: CIA, 2011.

Chang, G., *The Coming Collapse of China*, London: Random House, 2001.

Chang, H. J., *The Bad Samaritans*, London: Random House, 2008.

Chang, H.J., *Twenty-three Things They Don't Tell You about Capitalism*, London: Allen Lane, 2010.

Coe, D., and E. Helpman, 'International R&D Spillovers', *European Economic Review* 41 (1995).

Cuneo, P., and J. Mairesse, 'Productivity and R&D at the Firm Level in French Manufacturing', in *R&D, Patents and Productivity*, Z. Griliches (ed.), Chicago: University of Chicago Press, 1984.

D'Costa, A. P., 'Exports, University-Industry Linkages, and Innovation Challenges in Bangalore, India', World Bank Policy Research Working Paper no. 3887, World Bank, Washington, DC, April 2006.

Desai, M., *Marx's Revenge*, London: Verso, 2002.

Dollar, D., 'Poverty, Inequality and Social Disparities During China's Economic Reform', http://china.usc.edu/App_Images/Dollar.pdf, April 2007.

Dutz, A., and C. Dahlman, 'Promoting Inclusive Innovation', chap. 4 in *Unleashing India's Innovation*, M.A. Dutz (ed.), Washington, DC: World Bank, 2007.

Eberstadt, N., 'The Dying Bear', *Foreign Affairs* 90, no. 6, (November/December 2011).

The Economist, 'Nipping at Their Heels', 22 January 2011.

The Economist, 'An Old Enemy Rears Its Head', 22 May 2008.

The Economist, 'Tata for Now', 10 September 2011.

The Economist, 'What Do You Do When You Reach the Top?', 12 November 2011.

Eichengreen, B., D. Park and K. Shin, 'When Fast-Growing Economies Slow Down: International Evidence and Implications for China', National Bureau for Economic Research Working Paper no. 16919, NBER, Washington, DC, March 2011.

Englander, A. S., and A. Mittelstädt, 'Total Factor Productivity: Macroeconomic and Structural Aspects of the Slowdown', OECD Economic Studies no. 10, Summer 1988.

Erixon, F., and R. Sally, 'Trade, Globalisation and Emerging Protectionism since the Crisis', European Centre for International Political Economy Working Paper no. 02/2010, ECIPE, Brussels, 2010.

Evenett, S., *The Unrelenting Pressure of Protectionism: The 3rd GTA Report*, London: CEPR / Global Trade Alert, 2009.

Fanon, F., *The Wretched of the Earth*, London: Penguin, 1961.

Ferguson, N., *Civilization: The West and the Rest*, London: Allen Lane, 2011.

Financial Times, 'Ascent and Dissent', 12 July 2011.

Financial Times, 'Asia: Eastern Billions Can Still Join the World', 3 January 2011.

Financial Times, 'Beijing Builds to Hold US Power at Bay', 19 January 2011.

Financial Times, 'Beijing Frets As Local Injustices Swell the Tide of "Incidents"', 15 June 2011.

Financial Times, 'Beijing Will Not Come Riding to the Euro's Rescue', 21 September 2011.

Financial Times, 'Beijing Sacks Rail Officials As Crash Kills 35', 25 July 2011.

Financial Times, 'Brazil Credit Bubble Fear As Defaults Rise', 20 June 2011.

Financial Times, 'Brazil May Be Heading for a Subprime Crisis', 21 February 2011.

Financial Times, 'Brazil to Seek New Arms for Currency Battle', 20 September 2011.

Financial Times, 'China: A Democracy Is Built', 7 March 2011.

Financial Times, 'China Cements Role as Top of the BRICs', 14 April 2011.

Financial Times, 'China Fund Shuns Guns and Gambling', 13 June 2008.

Financial Times, 'China's Credit Growth', 30 April 2009.

Financial Times, 'China Launch Set to Boost Space Station Plan', 21 September 2011.

Financial Times, 'China's Rare Earths', 7 July 2011.

Financial Times, 'China to Ease Path for Foreign Investors', 19 December 2011.

Financial Times, 'Chinese Cities to Pilot Property Tax', 27 January 2011.

Financial Times, 'Chinese Trades Suggest Shift from US Dollar towards Euro Market', 21 June 2011.

Financial Times, 'Food Subsidy Bill to Test India's Finances', 19 December 2011.

Financial Times, 'How China Could Yet Fail like Japan', 15 June 2011.

Financial Times, 'Huawei Goes on Attack against US Restrictions', 17 October 2011.

Financial Times, 'Labour Unrest Sweeps China', 20 December 2011.

Financial Times, 'Outsourcing: Thick Skins Shrug Off Protectionist Rhetoric', 16 January 2011.

Financial Times, 'The Price of Tea in China', 15 June 2011.

Financial Times, 'Reject Sovereign Wealth Funds at Your Peril', 20 June 2008.

Financial Times, 'Rifts Emerge in WTO over Push for Pacts', 19 December 2011.

Financial Times, 'Talk of Currency Wars Fades As Emerging World Battles Inflation', 14 April 2011.

Financial Times, 'US Threatens to Retaliate at EU's Green Levy on Airlines', 20 December 2011.

Financial Times, 'War of the Worlds', 26 January 2011.

Financial Times, 'Workers Call the Tune in China', 22 February 2011.

Financial Times, 'Writing Is on the Wall', 22 March 2011.

Foellmi, R., T. Wuergler and J. Zweimuller, 'The Macroeconomics of Model T', Institute for Empirical Research in Economics of Zurich University Working Paper no. 459, Zurich, 2009.

Forbes, K., 'A Reassessment of the Relationship between Inequality and Growth', *American Economic Review*, no. 90 (2000): 869–97.

Fox, R., 'BRICs: Evolving Regional Security Trends', *Defence Systems* 13, no. 2 (October 2010): 97–9 (published by Royal United Services Institute).

Freeman, C., *Technology Policy and Economic Performance – Lessons from Japan*, London: Frances Pinter, 1987.

Fukuyama, F., *The Origins of Political Order*, New York: Farrar, Straus & Giroux, 2011.

Furtado, C., *Formacao Economica do Brasil*, Rio de Janeiro: Fundo de Cultura, 1959.

Galbraith, J. K., L. Krytynskaia and Q. Wang, 'The Experience of Rising Inequality in Russia and China during the Transition', UTIP Working Paper no. 23, UTIP, Austin, 2 February 2003.

Galor, O., and J. Zeira, 'Income Distribution and Macroeconomics', *Review of Economic Studies* 60 (1993): 35–52.

Geroski, P., 'Entry, Innovation and Productivity Growth', *Review of Economics and Statistics* 71 (1989).

Gokhberg, L., N. Gorodnikova, T. Kuznetsova, A. Sokolov and S. Zaichenko, 'Prospective Agenda for Science and Technology and Innovation Policies in Russia', chap. 3 in *BRICs and Development Alternatives*, J. E. Cassiolato and V. Vitorino (eds), London: Anthem Press, 2011.

Griliches, Z., 'Returns to R&D Expenditures in the Private Sector', in *New Developments in Productivity Measurement*, K. W. Kendrick and B. Vaccara (eds), Chicago: Chicago University Press, 1980.

Gruenwald, P., and M. Hori, 'IMF Survey: Intra-regional Trade Key to Asia's Export Boom', *IMF Survey*, 6 February 2008, International Monetary Fund, Washington, DC.

Guardian, 'China's Top Universities Will Rival Oxbridge', 2 February 2010.

Haas, E. B., *When Knowledge Is Power: Three Models of Change in International Organizations*, Berkeley: University of California Press, 1990.

Haas, E.B., 'Why Collaborate? Issue-Linkage and International Regimes', *World Politics*, no. 32 (April 1980): 357–405.

Halper, S., *The Beijing Consensus*, New York: Basic Books, 2010.

Harvey, D. I., 'The Prebisch-Singer Hypothesis: Four Centuries of Evidence', http://www.africametrics.org/documents/conference08/day2/session6/harvey_kellard_madsen_wohar.pdf, June 2008.

Helbling, T., and S. Roache, 'Rising Prices on the Menu', *Finance and Development* 48, no. 1 (March 2011).

Held, D., A. McGrew, D. Goldblatt and J. Perraton, *Global Transformations*, Cambridge: Polity Press, 1999.

Hirschman, A. O., and M. Rothschild, 'The Changing Tolerance for Income Inequality in the Course of Economic Development; with a Mathematical Appendix', *Quarterly Journal of Economics* 87, no. 4 (November 1973): 544–66.

Huang, Y., 'The Sick Man of Asia', *Foreign Affairs* 90, no. 6 (November/December 2011).

International Energy Agency, *International Energy Outlook*, Paris: IEA, 2010.

Jaffe, A., 'Real Effect of Academic Research', *American Economic Review* 79 (1989): 957–70.

Johnson, C., *Miti and the Japanese Economic Miracle*, Stanford, CA: Stanford University Press, 1982.

Joseph, K. J., and D. Abrol, 'Science, Technology and Innovation Policies in India', chap. 4 in *BRICs and Development Alternatives*, J. E. Cassiolato and V. Vitorino (eds), London: Anthem Press, 2011.

Kaletsky, A., *Capitalism 4.0*, London: Bloomsbury, 2010.

Kennedy, P., *The Rise and Fall of the Great Powers*, New York: Vintage, 1989.

Keohane, R., and J. S. Nye, *Power and Interdependence: World Politics in Transition*, Boston: Little, Brown, 1977.

King Whyte, M., *Myth of the Social Volcano*, Stanford, CA: Stanford University Press, 2010.

Koeller, P., and J. E. Cassiolato, 'Achievements and Shortcomings of Brazil's Innovation Policies', chap. 2 in *BRICs and Development Alternatives*, J. E. Cassiolato and V. Vitorino (eds), London: Anthem Press, 2011.

Kose, M. A., and E. S. Prasad, *Emerging Markets: Resilience and Growth amid Global Turmoil*, Washington, DC: Brookings Institution Press, 2010.

Kwa, A., *Power Politics in the WTO*, Bangkok: Focus on the Global South, 2003.

Li, H., and H. Zou, 'Inflation, Growth and Income Distribution: A Cross-Country Case Study', *Annals of Economics and Finance*, no. 3 (2002): 85–101.

Limao, N., 'The Clash of Liberalizations: Preferential Trade Agreements as a Stumbling Block to Multilateral Liberalization', comments prepared for the Conference in Honor of Jagdish Bhagwati's 70th Birthday at Columbia University, New York, 5–6 August 2005.

Lipman, J. K., 'Law of Yuan Price: Estimating Equilibrium of the Renminbi', *Michigan Journal of Business* 4, no. 2 (April 2011).

Liu, M., L. Xu and L. Liu, 'Foreign Investment in China: Firm Strategies', in *The Globalisation of the Chinese Economy*, S. J. Wei, G. J. Wen and H. Zhou (eds), Cheltenham: Edward Elgar, 2002.

Liu, X., and J. Liu, 'Science and Technology and Innovation Policy in China', chap. 5 in *BRICs and Development Alternatives*, J. E. Cassiolato and V. Vitorino (eds), London: Anthem Press, 2011.

Lopez, H., 'Pro-Poor Growth: Is There a Trade-off?', World Bank Policy Research Working Paper no. 3378, World Bank, Washington, DC, 2004.

Maddison, A., 'Background Note on Historical Statistics', www.ggdc.net/Maddison, March 2010.

Magnus, G., *Uprising*, London: Wiley, 2010.

Mairesse, J., and P. Cuneo, 'Recherche-Developpement et Performances des Entreprises: Une Étude Econometrique sur Données Individuelles', *Revue Economique* 36 (1985): 1001–42.

Mansfield, E., 'Industrial R&D in Japan and the United States: A Comparative Study', *American Economic Review* 78 (1988): 223–8.

Mirlees, J., 'An Exploration in the Theory of Optimum Income Taxation', *Review of Economic Studies*, no. 38 (1971): 175–208.

Moore, M., and H. White, 'Meeting the Challenge of Poverty and Inequality', chap. 3 in *States, Markets and Just Growth*, A. Kohli, C. I. Moon and G. Sorensen (eds), Tokyo: United Nations University, 2003.

Morgan Stanley, *Alphawise Evidence Series on Asian Inflation*, March 2011.

Morris, I., *Why the Rest Rules – for Now*, London: Profile Books, 2010.

Moyo, D., *How the West Was Lost*, London: Penguin, 2011.

Nadiri, M., 'Sectoral Productivity Slowdown', *American Economic Review* 70 (1980): 349–55.

Nadiri, M., and G. Bitros, 'Research and Development Expenditures and Labor Productivity at the Firm Level', in *Studies in Income and Wealth*, J. Kendrick and B. Vaccara (eds), Chicago: University of Chicago Press, 1980.

Nadiri, M., and T. Mamuneas, 'The Effects of Public Infrastructure and R&D Capital on the Cost Structure and Performance of US Manufacturing Industries', paper presented at NBER Summer Institute, 1991.

Nadiri, M., and I. Prucha, 'Comparison and Analysis of Productivity Growth and R&D Investment in the Electrical Machinery Industries of the United States and Japan', in *Productivity Growth in Japan and the United States*, C. Hulten and R. Norsworthy (eds), Chicago: University of Chicago Press, 1990.

Naughton, B., *The Chinese Economy*, Cambridge, MA: MIT Press, 2007.

Nelson, R. R., and S. G. Winter, *The Evolutionary Nature of Economic Change*, Cambridge, MA: Belknap Press, 1982.

Nye, J. S., Jr, *The Future of Power*, Washington, DC: Public Affairs, 2011.

O'Neill, J., 'Building Better Global Economic BRICs', Goldman Sachs Global Economics Paper no. 66, New York: Goldman Sachs, November 2001.

O'Neill, J., *The Growth Map: Economic Opportunity in the BRICs and Beyond*, London: Penguin, 2011.

Organisation for Economic Cooperation and Development, *Economic Survey of Brazil*, Paris: OECD, 2006.

Organisation for Economic Cooperation and Development, *Economic Survey of China 2010*, Paris: OECD, 2011.

Organisation for Economic Cooperation and Development, *Compendium of Patent Statistics 2008*, Paris: OECD, 2008.

Organisation for Economic Cooperation and Development, *OECD Review of Innovation Policy: China, Synthesis Report*, Paris: OECD, 2007.

Organisation for Economic Cooperation and Development, *OECD Science, Technology and Industry Outlook 2008*, Paris: OECD, 2008.

Packer, G., 'The Broken Contract: Inequality and American Decline', *Foreign Affairs* 90, no. 6 (November/December 2011): 20–31.

Pal, P., and J. Ghosh, 'Inequality in India: A Survey of Recent Trends', chap. 13 in *Flat World, Big Gaps*, K. S. Jomo and J. Baudot (eds), London: Zed Books, 2007.

Parello-Plesner, J., and P. Khann, 'Stop Fretting about Beijing as a Global Policeman', *Financial Times*, 29 December 2011.

Parent, J. M., and P. K. MacDonald, 'The Wisdom of Retrenchment', *Foreign Affairs* 90, no. 6 (November/December 2011).

Patel, P., and L. Soete, 'L'Evaluation des Effets Economiques de la Technologie', *STI Review*, no. 4 (1988): 133–83.

Pei, M., 'Think Again: Asia's Rise', *Foreign Policy*, July/August 2009.

Perotti, R., 'Growth, Income Distribution, and Democracy: What the Data Say', *Journal of Economic Growth* 1 (June 1996): 149–87.

Prahalad, C. K., *Fortune at the Bottom of the Pyramid: Eradicating Poverty through Profits*, Upper Saddle River, NJ: Wharton School Publishing, 2004.

Rodrik, D., *The Globalization Paradox*, Oxford: Oxford University Press, 2011.

Plender, J., 'The Code That Forms a Bar to Harmony', *Financial Times*, 9 January 2012.

Ravallion, M., 'Competing Concepts of Inequality in the Globalization Debate', World Bank Policy Research Working Paper no. 3243, World Bank, Washington, DC, March 2004.

Remington, T. M., *The Politics of Inequality in Russia*, Cambridge: Cambridge University Press, 2011.

Rodrik, D., *The Globalization Paradox*, Oxford: Oxford University Press, 2011.

Romer, P., 'What Determines the Rate of Growth and Technological Change?', Washington, DC: World Bank, Country Economics Department, 1989.

Rosen, D. H., and T. Hanemann, *An American Open Door?, Maximising the Benefits of Chinese Direct Foreign Investment*, Asia Society, May 2011.

Royal Society, *Knowledge, Networks and Nations: Global Scientific Collaboration in the Twenty-first Century*, London: Royal Society, 2011.

Saint-Paul, G., *Innovation and Inequality: How Does Technical Progress Affect Workers?*, Princeton, NJ: Princeton University Press, 2008.

Saith, A., 'China and India: The Institutional Roots of Differential Performance', *Development and Change* 39, no. 5 (2008): 723–57.

Sassenou, M., 'Recherche-Developpement et Productivité dans les Entreprises Japonaises: Une Étude Econometrique sur Données de Panel', doctoral diss., L'École des Hautes Études en Science Sociales, Paris, 1988.

Schumpeter, J., *The Theory of Economic Development*, Piscataway, NJ: Transaction, 1934.

Sengupta, R., and J. Ghosh, 'Understanding the Extent and Evolution of Inequalities in China', chap. 15 in *Flat World, Big Gaps*, K. S. Jomo and J. Baudot (eds), London: Zed Books, 2007.

Simai, M., 'Poverty and Inequality in Eastern Europe and the CIS Transition Economies', chap. 9 in *Flat World, Big Gaps*, K. S. Jomo and J. Baudot (eds), London: Zed Books, 2007.

Smith, P., *Somebody Else's Century*, New York: Random House, 2010.

Srinivasan, T. N., 'Economic Reforms, External Opening and Growth: China and India', Brookings-NCAER India Policy Forum 2007, New Delhi, 2007.

Srinivasan, S., 'Estimation of Own R&D, R&D Spillovers and Exogenous Technical Change Effects in Some US High-Technology Industries', University of Southampton Discussion Paper in Economics no. 9607, February 1996.

Stephens, P., 'Leaders Who Generate Diminishing Returns', *Financial Times*, 19 January 2012.

Stiglitz, J., 'Economics: Facing a Marked Global Reversal', *Financial Times*, 3 January 2011.

Stiglitz, J., *Globalisation and Its Discontents*, New York: Penguin, 2003.

Summers, L., 'Current Woes Call for Smart Reinvention Not Destruction', *Financial Times*, 9 January 2012.

Teune, H., 'Is Globalization an American Ideology?', prepared for the XV World Congress of the International Sociological Association, Brisbane, 7–13 July 2022.

Times (London), 'Britain Can Learn from India's Assembly-Type Heart Operations, Says Doctor', 14 May 2010.

United Nations Conference on Trade and Development, *World Investment Report 2010*, Geneva: UNCTAD, 2010.

Van Agtmael, A., *The Emerging Markets Century*, London: Free Press, 2007.

Vasiliev, S., *Ten Years of Russian Economic Reform: A Collection of Papers*, London: Centre for Research into Post-Communist Economies, 1999.

Verspagen, B., 'R&D and Productivity: A Broad Cross-Section Cross-Country Look', *Journal of Productivity Analysis* 6 (1995): 117–35.

Wade, R. H., 'The Invisible Hand of the American Empire', *Ethics and International Affairs* 17, no. 2 (2003): 77–88.

Wade, R.H., 'The Ringmaster of Doha', *New Left Review*, no. 25 (January-February 2004).

Wilson, D., and R. Purushothaman, 'Dreaming with BRICs: The Path to 2050', Goldman Sachs Global Economics Paper no. 99, New York, October 2003.

World Economic Forum, *Global Competitiveness Report 2010–11*, Davos: World Economic Forum, 2010.

World Trade Organization, *Overview of Developments in the International Trading Environment*, Geneva: WTO, A3–A46.

Wu, S., and K. Zou, *Maritime Security in the South China Sea*, Farnham: Ashgate, 2009.

Yang, Y., 'Beijing Will Not Come Riding to the Euro's Rescue', *Financial Times*, 21 September 2011.

Yu, B., *Pattern of Indigenous Innovation: The Case of HPEC[R]*, Beijing: NSFC, 2007.

Zhang, Y., and T. Eriksson, 'Inequality of Opportunity and Income Inequality in Nine Chinese Provinces', 1989–2006, Aarhus University Department of Economics Working Paper no. 09–18, Aarhus, 2009.

Zhao, M., Conducting R&D in Countries with Weak Intellectual Property Protection, http://www.carlsonschool.umn.edu/Assets/45555.pdf, 2006.

Index